PUBLIC FACES, SECRET LIVES

Public Faces, Secret Lives

A Queer History of the Women's Suffrage Movement

Wendy L. Rouse

NEW YORK UNIVERSITY PRESS

New York

NEW YORK UNIVERSITY PRESS
New York
www.nyupress.org

References to Internet websites (URLs) were accurate at the time of writing. Neither the author nor New York University Press is responsible for URLs that may have expired or changed since the manuscript was prepared.

Library of Congress Cataloging-in-Publication Data
Names: Rouse, Wendy L., author.
Title: Public faces, secret lives : a queer history of the women's suffrage movement / Wendy L. Rouse.
Description: New York : New York University Press, [2022] | Includes bibliographical references and index.
Identifiers: LCCN 2021035988 | ISBN 9781479813940 (hardback) | ISBN 9781479830947 (paperback) | ISBN 9781479813957 (ebook) | ISBN 9781479813964 (ebook other)
Subjects: LCSH: Women—Suffrage—United States—History. | Suffragists—United States—History. | Lesbians—Political activity—United States.
Classification: LCC JK1896 .R68 2022 | DDC 324.6/230973—dc23
LC record available at https://lccn.loc.gov/2021035988

New York University Press books are printed on acid-free paper, and their binding materials are chosen for strength and durability. We strive to use environmentally responsible suppliers and materials to the greatest extent possible in publishing our books.

Manufactured in the United States of America

10 9 8 7 6 5 4 3 2
Also available as an ebook

CONTENTS

FIGURES

Introduction

In 1873, Dr. Mary Edwards Walker, dressed in one of her characteristi-
cally gender-defying outfits, boldly walked onto the stage at the National
Woman Suffrage Association (NWSA) convention in Washington, DC.
She stood there silently, waiting for Susan B. Anthony to yield the floor
to her. Elizabeth Cady Stanton was visibly annoyed at Walker's presence and believed that since she was not on the program she should not
be allowed to speak. Anthony, recognizing Walker's popularity with the
crowd, eventually acquiesced and invited her to make remarks. Walker
took the floor and immediately launched into a scathing critique of
NWSA leadership for their failure to push for broader social reforms.

Walker specifically called out Stanton and Anthony for abandoning
dress reform. Dress reformers advocated for women's right to wear comfortable and practical clothing, such as bloomers. Walker had endured
multiple arrests in her commitment to the cause. She noted that Stanton
and Anthony had given up dress reform because they lacked the courage to continue the fight. Walker told reporters that suffragists had now
snubbed her because of her gender queer appearance: "These women
have shaken me off because I wear pants."[1] She went on to criticize the
NWSA's approach to winning the vote, insisting that there were more efficient and expedient ways. Later, in a letter to Martha Coffin Wright, Stanton complained: "I endured untold crucifixion at Washington. I suppose
as I sat there I looked patient & submissive but I could have boxed that
Mary Walker's ears with a vengeance."[2] This type of confrontation between Walker and NWSA leaders would become a recurring event, cul-
minating at one point with Anthony's call for the police to arrest Walker
when she again interrupted a suffrage convention. After police arrived,
Walker relented rather than endure another arrest. Taking her seat, she
told Anthony, "You are not working for the cause, but for yourselves."[3]

Walker's queer gender expression, unwavering commitment to dress
reform, love of the spotlight, and condemnation of suffrage leaders and

their methods, elicited the ire of mainstream suffragists. Walker was a Civil War surgeon and Medal of Honor recipient who spent her entire life fighting for women's rights and suffrage. Her choice to wear the reform dress and, later, "men's clothing" made her a target of open ridicule and harassment both inside and outside the movement. As an individual who stretched the limits of conventional notions of gender, Walker's life highlights both the marginalization of queer individuals and the centrality of queerness in the women's suffrage movement. But, this history has been largely erased.

The reality is that the women's suffrage movement was very queer, and queer suffragists were central figures in the movement. It is time that we tell their story. Scholars have extensively documented how the narrow focus on the stories of middle- and upper-class white women in the narrative of women's suffrage history ignores the important role of Black women, Indigenous women, working-class women, immigrant women, and women of color fighting for the vote.[4] Similarly, I argue here that the narrow focus on cisgender heterosexual women erases the existence of queer suffragists—individuals who transgressed normative notions of gender and sexuality. A reframing of the traditional narrative of suffrage history can help recover the stories of queer suffragists and their significant role as changemakers in the suffrage movement while illuminating the factors that led to the marginalization of some of these individuals and the erasure of their queerness from the historic record.

I use the term "queer" throughout this book as an umbrella term to refer to suffragists who were not strictly heterosexual or cisgender. My use of the term "queer" is not in any way intended to obscure or conflate individual sexual or gender identities but is used to provide a concise way to discuss those suffragists who transgressed norms. This term includes individuals who, if they were alive today, might identify as lesbian, gay, bisexual, transgender, intersex, asexual, aromantic, pansexual, non-binary, gender queer, or gender non-conforming. The language we use changes over time and although these labels are common today, individuals in the past did not use these terms to identify themselves. Sexuality and gender as individual or collective identities were only beginning to emerge at the time under study.[5] Yet, individuals expressing a range of genders and sexualities lived during this era. Queer people always have and always will exist.

In addition to the focus on recovering the lives of queer suffragists, this book also seeks to queer the history of the women's suffrage movement as a whole. The act of queering history allows us to disrupt the traditional framing of a topic and consider it from different perspectives. Scholars have already begun queering the history of the women's suffrage movement by deconstructing the dominant narrative and creating a more nuanced analysis through a discussion of race and class. Queering the suffrage movement can also help us move beyond a framework that privileges a cisheteronormative perspective to consider how suffragists challenged white, middle-class sexual and gender conventions while navigating the complexities of respectability politics.

Dr. Mary Edwards Walker was not always on the fringe of the suffrage movement. In the mid-nineteenth century, Elizabeth Smith Miller and Amelia Bloomer advocated dress reform as a way of freeing women from the physical restrictions imposed by their clothing. The new outfit typically consisted of some sort of pants worn underneath a shortened dress, thus freeing women from heavy petticoats and corsets that constricted their internal organs and damaged women's health. Elizabeth Cady Stanton, Lucy Stone, and Susan B. Anthony also eagerly adopted "bloomers" as symbolic of their efforts to liberate women from the larger subjugation they faced in society. However, opponents of women's rights and of dress reform mocked and assaulted women who appeared in public dressed in bloomers, deriding them as "mannish" women. These insults, combined with pressure from peers who objected to the negative publicity generated by the outfit, eventually forced most women's rights reformers to capitulate and abandon the attire in order to focus solely on the goal of women's suffrage. But others, like Walker, continued to advocate for a radical restructuring of societal gender norms beyond simply winning the vote.[6]

Walker was arrested many times for her queer appearance. In the early years, she wore a short dress over pants. Gradually she transitioned simply to wearing pants and a man's coat. She cut her hair short in the fashion of men of the era. Critics disparaged her as a "she-man," a "man-hater," and an "Amazon." Her gender, sexuality, and sanity were all called into question. Despite personal attacks on her womanhood, repeated arrests, and physical assaults, she refused to conform to preconceived views of how a woman should look, insisting: "I don't wear men's clothes, I wear my own clothes."[7] Walker's fame as a reformer, her whiteness, and her class status somewhat protected her from attempts to dismiss her as a sexual deviant. A police officer apologized profusely after her arrest in Baltimore in 1873, commenting that he did not know she was a prominent and famous doctor. Walker replied, "It should make no difference who I am. Any woman has the right to wear this costume."[8] But, Walker later admitted that this commitment took a toll on her emotionally:

> I have never seen the day when it was not a trial to me to appear in public in a reform dress. Every jeer has cut me to the quick. Many times have I gone to my room and wept after being publicly derided. No one knows, or will ever know, what it has cost me to live up to my principles, to be consistent with my convictions and declarations; but I have done it, and am not sorry for it.[9]

She continued to push back against gendered expectations of ideal femininity, often at great personal cost.

The most painful criticism, however, came not from outsiders but from those within the women's movement. In January 1873, Susan B. Anthony noted in her diary that Elizabeth Cady Stanton and Matilda Joslyn Gage were writing a report summarizing the recent national convention and that "Mrs. Stanton would not allow Dr. Walker's named to be mentioned in it." Anthony, who respected Walker, objected to no avail.[10] Years later they wrote the *History of Woman Suffrage*, documenting the movement through the lens of elite white womanhood and highlighting their role as powerful political leaders. They deliberately sought to conceal the queerness of the suffrage movement. Disdain for Walker, specifically, was evident throughout multiple volumes of the book. Walker's role was reduced to that of a minor player, stating simply that she had served in the Civil War as a volunteer physician. In another section, they reprinted Sarah Clarke Lippincott's (Grace Greenwood) biting description of Walker at the 1869 Woman's Suffrage Convention in Washington, DC, originally printed in the *Philadelphia Press*. Lippincott poked fun at Walker's "emancipated garments and Eve-like arrangement or disarrangement of hair."[11] Other suffragists proved even more cruel, attacking Walker in the press. Leila Crum Gardner published a February 1974 article:

There stalks about our city unmolested by the police a curious compound of flesh and blood which has the appearance of being "neither man nor beast," but altogether ghoul. It is clad in pants cut like a man's, and a half-fitting basquine with a skirt reaching to the knee; a head of short curls is surmounted by a woman's hat. The wearer of the promiscuous dress is called Dr. Mary Walker.[12]

Suffrage leaders thus invalidated and dehumanized Walker, seeking to purge her from their movement.

More than forty years later, Walker had been completely ostracized. In 1913, Anna Howard Shaw, who was president of NAWSA at the time, fervently objected to Walker speaking alongside NAWSA suffragists in a Senate hearing. Shaw wrote to Alice Paul, who was heading NAWSA's Congressional Committee, to insist that Paul prevent Walker from speaking or Shaw would refuse to speak alongside her. Shaw explained that NAWSA had long since denied Walker's membership applications on account of her personal attacks on NAWSA leaders. She further noted that "we don't want our Hearing made ridiculous by her presence."[13] Shaw expressed concern that Walker would detract from their point and attract the full attention of the press with her eccentricities. Indeed, the press was enamored with Walker and spent a great deal of time describing her masculine clothing rather than reporting on the suffragists' points. Most people admired Walker's gumption, and she was famous around the country as a woman's rights advocate. But mainstream suffragists viewed queer suffragists like Walker as altogether too radical and tried to silence them, publicly disassociate themselves and their organizations from them, and erase them from their histories.

Queer suffragists who transgressed boundaries through their clothing, appearance, and behavior represented a challenge to suffrage leaders. Responding to criticism and seeking a broader base of support, major suffrage organizations increasingly sought to frame the women's suffrage movement within the confines of cisheteronormative respectability. The phrase "respectability politics," as articulated by historian Evelyn Brooks Higginbotham, has been used to describe the efforts of Black women leaders of this era to distance themselves from harmful and disreputable stereotypes by conforming, or at least appearing to conform, to white middle-class norms of femininity and domesticity.[14] Queer individuals

Figure 1.1. Dr. Mary Walker's gender non-conforming dress, advocacy of dress reform, and vocal critiques of suffrage leaders put her at odds with mainstream suffrage organizations. Walker, Dr. Mary [graphic]. [between 1873 and ca. 1916]. C. M. Bell, photographer. Library of Congress, Washington, DC.

have historically adopted similar strategies to gain some acceptance in society. Suffragists who outwardly conformed to white, middle-class norms of cisheterosexual femininity and domesticity found a much greater degree of acceptance and tolerance in the movement.[15] There was no organized movement of queer suffragists, nor was there a single unified position about how to express their queer genders and sexualities. Thus, while some vocally resisted and demanded immediate reform, others found ways to subtly resist by crafting separate public versus private lives.

Appearance definitely mattered and nobody understood this better than Dr. Reverend Anna Howard Shaw. Even as times changed and the "new woman" of the late nineteenth and early twentieth centuries began to adopt more modern styles of fashion that blurred the lines between men's and women's clothing, suffrage leaders believed that staying within the bounds of acceptable femininity helped keep the focus on the vote. As a member of NWSA, and later as president of NAWSA, Shaw had personally experienced attacks about her mannish clothing throughout her career. Biographer Trisha Franzen explained that Shaw kept her hair cropped short in her youth, no doubt earning her the nickname of "Annie boy" in college. But in her work as a preacher and public speaker on behalf of women's rights, Shaw began to learn the importance of cultivating "the 'feminine charm' of her public persona." Aggravated by the criticism about her mannish gender presentation, Shaw decided to grow her hair long and adopt a new fashion style that exuded a conservative professionalism. Still she could not entirely escape public opinion. When she visited the beach with a group of suffragists, a *New York World* reporter noted that their choice of bloomers for swimwear appeared rather masculine. The article mortified her.[16] This only solidified her philosophy that "no woman in public life can afford to make herself conspicuous by any eccentricity of dress or appearance. If she does so she suffers it herself, which may not disturb her, and to a greater or less degree she injures the cause she represents, which should disturb her very much."[17] Shaw suggested other suffragists similarly conform to accepted standards of femininity to avoid unnecessary criticism. But, this approach sacrificed some of the goals and marginalized the most radical voices in the women's rights movement.

Similarly, the queer relationships of many suffragists were hidden from public view and their lives straight-washed to appear to align with

Figure I.2. Anna Howard Shaw gradually abandoned the gender non-conforming style of her youth as she became more active in public life because she feared that it hurt the cause. Anna Howard Shaw, 1875. Box 1, Folder 1. Anna Howard Shaw Papers. Archives and Special Collections, Stockwell-Mudd Library, Albion College, Albion, Michigan.

accepted norms. Anna Howard Shaw was just one of many suffragists who had romantic relationships with other women. Lucy Elmina Anthony, Susan B. Anthony's niece, became Shaw's intimate companion. They wrote flirtatious love letters to each other and later moved in together. They remained committed to each other for more than thirty years. Lucy Anthony was at Shaw's bedside when she died and acted as executrix of her estate. Yet, their relationship was downplayed in public and Anthony was listed only as her secretary in Shaw's obituaries.[18]

Queer relationships were crucial to the history of the suffrage movement. Historians have speculated about the queer lives of suffrage leaders such as Susan B. Anthony and have documented the queer romantic partnerships of suffrage couples like Carrie Chapman Catt and Mary Garrett Hay, Frances Willard and Anna Adams Gordon, Alice Stone Blackwell and Kitty Blackwell, Jane Addams and Mary Rozet Smith, Sophonisba Breckinridge and Edith Abbott, and M. Carey Thomas and Mary Elizabeth Garret.[19] These queer relationships, typically referred to as Boston marriages, were ubiquitous in the suffrage ranks and essentially powered the movement. Because the lives of these leaders have been well-documented by biographers, I have chosen in this book to spotlight lesser-known queer suffragists. I believe this focus on the average suffragist especially highlights just how queer the suffrage movement really was.[20]

In part because these relationships between suffragists were so common, anti-suffragists pointed to examples of these unmarried and cohabiting women as evidence of the abnormality of suffragists and the dangers of independence for women. An anti-suffrage writer to the *Houston Post* attacked Anna Howard Shaw, claiming that she "has not known a woman's normal life and she is not competent to advise women who are wives and mothers . . . she has lived in the open under conditions usual to men."[21] Although these couples were very open about their relationships with other suffragists, each adopted their own strategy for navigating their personal and professional lives, often increasingly choosing over time to conceal their personal relationships from public view.

Black queer suffragists, who were tokenized, marginalized, or entirely shut out of mainstream suffrage movements, were especially concerned about presenting a respectable public image, not only to defend against sexism and homophobia but also to protect themselves against racist attacks. In the post-Reconstruction era, Black Americans witnessed the emergence of Jim Crow, disenfranchisement, and an increase of racialized violence against their communities. They advocated for their rights based on their multiple intersecting identities. Gendered and racialized stereotypes about Black women focused on their alleged criminality and sexual immorality. Black suffrage leaders therefore sought to highlight their cisheterosexual respectability to deflect criticism. Alice Dunbar Nelson worked as a speaker and organizer for the Congressional Union in the 1910s. Publicly, she cultivated an image as "Mrs. Paul Laurence Dunbar, widow of the famous poet." She used Dunbar's name for the status it afforded her as a married woman. Although she maintained this public face of respectable heterosexuality, privately, she engaged in romantic and sexual relationships with men and women throughout her single and married life (see chapter 2).[22]

The decision by many suffragists to obscure their private lives and to present a heteronormative public image was in part a reaction to suffragists who outright challenged normative heterosexuality and faced harsh backlash as a result. Victoria Woodhull was a well-respected and famous suffrage speaker in the NWSA and popular with mainstream leaders like Elizabeth Cady Stanton. However, she made quite a stir in the suffrage ranks as a result of her unconventional life and beliefs. Woodhull and her sister Tennessee Claflin established a brokerage firm on Wall Street and published their own radical newspapers advocating women's rights, spiritualism, and free love. Claflin's gender-defying behaviors such as wearing men's clothing and smoking cigars also earned the sisters notoriety. Woodhull married at age fourteen, divorced, and remarried. She scandalously lived in the same house with her ex-husband and new husband. Woodhull argued that marriage, as it had been traditionally construed, was a form of oppression for women, binding them economically and legally to men. Rejecting strict societal and governmental constraints that confined love and sex to traditional marriage, she asserted that individuals should be free to have sex, marry, divorce, or have children at their own choosing. She also argued that women should be taught about their bodies. Woodhull encouraged the expression of women's sexuality and disconnected sexual intercourse from reproduction, insisting that sex was an expression of love and was therefore natural and good. Critics accused her of advocating infidelity and polygamy in part because of a speech she gave in New York City in 1871 in which she articulated the more radical ideas of free love:

> Yes, I am a free lover. I have an inalienable, constitutional and natural right to love whom I may, to love as long or as short a period as I can; to change that love every day if I please.[23]

Although in later statements she advocated for largely monogamous heterosexual relationships, Woodhull's ideas were radical because she challenged the necessity of legal marriage and insisted on the right to love and divorce free of social ostracization. She also objected to the sexual double standard that punished and condemned women for extramarital affairs but largely ignored the adulterous relationships of men. Like many other suffragists of the era, Woodhull insisted on a single sexual standard that applied to both sexes. Elizabeth Cady Stanton and Susan B. Anthony therefore allied with Woodhull because they agreed that marriage, as it was legally construed at the time, oppressed women. The anti-suffrage reaction against Woodhull and the free love philosophy reflected fears that women's suffrage and women in powerful political positions would lead to the end of marriage and family life. They believed that suffragists like Woodhull would usher in an era of divorce and promiscuous lust.[24]

The publicity generated by Woodhull's public speeches, and especially by her decision to criticize a prominent clergyman for his adultery, led to a scandal that resulted in backlash against her and against the suffrage movement as a whole. Henry Ward Beecher was an eminent clergyman and suffragist who frequently railed against Woodhull and her "free love" philosophy in his sermons. In an effort to make her case against traditional marriage and highlight the hypocrisy of so-called respectable Christian men like Beecher who practiced free love in their own personal lives, Woodhull published a detailed account of Beecher's affair with a congregant named Elizabeth Tilton. Federal officials arrested and filed obscenity charges against Woodhull for sending the publication through the United States Postal Service. The story of the scandalous affair, its distribution by Woodhull, and the resulting obscenity trial proved an embarrassment to suffrage movement leaders. They had previously celebrated Woodhull as a champion of women's rights. But the backlash generated by the Beecher scandal and Woodhull's advocacy of free love led to increased criticism of suffragists as abnormal and dangerous sexual deviants. Anti-suffragists linked Woodhull and free love directly with the suffrage movement. Suffrage leaders feared that Woodhull's disreputable image would pull the whole movement down. Furious at the gossip circulating about her among suffragists, Woodhull threatened to expose details about the private sexual relations of some prominent women's rights advocates. Although still respected by suffragists like Stanton, others, including Anthony, argued for the need to distance their organization from Woodhull and begin repairing the damage to the suffrage movement's reputation. For years after this incident, however, suffragists continued to be associated with the idea of free love.[25]

In 1930, reflecting back on the history of the suffrage movement, Carrie Chapman Catt attempted to distinguish suffragists like Woodhull as the "lunatic fringe" of the movement. Using the term queer as it was used at the time to denote someone as odd or outside the norm, Catt insisted that "queer folk dropped into suffrage circles unceremoniously from time to time and no one knew from whence they came nor whither they were going, but when they were very queer, they never staid long. Eventually the door was opened and they were shown the way out."[26] Thus, Catt argued that these individuals were not like more respectable suffragists and were therefore ejected from the movement.

Partly in response to the negative publicity generated by controversial figures like Dr. Mary Edwards Walker and Victoria Woodhull, leaders of mainstream suffrage organizations sought to publicly counter anti-suffrage accusations that women suffragists were sexually deviant free lovers or "mannish," "man-hating," and "abnormal" women by staging public performances of white middle-class gender normativity and heterosexual domesticity.[27] Although this embrace of respectability politics was somewhat effective in helping gain public support for women's right to vote, these performances concealed from public view suffragists who deviated from the accepted norm.[28] This resulted in greater policing of suffragist behavior as leaders promoted conformity to gendered views of acceptable appearance and behavior. The problematic effect was to hide the movement's queerness and reinforce a patriarchal, cisheteronormative standard of ideal womanhood and manhood in order to make suffragists and women's suffrage more palatable to voters. But, queerness and queer suffragists were central to the history of the women's suffrage movement.

The remainder of this book is organized thematically and covers a period of time from roughly the late nineteenth century up to the ratification of the Nineteenth Amendment in 1920. Chapter 1 examines how anti-suffragists framed suffragists as sexual and gender deviants who were dangerous to society. These depictions of suffragists as mannish women and feminine men prompted suffrage leaders to create a counter propaganda campaign to recast suffragists as womanly women and manly men. This strategy helped normalize suffragists in the popular imagination and win support from a mainstream audience often at the expense of the queer suffragists in the movement.

Beginning with chapter 2, the focus shifts primarily to the stories of the private lives of individual suffragists. This is especially crucial to the goal of recovering the life stories of previously marginalized queer suffragists. Chapter 2 highlights the various ways that suffragists queered concepts of heteronormative domesticity through their living arrangements. Suffragists established a diversity of queer domesticities ranging from spinster households to Boston marriages.

Chapter 3 examines how suffragists created queer chosen families and communities that nurtured and sustained them in their activism. These families provided crucial financial, medical, legal, and emotional love and support. Queer suffragists also created extended networks of like-minded individuals who protected and shielded one another from attacks from the outside world. These relationships fueled the suffrage movement.

Chapter 4 pulls back to consider a broader geographic perspective by examining how suffragists forged queer transatlantic alliances. American suffragists learned from and allied with British suffragists. Through their professional collaborations and personal romantic partnerships, queer suffragists built powerful coalitions that were crucial to propelling the global women's rights campaign forward. This often overlooked perspective allows for a broader understanding of the fluidity of individuals and ideas across borders and between suffrage movements. Women's friendships, romantic attachments, and intimate relationships played an important key role in the formation of these international coalitions.

Chapter 5 explores how suffragists found ways to come together outside of normative spaces to socialize, bond, and build community. This chapter illustrates how queer spaces served as sites for radical discussion and debate that deviated significantly from middle-class norms and allowed greater freedom for suffragists to express their gender and sexuality. This chapter also considers how suffragists transformed public sites—some of which were spaces formerly used to marginalize, restrain, or control them—into sites of queer resistance.

Chapter 6 examines how suffragists queered traditional death rituals and enacted queer modes of grieving. Death rituals not only functioned to allow the bereaved to move through their grief, but also, in some cases, served as significant acts of resistance through the public declaration of queer love. Public mourning and commemoration practices took on especially significant meanings for suffragists who lived nonnormative lives. By exploring how suffragists concealed, memorialized, and/or codified their queer relationships in death, we can come to a better understanding not only of the significance of queerness in the suffrage movement but of how that queerness was remembered.

The concluding chapter examines the historical processes that have led to the erasure of queerness in the history of the suffrage movement and the consequences of that erasure. Here I turn to a discussion of the strategies used to interpret the archival silences and read between the lines of historic documents in order to begin the process of recovery. This chapter concludes by offering reflections on the overall significance of the queer history of the suffrage movement and the necessity of continuing the work of resurrecting the life stories of queer suffragists.

In many ways, the suffrage movement was remarkably inclusive—providing sanctuary to individuals reflecting a wide range of gender expressions, gender identities, and sexualities while fostering the formation of a variety of queer relationships. But queer suffragists had to develop complex strategies for survival in a movement concerned with public image and focused solely on one goal. By strategically embracing selective aspects of respectability politics, queer suffragists created innovative strategies to allow them to remain active in the movement while preserving and protecting their most intimate relationships from public scrutiny. However, this masked life had significant long-term implications for individuals and movements for generations to come.

1

Mannish Women and Feminine Men

In the campaign for the vote, suffragists sought to win the support of Congress and President Woodrow Wilson. But Wilson initially refused to support a federal women's suffrage amendment. Wilson confessed his concerns to a friend: "Suffrage for women will make absolutely no change in politics—it is the home that will be disastrously affected." He further expanded on his theory by resurrecting the archaic notion of separate spheres: "Somebody has to make the home and who is going to do it if the women don't?"[1]

The passage of a federal women's suffrage amendment met with direct opposition from anti-suffragists who, like Wilson, feared the effects of granting women the right to vote. In the minds of many Americans, women's political empowerment threatened to upend existing gender norms and destroy the family. The nineteenth-century concept of separate spheres suggested that a woman's ideal place was in the domestic sphere where she held significant responsibilities as wife, mother, and guardian of the home and family. She was expected to embody the traits of true womanhood through purity, piety, domesticity, and submissiveness while creating a model Christian household. The home was supposed to provide a haven from the harsh realities of the outside world. Men, in contrast, occupied the public sphere, economically supporting the family while also navigating the dangers of the cities. Men were expected to embody the traits of moral courage, physical strength, and chivalry. This notion of separate spheres, however, was only ever an ideal rather than a strict reality. Most families, and working-class families in particular, rarely adhered to this middle-class vision of domesticity. Nevertheless, the idea of separate spheres held great influence in the popular imagination.[2]

Anti-suffragists blamed the suffrage movement for disrupting the so-called natural order. They pointed to allegedly increasing rates of divorce, juvenile delinquency, and sexual immorality as evidence of the effects of women abandoning their duties in the domestic sphere to engage in politics in the public sphere. These beliefs were prevalent among the majority of the population, and some of the most educated and powerful individuals in society vocally expressed these ideas—including the president of the United States. Anti-suffragists propped up the menacing specter of mannish women and feminine men as the most extreme manifestations of the suffrage movement. In the minds of anti-suffragists, these gender and sexual deviants represented the vanguard of a new era that would destroy the heteronormative family. Suffrage leaders, seeking mainstream support for their movement, therefore created a counter-narrative to try to normalize suffragists and their demands for political equality without stepping too far outside the existing gendered construct. But this had consequences for the queer history of the suffrage movement.[3]

Mannish Women

Anti-suffragists constructed images of the woman suffragist as a mannish, abnormal aberration bent on disrupting the harmony of heterosexual domesticity. Advice books of the era recommended that respectable women avoid discussing and especially getting unduly excited about politics. They were not supposed to speak to strangers or call unnecessary attention to themselves in public. Women were also expected to wear conservative attire and to avoid extremes of fashion or eccentric styles.[4] Anti-suffragists pointed to the tactics adopted by some suffrage organizations as inappropriate for women. Public speeches, parades, and pickets were activities typically associated with men. They criticized suffragists' adoption of such tactics as unfeminine, even as they themselves ironically employed similar tactics to make their point. Anti-suffragists pointed to real-life examples of gender non-conforming suffragists who cut their hair short or dressed in "masculine" clothing as evidence that women who desired the vote were "unnatural."[5]

The specter of the "abnormal mannish" woman thus haunted suffragists. As discussed in the introduction, Dr. Mary Edwards Walker's career as a dress reformer subjected her to repeated attacks that not only criticized her commitment to dress reform, but attacked her womanliness and sexuality. Anti-suffragists caricatured Walker as the quintessential mannish suffragist.[6] Although Walker was a woman, anti-suffrage attacks against her focused on her gender presentation, accusing her of wanting to be a man. Subsequent anti-suffrage imagery appeared to caricature the caricatures of Walker. Even in the early twentieth century, when women enjoyed more freedom in blurring the boundaries between men's and women's fashions, the characterization of suffragists as mannish was still employed to imply gender deviancy. Concern about gender and sexual deviance was apparent in postcard images of suffragists. One postcard warned young women not to become mannish or they would never find a man to marry:

MISS MANNISH
Do you suppose that mannish clothes
And Turkish cigarette
Make you a prize in young men's eyes?
No, no, not soon, nor yet!
Leave all such joys to college boys
Get girlish, or too late
You'll find that men choose girl girls when
They're looking for a mate.[7]

Another postcard explicitly expressed the fear of lesbianism as a direct outcome of suffrage. The depiction of two women kissing included the caption "I don't like to see a woman do a man's work."[8]

Emerging theories about "sexual inversion" influenced the creation of these images. Sexologists such as Richard von Krafft-Ebing and Havelock Ellis conflated gender and sexuality by categorizing both women who dressed in clothing that was considered "men's attire" and women who exhibited a sexual desire for other women as "sexual inverts." Many of these sexologists sought to destigmatize sexual inversion by describing gender and sexual variation as common. Others, like Edward Carpenter and Magnus Hirschfeld, openly advocated for acceptance of gender and sexual diversity. But in most medical discourse and in the popular interpretation of the sexologists' writings, sexual inversion was generally viewed as a congenital defect or an abnormal psychological development that required diagnosis and treatment. White, middle-

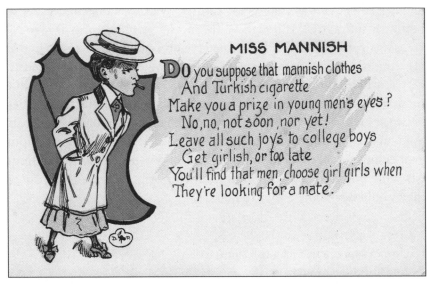

Figure 1.1. Postcards depicted suffragists as "mannish" women and, conflating gender with sexuality, suggested that suffragists were also sexually abnormal women. "Miss Mannish." Chicago: H.G. Zimmerman & Co. Date unknown. Catherine Palczewski Suffrage Postcard Archive, University of Northern Iowa, Cedar Falls, Iowa.

class, cisgender, and heterosexual bodies were depicted as the norm, and bodies that deviated from that norm were pathologically disordered.[9]

The focus on the physical appearance of suffragists then was associated with this shift to a medical model that defined sexual inversion as a biological defect. Doctors subjected women's bodies, and especially the bodies of queer women and women of color, to meticulous inspection in an attempt to classify them as either normal or abnormal. Relying on evolutionary theories and racial hierarchies rooted in scientific racism, doctors sought to identify alleged common biological anomalies in non-white and non-cisheterosexual women. To these theorists, abnormal markers allegedly signified evolutionary inferiority but also degeneracy and pathology. The scrutiny of the physical bodies of suffragists then was an attempt to diagnose them based on the extent of their deviation from the appearances of so-called normal women.[10]

Several sexologists were more straightforward in suggesting a direct association between sexual inversion and the suffrage movement. In his writings, Havelock Ellis made a correlation between women's growing emancipation and allegedly increasing rates of sexual inversion. Ellis, however, was not arguing that feminism directly caused sexual inversion. Instead, he believed that sexual inversion was a congenital anomaly associated with women of high intelligence and that these educated women, many of whom were active in women's rights campaigns, might influence other women toward lesbianism.[11]

This purported association between sexual inversion and suffrage was made more explicitly clear and was more directly condemned in the writings of other sexologists. Physician William Lee Howard wrote extensively on the topic. In several articles and in his 1901 book, *The Perverts*, he argued that the "female possessed of masculine ideas of independence," the woman who demands higher education and freedom for women, and "the female sexual pervert" are all "degenerates." Howard took it a step further, arguing that the progeny of the "new woman" would be "human misfits"—effeminate men and masculine women.[12] Sexologists like Howard argued that suffragists and women who desired equality in education and the professions were biologically abnormal. These assertions therefore justified gender inequality based on biological determinism and contributed to the continued subjugation of women.

Sigmund Freud's theories, emphasizing parental influence and environmental factors in shaping development, cast even more suspicion on suffrage as a cause of sexual inversion. Freud's belief in acquired homosexuality contributed to existing fears about all-women environments and social movements. The popularization and dissemination of Freud's theories among both scholars and non-scholars led to further scrutiny of feminists. Medical professionals thus often diagnosed suffragists as deviant, mentally disturbed, or suffering from gender confusion resulting from their desire to be men. The implication was that normal women did not behave in this way and therefore women who desired equality with men were not normal.[13]

Anti-suffragists adopted these so-called scientific arguments associating suffrage with sexual inversion to condemn the women's suffrage movement. Religious beliefs added further credence to the suggestion that suffragists were unnatural or ungodly abominations. In 1915, the Pennsylvania Association Opposed to Woman Suffrage quoted the Rev. Lyman Abbott: "If man attempts woman's functions, he will prove himself but an inferior woman. If woman attempts man's functions, she will prove herself an inferior man. Some masculine women there are; some feminine men there are. These are the monstrosities of Nature."[14] This quote was widely distributed by the organization through paid ads featured in several Pennsylvania newspapers.

These attacks were especially harmful to Black suffragists who faced racialized constructions of Black women as sexual deviants. Anti-suffragists criticized Mary Church Terrell and other Black suffragists by attacking their femininity. Both Black and white anti-suffragists attacked Black suffragists as mannish and sometimes derogatorily referred to suffragists as men. But, white critics based their depictions of Black suffragists on racist stereotypes of Black women as hypersexual and criminally deviant women. These stereotypes, intertwined with caricatures of suffragists as mannish, implied overall degeneracy.[15]

In addition to the criticism that suffragists faced for allegedly inverting gender and sexual norms, suffragists were often also described as entirely sexless. Individual suffrage leaders like Susan B. Anthony were derided as Amazons, hermaphrodites, and members of a third sex. These three phrases were used in association or interchangeably to suggest that suffragists were asexual women who had selfishly chosen to reject a life devoted to husband and home. With the expansion of the suffrage movement, critics increasingly applied these terms to the emancipated "new woman." A woman's choice to remain unmarried and/or childless reduced her to the status of a "desexualized neuter" representing a threat to the perpetuation of the human race.

An incendiary article in the 1918 *New York Times* defining the so-called third sex sparked widespread debate. William W. Gregg, a lawyer and eugenicist, decried suffrage as the cause of the increasing numbers of unmarried or childless white women in society. Gregg condemned these women as "subnormal" members of society. This third sex, he declared, stood in direct contrast with the "normal" woman who "meets her social obligations as child bearer and rearer and as home maker." He further chastised elite and educated couples who chose to not have children. Gregg also classed them as members of the third sex for failing to perpetuate the survival of the white race. Reiterating the common arguments about the dangers of women stepping outside the domestic sphere, he blamed the war, suffrage, and feminism. Gregg insisted that the "leaders of the various woman's movements almost always belong to this third sex" and thus

Figure 1.2. Postcards revealed underlying fears that suffrage would lead to homosexuality. "I Don't Like to See a Woman Do a Man's Work," The Dovie Horvitz Collection, The Gender and Women's Studies Collection, University of Wisconsin–Madison Digital Collections.

did not represent the interests of the average married woman. He blamed these women for fomenting antagonism between the sexes and convincing otherwise normal women to be dissatisfied with their status in society.[16]

Eleanor Kinsella McDonald, a suffragist and *New York Times* reader, responded with a retort that illustrates the strategies that suffragists had adopted to deflect these types of accusations. In a letter to the editor, McDonald suggested that Gregg educate himself on the history of the suffrage movement. She argued that the interests of the suffragists have always reflected the interests of married women. "Mrs. Stanton had seven happy children and Mrs. Mott six. Both were noteworthy house-keepers, and had devoted husbands." She went on to describe Susan B. Anthony's sacrifices of her "woman heart" and tireless devotion to the cause for the purpose of improving the lives of married women and chil-dren. This coupled with the image of Stanton and Anthony hard at work after "Stanton's children had been put to bed" helped prop up an image of suffragists as noble heterosexual or self-sacrificing unmarried women exuding motherly virtues. McDonald's strategy reflected what had be-come a common defensive tactic among suffragists.[17]

Feminine Men

Another common theme in anti-suffrage arguments was the implication that women's suffrage would entirely reverse existing gender roles, effec-tively emasculating men. Anti-suffragists feared that men would become weak and unmanly and the results would be devastating to society. Man-nish, overbearing suffragist mothers, sisters, or wives would browbeat their men into submission. In 1915, Mrs. Simeon H. Guilford, a member of the Pennsylvania Association Opposed to Woman Suffrage, argued: "We cannot have manly men unless we preserve womanly women—it is simply not in the nature of things. No real woman admires or respects an effeminate man, the more 'lady-like' he becomes, the more she despises him." Relying on the conclusions of Cesare Lombroso, an Italian crimi-nologist who linked the masculine woman with criminality and insanity, Guilford argued that the masculine suffragist was inherently defective, as was her "sissy" man counterpart.[18]

If suffrage emasculated men, then the most feminine of all men, ac-cording to the anti-suffragists, were the men who openly advocated for women's suffrage. Suffragists were described as "the mannish female politician and the little effeminate, sissy man."[19] The term "suffragent" was used to make fun of men who supported women's suffrage and it often appeared along with the derogatory term "suffragette" which was initially used to mock the militant suffragists in England but began to be more widely used to denigrate suffragists in the United States as well. Men and boys who marched in support of women's suffrage in New York City directly experienced the hostility of anti-suffragists. They were greeted with emasculating insults. Anti-suffrage hecklers shouted to the men: "Hold up your skirts, girls!" Rabbi Stephen Wise marched along with his ten-year-old son and other men and boys representing the Men's League for Woman Suffrage in the 1912 parade. Wise recalled encounters with an aggressive crowd who called the men names like "long-haired Susan" and sarcastically asked them, "Who's taking care of the baby?"[20]

In the rhetoric of anti-suffragists, pro-suffrage men represented the worst example of their sex. In 1909, anti-suffragist James Stubbs publicly attacked pro-suffragists including his son, Francis Gurney Stubbs, who was the husband of Chicago suffragist Jessie Belle Hardy Stubbs. In a letter to the Illinois Legislature James Stubbs called men like his son "male women" and "female men." He primarily blamed "childless, barren and motherless women and spinsters" for the suffrage agitation. But he specifically condemned men who supported women's suffrage as "sissy men" who were mere "half men" entirely subjugated by "henpecking," hiding their heads "under a petticoat." Stubbs declared that "the man who is not the head of his house and home is not worthy of one." Jessie Belle Hardy Stubbs dismissed the insults, declaring to reporters that her father-in-law was old and out of touch with new ideas while her husband represented the new generation of modern men who were ardent suffragists.[21]

But these types of gendered insults against men who supported women's suffrage did not entirely disappear over time. Eight years later, in February 1917, Representative Stanley Beard declared in a speech before the Texas House of Representatives that all men in favor of woman's suffrage were "sissies" and "willy-boys."[22] Derided as "she-men," "he-women," and "mollycoddles," men who supported suffrage faced assaults against their masculinity and their sexuality.

Womanly Women

Beginning in the late nineteenth century, the leaders of the women's suffrage movement recognized the necessity of countering anti-suffrage propaganda by staging public performances of middle-class gender normativity and heterosexual respectability. Local, state, and national suffrage organizations launched publicity campaigns that defensively sought to combat negative depictions of suffragists. Regardless of their own personal lives or their private views on the issues, they tried to refute accusations of mannishness and sexual abnormality.

Some suffragists attempted to deflect criticism by turning the stereotype of the mannish suffragist back on the anti-suffragists. Journalist and suffragist, Nixola Greeley-Smith, was a popular writer whose column appeared across the country in Joseph Pulitzer's newspapers. Greeley-Smith noted that the "manly and insistent" women were "found much more frequently among anti-suffragists." She further decried the anti-suffragist masculine woman, noting that such women opposed the ballot for women because the "man's soul we know she possesses clings naturally to its ancient prejudices, and the mere fact that Fate has lodged it in a feminine body cannot be expected to alter its point of view." The effect of this reversal was to demonize both the anti-suffragist for her failure to support the vote and gender non-conforming women for their failure to live up to a cisheteronormative ideal of feminine beauty.[23]

Leaders in mainstream suffrage organizations increasingly promoted conformity as part of their key strategy. Ella M. Sexton, a delegate from California and a member of the Pacific Coast Woman's Press Association, spoke out at the April 1913 Mississippi Valley Suffrage Conference in St. Louis. Sexton encouraged suffragists to: "Be as attractive, as charming and as lovable as you possibly can. That is the way to win equal suffrage from men." Mrs. Sexton further stated:

> The fear of man when equal suffrage was first proposed was that it would turn his women folk into bifurcated females. Something strenuous in talk and unlovely to look on . . . Taste in dress, charm in manner, a lovable disposition, all the thousand and one little methods of making herself attractive that woman has at her command should be used, not only as a means to gain suffrage but to help in correcting man's wrong impression.[24]

Suffragists like Sexton believed that feminine clothing and behavioral codes of conduct would win support for the vote. Although they rarely formally imposed a written dress or conduct code, suffrage organizations highly recommended appropriate attire and behavior. They applied social pressure to ensure conformity among their membership.[25]

Because phrases such as "mannish" or "masculine" suggested both gender deviancy and lesbianism, suffragists hoped that fashionable feminine apparel would counter concerns about their femininity and sexuality. In 1912, a writer for the *Pittsburgh Post* interviewed a group of suffragists who gave a series of suffrage speeches to an unsuspecting audience at the Grand Opera House. Accompanying illustrations depicted the elegant gowns worn by the women. A young suffragist explained that "we have got to stop those caricaturists from picturing us suffragists as 'frumps.'" The reporter noted that the "stylish gowns, very feminine" that were worn by suffragists were intended to "prove they are not 'Frumps' and also that they are not tending toward masculinity."[26] The new public image suffragists created assured viewers of the femininity and therefore implied heterosexuality of suffrage women.

Alva Vanderbilt Belmont, the wealthy benefactor of the New York suffrage campaign, was especially concerned about appearances. Belmont established a Department of Hygiene within the building she purchased to serve as the headquarters of the New York Political Equality Association in 1911. Belmont wrote that the purpose of the Department of Hygiene was to teach "women (particularly working women) how to care for their health."[27] Women doctors were enlisted to provide consultations and lectures for specific topics related to women's physical health. But the newspapers described this as an effort to make over suffragists as a way to make them look more feminine. The Department of Hygiene sold various cosmetics and toiletries such as soap, skin cream, toothpaste, powders, and hair tonics. Journalists dubbed it a "beauty shop for suffragists." One journalist snidely commented that the "clearer the complexions, the niftier the clothes, the smarter the personalities of the 'getties,' the sooner the victory."[28]

Not all suffragists supported this extreme attempt to make over their image. Several of the women physicians who had initially agreed to volunteer their services to provide health lectures balked at the idea of a "suffragist beauty shop." Following the press coverage announcing Belmont's Department of Hygiene, some of the women doctors recorded their objection. Dr. Mary Crawford noted that "our agreement merely to give scientific health talks to the girls once a week has been violated . . . I most decidedly object to having my name exploited in connection with a 'beauty parlor.'"[29] Despite these concerns, Belmont carried on with her plan, ignoring the women doctors and instead expressing frustration with the negative press coverage. The Department of Hygiene continued to sponsor a weekly advice column in the *New York World Magazine* offering health and beauty tips. Suffragist Mary Donnelly resigned from her position at the suffrage headquarters, insisting that "every woman ought to try to be as beautiful as she can . . . But I'm for suffrage first, last and all the time, and when it comes to suffrage being swamped in face creams I'm done."[30]

Although they disagreed on the best tactics to win the vote, the leaders of major national organizations agreed on the importance of public perception. Suffragists in these organizations transgressed normative bounds of acceptable womanly behavior through their political tactics. Yet, they insisted that the suffragists in their ranks try to present an appearance of cisheterosexual femininity. The National American Woman Suffrage Association (NAWSA), the National Association of Colored Women (NACW), and the National Woman's Party (NWP) all developed public relations campaigns to promote a favorable image of suffragists that appealed to a wide audience. As a whole, they highlighted images of attractive, young, affluent suffragists and positioned the prominent wives and mothers in the forefront of the movement to rally public interest and support for women's suffrage. NAWSA emphasized a feminine and maternal image of suffragists that focused specifically on upper- and middle-class white women. The NACW adopted a similar approach while also attempting to fight deeply embedded sexist and racist views of Black women by cultivating an image of Black suffragists as educated and worthy citizens who represented respectable wives and mothers. The NWP projected an image of a beautiful, youthful generation of feminine, heterosexual white suffragists who boldly intended to claim the same rights as men.[31]

Similar tactics had been deployed by suffrage organizations since the mid-nineteenth century. One early strategy was to defend the unmarried women in the movement from attacks by lauding their virtues as womanly women. Susan B. Anthony wrote a speech in 1877 describing the "Homes of Single Women." In response to suggestions that spinsters were unnatural women with no home instincts, Anthony argued that unmarried women tended to their homes just as meticulously as did married women. More radically, Anthony argued that the single suffragist was not creating a home for a man, but for herself. Although the unmarried suffragist had committed her life to reform work to benefit others, this sacrifice was made without sacrificing her womanliness. Anthony hoped to counteract negative caricatures of the mannish unnatural suffragist by declaring that even the unmarried woman was a womanly woman. Over time, however, suffrage leaders shifted tactics, focusing less publicly on the spinsters in the movement and instead emphasizing the married (or soon to be) wives and mothers in their organizations.[32]

Suffragists relied on the image of motherhood and used a maternalist argument to justify their right to the vote. Lucy Stone's suffragist newspaper *Woman's Journal* consistently praised "womanly" women and offered examples of exemplary womanliness to refute popular assumptions of mannish suffragists. This framing of womanhood was fairly consistent throughout the nineteenth century until the early twentieth century, when suffragists began to use more visual imagery to make their point. Praising the mothers in the movement, the *Woman's Journal* began to feature photographs of suffragists surrounded by their children.[33] They used this rhetoric of motherhood and womanliness to argue that a woman's natural tendency to nurture and protect her children would enable her to become a mother to all by advocating for laws to nurture and protect all children. Suffragists therefore rationalized women's political involvement by insisting that they would serve as social housekeepers—extending their sphere of influence beyond the home to help clean up the problems in society. They stated that they did not want to disrupt existing gender norms but only to expand women's maternal influence so that they could become better wives and mothers.[34]

By the early twentieth century, the central point of all of the publicity campaigns crafted by suffrage organizations promised that the vote would not turn women against men, marriage, or motherhood. This was the main theme in most of the pro-suffrage rhetoric and was picked up by journalists who were supportive of the cause. In 1913, a suffrage-supporting writer for the *Denver Post* promised that suffragists would continue to fulfill their maternal duties:

> To those people who loudly argue that suffrage is only for the masculine female and does not interest the home-loving woman there will be nothing consoling in the statement of Mrs. Edward F. Dunne of Illinois. Mrs. Dunne is the mother of 13 children. She is also the wife of Governor Dunne who signed the Illinois suffrage statue . . . the mannish suffragist exists only in the imagination of those who fight the reform.[35]

The writer sought to counter the negative stereotype of the abnormal, mannish suffragist by emphasizing the heteronormativity of suffragists like Dunne. Images of babies helped solidify the theme. Suffragists sometimes literally paraded their commitment to heteronormative domesticity. The 1915 New York suffrage parade included wagons of babies to show that suffragists were devoted mothers.[36]

Even on the picket line, suffragists highlighted their maternal domesticity and cishetereosexuality. The women of the Congressional Union (CU), later the NWP, invited public censure by engaging in public protests and pickets of President Woodrow Wilson. Beginning in January 1916, the CU initiated a picket at the White House gates. Suffragists stationed as "silent sentinels" held banners calling out Wilson for hypocrisy and demanding his support of a federal suffrage amendment. Montana suffragist Hazel Hunkins's correspondence with her mother reveals the ways that militant suffragists were redefining appropriate feminine behavior. Anne Hunkins objected to her daughters' unfeminine behavior, disparaging her suffragist friends as radical "short haired women and long haired men."[37] But Hunkins and other suffragists recognized the importance of presenting a cisheteronormative face especially before the press. Hunkins noted that an anti-suffragist approached the pickets commenting, "Why, they don't look so bad" and asked them directly if they were "man-haters." One of the women retorted: "some of us are married and I have two children."[38] Suffragists were challenging gendered notions of acceptable feminine behavior at the same time that they were attempting to demonstrate their conformity to existing gendered norms to demand their right to the vote.

The image of suffragists marketed by NAWSA, NWP, and their state affiliate organizations was also notably and explicitly white. Suffrage organizations highlighted white women in their promotional efforts to assuage the anxieties of white men voters and attract the allegiance of white women. Suffrage organizations purposefully ignored the concerns of Black suffragists, Indigenous women, and women of color. At other times, suffrage organizations tokenized these women. Major suffrage organizations selected a few, beautiful and feminine, Asian, Indigenous, or Black suffragists as so-called exemplars of their race to highlight and exoticize in their parades (see chapter 5). More commonly, however, suffragist publicity directors pitched stories that focused exclusively on attractive, affluent white suffragists. Inez Milholland, the white attorney and suffragist who led the 1913 Washington, DC suffrage march on horseback, became a symbol of the movement. The physical positioning of Milholland and white suffragists at the head of the 1913 parade, combined with the racist request that Black suffragists be denied the right to march or be segregated in the parade, reflected the efforts of suffragists to whitewash the movement. The press often emphasized Milholland's whiteness, lauding her as the most beautiful suffragist.[39]

Leaders of the NACW launched their own publicity campaigns to counteract negative depictions of Black suffragists. At the same time that they were organizing against the disenfranchisement of Black men and fighting Jim Crow laws and racialized violence against their communities, Black women also demanded their own right to the franchise. They recognized the importance of highlighting the respectability of Black suffragists as essential not only to combatting sexist depictions of suffragists but to countering racist perceptions of Black women as hypersexualized and deviant women.

In 1895, a general call for a national convention of Black club women followed the publication of an inflammatory letter written by a Southern white man attacking the sexual morality of Black women. John Jacks, president of the Missouri Press Association, penned a letter to Florence Balgarnie, Secretary of the Anti-Lynching League of London, that slandered Black people in the United States as "wholly devoid of morality" and Black women as "prostitutes" and "natural liars and thieves."[40] In response, Josephine St. Pierre Ruffin and the Woman's Era Club of

Boston organized the First National Conference of Colored Women in America to meet in July 1895. Delegates representing the leaders of Black women's clubs from all over the country gathered in Boston to condemn the Jacks letter and mobilize for concerted action. Each organization recorded its outrage. Their letters and resolutions cited evidence of respectable femininity and heterosexual domesticity in their defense of Black womanhood. John Albert Williams, rector of the Church of St. Philip in Omaha, Nebraska reflected the common sentiment of the delegates when he wrote: "What vindication needs Negro womanhood? Look at our happy and virtuous homes. If our womanhood is depraved by what miracle are our homes preserved?"[41] The Boston convention led to the formal creation of the NACW the following year in Washington, DC. The organization formalized its goals and declared its purpose: "the elevation of the race, the ennobling of womanhood, and the concentrated effort toward improving the standard of home life among the masses."[42] The NACW promoted strategies of racial uplift by advocating for education, job training, and domestic skills courses. They created an image of Black suffragists as sexually restrained, moral, and educated community leaders.[43]

As the editor of *The Woman's Era* (1894–1897), the first national newspaper for Black women, Josephine St. Pierre Ruffin published articles that promoted a positive public image of the lives and work of Black women. The magazine included a feature called "Eminent Women" that highlighted prominent Black women intellectuals and reformers. *The Woman's Era* also published recurring columns on "domestic science" that emphasized the significance of women's role in the home as wives and mothers and focused on educating women on the so-called proper way to care for their family and homes. Features on "social etiquette" and "health and beauty" stressed the necessity of cultivating refined habits and beautiful appearances. Clothing also mattered. In 1914, the NACW passed a resolution at their annual convention urging young women to "refrain from indulging in . . . extreme and extravagant display of finery." Rather than follow "the extremes of fashion" that "invite criticism upon their moral integrity," young Black women were urged to "adopt a more sensible and more modest attire that will be indicative of true womanhood."[44] Thus, fashion could deflect criticisms about Black suffragists' sexual morality.

Emphasizing the womanliness, and implied cisheterosexuality, of Black suffragists was just as important as emphasizing their middle-class status. In February 1900, the *Colored American*, a Black newspaper based in Washington, DC, reported on the annual national women's suffrage convention. The author decried the mannishness of a previous generation of suffragists:

> There is nothing about the woman suffragist today to remind one of the agitator of a quarter of a century ago. The mannishly attired, short skirted, short haired woman, who, for so many years, was the butt of the satirist and the cartoonist, has been shoved off of the board, and in her place stands the cultured, womanly woman of the twentieth century. In her dress she keeps pace with fashion. She is in many instances a mother, and she boasts of it and the home which she ennobles.[45]

The author emphasized the cisheteronormative ideal of femininity and pointed to the purging of queer women from the suffrage movement as a good thing. Mary Church Terrell, speaking on behalf of the NACW and Black suffragists, embodied these ideals. The writer praised her as "the premier representative of our womanhood." Terrell's speech was not only "scholarly and logically put" but "was delivered with that ease and grace of bearing, that ineffable charm and magnetism of manner, and dignity and force that are characteristic of all Mrs. Terrell does or says."[46] Thus, Black suffragists, like Terrell, were expected to rise above the rest by exhibiting beauty, charm, and womanliness. Black suffrage leaders believed this was essential to combatting sexist and racist stereotypes. More conservative Black suffragists therefore objected to radical suffrage tactics for fear they reflected a masculinized image of suffragists as a whole. Margaret Murray Washington, a founder and president of the National Association of Colored Women (NACW), specifically objected to Black women "parading the streets in men's attire" to win the vote.[47] These criticisms reflected concerns about presenting a respectable image of Black womanhood.

Evelyn Brooks Higginbotham's notion of the "politics of respectability" and Darlene Clark Hine's idea of "cultural dissemblance" are useful in understanding the strategies that suffragists, and especially Black suffragists, employed in making their movements more acceptable to the mainstream. Higginbotham used the phrase "politics of respectability"

to describe the strategies that Black women in this era used to build political power and resist racial injustice. These strategies included sometimes playing into a white middle-class conception of appearance and
behavior. Hine emphasized how the "culture of dissemblance" among
Black women who concealed their innermost thoughts and feelings from
public view protected them somewhat from public criticism of their sexuality and physical assaults on their persons.[48] However, Brittney Cooper warned against an oversimplified analysis of respectability politics
and the culture of dissemblance by demonstrating how Black suffragists
simultaneously conformed to and challenged these very notions in their
writings, speeches, and actions. In the 1910s, for example, Mary Church
Terrell was the first president of the NACW; she promoted uplift strategies as a means of countering critics and combating both sexism and
racism. But, Cooper argues that over time Terrell increasingly embraced
a strategy of "dignified agitation" transcending the limits of respectability politics. This approach required a sustained and unrelenting challenge to violations of rights. While the NACW focused on racial uplift
projects like raising money for schools and settlement houses, they also
called attention to and vociferously demanded an end to segregation
and lynching. Thus, they were fighting a multi-front war against sexism
and racism that extended well beyond simply winning the vote. More
recently, scholars such as Martha S. Jones and Allison M. Parker have
highlighted how Black suffragists understood the complexities of the in-
tersectionality of race, class, and gender in their women's fight for justice
and engaged in militant civil rights activism throughout their lives.[49]

Manly Men

Just as suffrage leaders recognized the necessity of promoting suffragists as "womanly women," they likewise believed in the importance of
portraying men who advocated for women's suffrage as "manly men."
Minnie J. Reynolds of Utah, speaking in front of the Pennsylvania state
legislature in 1911, declared that the men who supported women's suffrage were "neither sissies nor fools."[50] Manliness as defined in the late
nineteenth and early twentieth centuries embodied chivalry, moral character, and physical strength.[51] Women suffragists, like Reynolds, relied
on this definition of manliness to laud men who supported suffrage as

exemplary, manly men who represented the true gentlemanly virtues of chivalry and moral character.

In 1914, Dr. Frederick Peterson, a professor at Columbia University, similarly constructed a cisheteronormative defense of suffrage by defending women suffragists against charges of mannishness and pro-suffrage men against charges of effeminacy. Peterson was responding to an article in the *New York Times* about William T. Sedgwick, a biologist at the Massachusetts Institute of Technology. Sedgwick had argued that:

> It is not surprising that it seems to be these very masculine women, these mistakes of nature, aided and abetted by their counterparts, the feminine men, who are largely responsible for the feminist movement.[52]

Sedgewick further argued that it was these "half-women" who achieved leadership in the movement and exerted their influence over "normal women." Although others predicted the total destruction of the family and an embrace of "free love" or "universal polygamy," Sedgwick optimistically believed that man would suppress the rebellion and "firmly shut down . . . feminist activities, and, putting the women back in their homes, say: 'That is where you belong. Now stay there.'"[53]

Sedgwick's archaic view of the relations of men and women and caricature of the feminist movement elicited outrage from suffragists. They responded with a flurry of letters to the *New York Times*. Peterson offered a forceful and direct retort to Sedgwick in an article, "Woman's Uplift Means Man's Uplift." He argued that suffragists sought not the destruction of the family but the protection of the family. He argued that the use of the derisive term "masculine women" was "an affront to the great body of able and dignified women who are supporting this movement." More personally, Peterson insisted that the "feminine men" who supported votes for women "need not be ashamed" since they could console themselves that they were in the company of great philosophers and leaders such as Plato, William Garrison, and Abraham Lincoln. "If these are types of 'feminine men,' we may rest content to wear the label."[54] Thus, Peterson reframed the image of suffragist men by placing them alongside educated and morally virtuous men in history. The NAWSA later reproduced and widely redistributed Peterson's article under the new title "Normal Women Not Neurotic."[55]

Men who supported women's suffrage developed a number of strategies for deflecting attacks against their manhood. Max Eastman, founder of the Men's League for Women's Suffrage in New York, insisted that he was secure enough in his manhood that he did not feel the need to assert it. "I am not such a sissy that I dare not champion the rights of women."[56] Thus, he inverted the arguments used against men who supported women's suffrage by implying instead that men who refused to support women's suffrage were the true sissies. Both anti-suffragists and suffragists then denigrated gender non-conforming and homosexual men as not "real men."

Suffragists praised men and boys who publicly supported women's suffrage by calling them manly men. Men who marched in the 1913 suffrage parade in Washington, DC experienced violence and personal attacks on their manliness. As the parade progressed along its route, the crowd grew increasingly aggressive. Spectators pushed their way into the streets, nearly blocking the path of the floats and marchers. Anti-suffragists hurled insults at marchers. Suffragists of all ages were heckled, harassed, and physically assaulted by the angry spectators. A group of young men from the Maryland Agricultural College tried to help quell the crowd and allow the marchers to proceed unimpeded. Approximately 1,500 Boy Scouts had volunteered to keep the path open during the suffrage parade. Stationed along the route, they used their staffs to push the crowd back. They also administered first aid to the injured suffragists. These boys and young men soon found themselves caught in violent encounters with an unruly mob. Eventually the Boy Scouts called for help from the federal government. The Pennsylvania and Massachusetts National Guard and a cavalry troop stepped in to clear a path for the suffragists. The organizing committee of the parade leveraged the press reports of the violence to draw public attention to the plight of women and the issue of suffrage. They demanded a congressional investigation into the inaction of the police. The NAWSA made heroes of the boys who participated in the parade, distinguishing them as models of ideal masculinity. The suffragists ordered bronze medals for each Boy Scout who participated in the event and insisted that they be formally honored for their efforts in protecting the marchers from the violent crowd.[57]

Black men who supported women's suffrage endured gendered and racialized assaults from anti-suffragists. White suffragists were little better. They made problematic statements that relied on white constructions of manhood to praise Black men who advocated for suffrage. Following the chaos of the 1913 parade in Washington, DC, women suffragists testified to the violence they endured from white anti-suffrage men. A white woman suffragist remarked with some surprise (that revealed her own racialized views) that not one of the Black men along the parade route "was boisterous or rude." She contrasted Black men's behavior with the "insolent, bold white men," noting that the Black men were "quiet and respectable and earnest, and seemed sorry for the indignities which were incessantly heaped upon us . . . I thank them in the name of all women for their kindness."[58] She thus shamed white men who were supposed to be exemplars of the civilized race by contrasting their behavior to that of Black men.

The leaders of the National Association for the Advancement of Colored People (NAACP) also took the opportunity to construct an argument about race and manliness. They used the evidence of white men's violence against the suffragists at the 1913 parade to attack the manliness and so-called racial superiority of white men. W.E.B. Du Bois, the editor of NAACP's *The Crisis*, sarcastically called out white men for their conduct:

> Hail Columbia, Happy Land! Again the glorious traditions of Anglo-Saxon manhood have been upheld! Again the chivalry of American white men has been magnificently vindicated. Down on your knees, black men, and hear the tale with awestruck faces: Learn from the Superior Race.[59]

The article went on to quote a white newspaper's account of the insults and injuries inflicted on the suffragists by the white men in the crowd. Returning to his commentator, the editor sarcastically asked the reader:

> Wasn't it glorious? Does it not make you burn with shame to be a mere black man when such mighty deeds are done by the Leaders of Civilization? Does it not make you "ashamed of your race"? Does it not make you "want to be white"?[60]

Skewering white men for their lack of chivalry and their violent behavior, Du Bois directly attacked their manliness. To further prove his point about the unmanly and uncivilized behavior of white men and the manliness of Black men, the editor quoted white suffrage women who praised the behavior of the Black men at the parade. He concluded by critiquing white fears of the advancement of women. Black men who supported the franchise for women were thus heralded as manlier men.

Conclusion

Anti-suffrage campaigns to construct suffragists as mannish women or feminine men were intended to discredit the suffrage movement by implying gender deviance and sexual abnormality. The efforts of local, state, and national suffrage organizations to combat these negative depictions of suffragists had the effect of creating a counter-narrative of women suffragists as feminine wives and mothers and manly men. White suffragists especially racialized this narrative to promote an image of suffragists as affluent, educated white womanly women. Black suffragists fought against both sexist and racist depictions by promoting their own images of cisheteronormative womanhood and manhood.

This emphasis on binary gender and sexual norms marginalized queer suffragists and, in many ways, erased the queerness of the suffrage movement. In the 1930s, queer Black civil rights activist Pauli Murray coined the term Jane Crow to critique a racist, cissexist, and homophobic system that favored the public presentation of a white, heteronormative definition of respectability. Those who did not conform were isolated and ostracized.[61] We can see the clear roots of Jane Crow in the suffrage movement. This concept, along with historian Brittney Cooper's concept of "dignified agitation," is helpful in informing an analysis of the ways in which queer suffragists, and especially Black queer suffragists and suffragists of color, resisted Jane Crow and negotiated the boundaries between conforming to and transgressing gender and sexual norms. The remainder of this book will attempt to reconstruct the queer history of the suffrage movement through an examination of the lives of individual suffragists and an exploration of the complicated strategies they developed to navigate their public and private lives.

2

Queering Domesticity

National American Woman Suffrage Association (NAWSA) president Carrie Chapman Catt presented a public front of heterosexual respectability. But, her private domestic arrangement was very queer. Catt had been twice married to men before her long-term committed relationship with Mary (Mollie) Garrett Hay. Catt and her second husband had agreed to a marital arrangement that freed her to pursue her suffrage work. She spent many months of the year traveling and working for the cause. During the summer of 1895, Hay moved in with Catt while her husband was away on business. The two women continued to travel together in the years after, spending most of their time staying in the same room at hotels while campaigning for suffrage. After Catt's husband died in 1905, she moved in permanently with Hay. Catt continued to use the title Mrs. Catt in her public life because she believed that it enhanced her status and reputation. The public assumption of her heterosexuality thus shielded her from scrutiny into her private life and specifically her queer relationship with Hay.[1]

In this chapter, I will explore how suffragists like Catt and Hay disrupted normative concepts of heterosexual domesticity through their queer domestic arrangements. Historian Nayan Shah coined the concept of queer domesticity in his study of epidemics and race in San Francisco's Chinatown to refer to the "variety of erotic ties and social affiliations that counters normative expectations" disrupting "the strict gender roles, the firm divisions between public and private, and the implicit presumptions of self-sufficient economics and intimacy in the respectable domestic household."[2] Applying this definition to the history of the women's suffrage movement, I examine how suffragists queered white middle-class notions of respectable domesticity. Suffragists formed a variety of non-heteronormative domestic arrangements to suit their economic, emotional, and sexual needs. Shah's definition of queer domesticity was not limited exclusively to homosexual households. For purposes of this discussion, I will also take a broader view to consider how suffragists (queer or not) queered domesticity. Some suffragists, for example, rejected marriage, choosing to remain single and live the spinster life for personal and/or political convictions. They created queer homosocial domestic arrangements with other suffragists or lived entirely on their own. The itinerant nature of suffrage work also facilitated a variety of temporary queer domesticities. Other suffragists relied on presumptive heterosexuality and an appearance of normative domesticity as cover for their queer lives.

This chapter also highlights the significance of "Boston marriages." These relationships were particularly common queer domestic arrangements among suffragists. The term Boston marriage was coined in the late nineteenth and early twentieth centuries to describe a pairing between two women who formed a long-term, committed relationship with one another. These often simultaneously represented friendships, professional partnerships, creative collaborations, and lesbian romances. The history and significance of these relationships, especially among educated middle- and upper-class urban reformers, has been well-documented by historians.[3] Here, I will build on this existing scholarship to consider how suffragist couples in Boston marriages leveraged their class status and downplayed their perceived queerness to earn a degree of acceptance in mainstream society. I will also go beyond relatively well-known cases of elite suffragists to consider some lesser-known examples of Boston marriages and discuss those relationships within the context of the suffrage movement specifically.

Spinster Life

Suffragists who chose to live a spinster life queered domesticity by rejecting heterosexual marriage and forming alternate domestic arrangements. Chicago suffragist Viola Belle Squire challenged conventional views of marriage in 1913 when she declared to a *Chicago Tribune* reporter that she would rather have a vote than a husband. Squire criticized marriage because it reinforced heteropatriarchal hegemony. Suffragists, like Squire, who chose to remain single may have been motivated by a variety of complicated factors including coming to terms with their own sexuality. But publicly, they often framed these decisions within the context of the larger fight for women's equality.[4]

Choosing not to marry in this era was an especially radical act. However, it was an option open only to a few privileged women whose access to higher education and professional careers afforded them the economic independence to reject marriage. The "new woman" emerged in the 1890s. The next three decades saw a surge in the number of college-educated and career-oriented women. Whereas in 1890, women constituted only 35 percent of university students, by 1920, women made up 47 percent of the college population. This was an elite group of women, however, since only 8 percent of college-aged women were attending college in 1920. This generation also included more never married white women than any generation before or after it.[5] According to historian Trisha Franzen, this was essentially a "golden age for independent women."[6]

Anti-suffragists, however, attacked the "new woman" and the suffrage movement as threats to the traditional family. Suffragists who chose to eschew marriage and motherhood were therefore depicted as particularly deviant. The eugenics movement fueled anti-suffrage arguments by insisting that white women must ensure the perpetuation of the white race. Eugenicists worried that the increasing birthrates of immigrant and non-Anglo populations compared with the declining birthrates of the native-born Anglo population would lead to race suicide. Nativists further feared that the mingling of non-white people with white people threatened the purity and stability of the Anglo race. They therefore encouraged middle-class white women to procreate and do their part to strengthen the race.[7]

To anti-suffragists, then, spinsters represented the ultimate worst-case outcome of granting women the vote. They viewed women who chose not to marry or have children as a danger to society as a whole. But this was an old argument. Since the inception of the women's suffrage movement, suffragists had been scorned as man-hating spinsters. These cultural assaults on never-married suffragists reflected deeply ingrained anxieties that the vote would turn women away from men, marriage, and motherhood. Suffragists attempted to counter these attacks by arguing that the decision of single women to commit their lives to suffrage rather than to matrimony was the ultimate self-sacrifice. When this argument ceased to be effective, later suffrage leaders defensively propped up wives and mothers as the symbol of the suffrage movement.[8]

Thus, when Belle Squire announced her refusal to marry in 1913, she was both affirming anti-suffragists' perception of suffragists as spinsters and radically departing from the preferred message of heteronormative conformity touted by suffrage movement leaders. Squire eagerly embraced her identity as a spinster suffragist. But this deviated from the suffrage movement's new public relations campaign that focused on suffragists as happily married mothers. Her anti-marriage stance put her on the margins of the suffrage movement.

Squire launched her assault against marriage by pointing to married women's subordinated status. She noted that women had been brought up on the philosophy that it did not matter what they wanted from a potential mate. They were taught that all that mattered was what men wanted from women. Squire noted that little girls were trained to suppress their own desires and to be charming and demure in order to win a husband.[9] Women were therefore often trapped in unhappy, loveless marriages and were denied the right to pursue their passions.

Squire's attack on marriage may seem entirely in line with the growing acceptance of companionate marriage. This early twentieth-century view of marriage envisioned a more loving and egalitarian relationship between husband and wife.[10] But, Squire further queered convention by rejecting even companionate marriage and firmly expressing her intention to never marry on the grounds that women gained nothing from marriage. When a reporter asked if she would rather have a husband or a vote, she definitively insisted on the vote: "With a vote a woman's wages, dignity and position are raised; with a husband they may be lowered."[11] She made her point by highlighting the power differentials inherent in marriage.

Squire also resented the assumption that marriage alone made a woman worthy of respect. She challenged the heteropatriarchy by assuming the title Mrs. Squire:

Why should a woman remain Miss until death or marriage? The boy changes his title from master to mister as soon as he wishes . . . They say it's confusing. They will not know then whether we are single or married. I don't think it is anybody's business what we are. Why should we be obliged to print our marital relations on our business cards? Men don't.[12]

Rather than force herself into marriage, Squire preferred to "take the title 'Mrs.' without the man."[13] She was attempting to call attention to the double standard that automatically afforded men respect at adulthood but only granted women respect at marriage.

Squire faced resistance from conservative suffragists who rejected her radical idea. Laura G. Fixen, representing married suffragists, objected to Squire's proposition, declaring that unmarried women who used the title Mrs. were "parading on married women's preserves." Squire retorted: "We do not have to wait for any man to give it to us. Mrs. Fixen had to have a man give it to her. I took it myself." Another spinster suffragist, Virginia Brooks, backed up Squire's claim to the title. Brooks suggested they go even further and disregard gendered distinctions altogether.[14] This rejection of marriage and demeaning titles was a powerfully queer protest against society's expectations for women that put these suffragists on the extreme edge of the suffrage movement.

Aleda Briggs Richberg-Hornsby also rejected marriage and queered heteronormative domesticity, but only after having experienced matrimonial life first-hand. As the daughter and granddaughter of suffragists, she developed a strong commitment to women's rights and a stronger commitment to going against the grain.[15] In 1912, she secretly eloped with Hubert Primm Hornsby. This rejection of so-called proper courtship, engagement, and marriage rituals shocked her family. The short-lived marriage also defied notions of normative domesticity. The couple lived together for only three months before separating and living apart for more than two years. In January 1915, Richberg-Hornsby filed for divorce. Since divorce was generally viewed as a failure of a woman's ability to live up to her potential as a wife and mother, a woman who wanted a divorce had to demonstrate to the court that the breakdown of the marriage was through no fault of her own. She thus claimed that her husband failed to provide and requested a divorce on the grounds of desertion.[16]

After the divorce, Richberg-Hornsby once again defied norms by becoming the eighth woman in the United States to earn a pilot's license. She demonstrated her skill through a series of exhibition flights in New York and Chicago. In 1916, NAWSA enlisted her to fly over President Woodrow Wilson's yacht, dropping petitions for a federal suffrage amendment from women voters in the western United States.[17]

Figure 2.1. Ida Blair and Aleda Richberg-Hornsby on the flight to drop suffrage petitions over President Woodrow Wilson's yacht. Mrs. John Blair and Mrs. Richberg-Hornsby, Midland Beach, Staten Island, December 2, 1916. Unidentified photographer, PR 068, New-York Historical Society.

Richberg-Hornsby used the press coverage of her flights not only to advocate for women's suffrage but also to contest romantic notions of heterosexual domestic bliss. When a reporter asked about how she managed her fears while flying, she compared the experience to marriage. "I consider aviation as a career much less dangerous than matrimony." Reversing gendered stereotypes about "nagging wives," she argued that "marriage teaches a woman nerve control. A balky engine is nothing [compared] to a nagging man, believe me." Recalling an early brush with death when her plane engine failed, she noted that although it was scary, "I was ready to fly the next day," but, she added, "I'll never marry again. I just haven't the nerve."[18] Her divorce and public critique of marital life defied constructions of the home as a peaceful sanctuary. Her refusal to marry again suggested that marriage was not a necessity.

Suffragist Angelina Weld Grimké also decided that remaining single was the best choice for her life. Spinsterhood freed her to focus on her creative work as a feminist writer and activist. Born into a family of prominent abolitionists and suffragists, Grimké's activism was inspired in part by the legacy of her famous white aunts, Angelina Grimké Weld and Sarah Grimké. Her father, Archibald Grimké, was also an abolitionist and active suffragist who marched in suffrage parades and served as president of the Massachusetts Woman Suffrage Association. He was the son of an enslaved woman and a white enslaver who ran away to freedom. He married Sarah Stanley, a white woman, and together they had Angelina. They separated shortly after her birth. Angelina Grimké experienced a range of queer living situations in her youth, all deviations from a white middle-class ideal of heteronormative domesticity. At various points she lived with her mother, her father, and her extended family. Sometimes she lived as a boarder with other families, and sometimes she lived entirely on her own. These rich and varied experiences introduced her to people and ideas that inspired her commitment to racial and gender justice.[19]

Black communities had long viewed domesticity in less rigid terms than the heteronormative two-parent household model. They valued a broader definition of family and a collective sense of responsibility that was especially crucial to their survival under the oppressive conditions of enslavement, Jim Crow, and institutional racism. These outside factors led to the development of a range of single-parent, multigenerational, or extended-family households. Still, some Black middle-class leaders idealized the two-parent, heterosexual model of family and sought to conform, at least outwardly, to notions of respectable domesticity. Yet, the living situations of many Black suffragists like Grimké rarely adhered to this ideal.[20]

In Grimké's case, her non-traditional domestic arrangements allowed her the freedom to explore her queer desire. When her father was appointed to live and work in the Dominican Republic as a consul from 1894 to 1898, Angelina remained in the United States, attending a number of different schools around the country.[21] The close relationships she developed with other young women in these environments inspired both her activism and her queer poetry. At one point, Grimké lived in Washington, DC with her aunt and uncle while attending the M Street School. There she developed a romantic friendship with classmate and future suffragist, Mary Burrill. Grimké's father arranged to send her away to school after her aunt and uncle expressed concern over her generally rebellious behavior. When Grimké left to attend the Carleton Academy in Northfield, Minnesota in 1896, Burrill wrote Grimké to say how much she missed her. Recalling their past encounters Burrill wrote: "Could I just come to meet thee once more, in the old sweet way, just coming at your calling, and like an angel bending o'er you breathe into your ear 'I love you.'"[22] Burrill included a quote from a poem she had read that she said reminded her of Grimké:

> Farewell!—and never think of me,
> In lighted hall or lady's bower.
> Farewell!—and never think of me,
> In spring sunshine or summer hours.
> But when you see a lonely grave
> Just where a broken heart may lay
> With not one mourner by its sod
> Then and then only—Think of me![23]

Although the relationship with Burrill ended, Grimké continued to pursue romantic relationships with other young women.

At Carleton, Grimké developed a crush on white classmate Mary (Mamie) Edith Karn and drafted passionate letters to her:

> Oh Mamie if you only knew how my heart beats when I think of you and it yearns and pants to gaze, if only for one second upon your lovely face. If there were any trouble in this wide and wicked world from which I might shield you how gladly would I do it if it were even so great a thing as to lay down my life for you. I know you are too young now to become my wife, but I hope, darling, that in a few years you will come to me and be my love, my wife! How my brain whirls how my pulse leaps with joy and madness when I think of these two words, "my wife."[24]

But Karn apparently did not return Grimké's sentiments. Grimké eventually moved back to Massachusetts, where she lived as a boarder in another family's home while she attended the Girl's Latin School and then the Boston Normal School of Gymnastics in the years 1898 to 1902.[25]

Grimké expressed interest in both men and women as lovers. In 1903, she developed feelings for a man named Hinton Jones. But he did not return her affections. This caused her much heartbreak and may have been the motivation for Grimké's decision to never marry. However, her queer desire likely also played a significant role. Though she openly discussed the relationship with Jones in her correspondence with her father, Grimké chose to keep her desire for women private. Much of Grimké's poetry reveals her often-unrequited longings.[26] An example of one such poem is "Caprichosa," written 1901:

> Little lady coyly shy
> With deep shadows in each eye
> Cast by lashes soft and long,
> Tender lips just bowed for song,
> And I oft have dreamed the bliss
> Of the nectar in one kiss.[27]

Grimké's abundant body of work includes many examples of other poems that allude to her queer desire. Another example is an undated poem titled "Babette":

> I love Babette. You ask me why?
> Do winds know why the violet
> Is dear to them? Then why should I?
> I love Babette.
>
> Last night when in the fields we met
> She paused and shyly bade me tie
> Her britches-string. Was it a net?
>
> I only know as she slipped by
> She raised me eyes I can't forget.[28]

Although she was a prolific writer, she chose to keep the most intimate expressions of her queer desire obscured or unpublished. Societal proscriptions against homosexuality and bisexuality limited Grimké's willingness to share her writing. Grimké concealed her subjects by avoiding the use of pronouns in some of her poetry.[29] An undated poem about a kiss from a lover reveals her intense longing and desire for a subject whose gender remains unknown:

> I let you kiss my mouth.
> Quite through my curtained eyes
> I felt your eyes upon my eyes, my mouth
> Compellingly and hungrily you fed
> Against my will the curtains lifted from my eyes.
> One breathless space our souls clung each to each,
> And then I slipped into your arms
> Forgot all else but just your lips upon
> My mouth.[30]

Grimké's variety of queer domestic arrangements also inspired her advocacy for gender and racial equality. Around 1902, Grimké returned to live with her aunt and uncle, Charlotte Forten and Francis Grimké, in Washington, DC. Archibald and his brother, Francis Grimké, were both members of the National Negro Committee who helped found the National Association for the Advancement of Colored People (NAACP). As a family, they worked together to fight against racial segregation, discrimination, and violence targeting the Black community. Angelina Grimké wrote short stories and poems that drew attention these issues. She wrote the play *Rachel* in response to a call from the NAACP to rally public opinion against the racist portrayal of Black people and glorification of the KKK in the film *Birth of a Nation*. Her play, along with her other short stories and poems, revealed the horrors of lynching.[31]

Grimké's aunt, Charlotte Forten, played a significant role in shaping her feminism. Forten grew up in a free northern Black family that was active in abolitionist causes. She also advocated for gender equality by helping to form the Washington, DC Colored Women's League. In 1896, Forten was also one of the founders of the National Association of Colored Women (NACW), the most important national suffrage organization advocating for Black women's right to vote. The Forten-Grimkés hosted suffrage meetings in their home with well-known activists such as Mary Church Terrell and Anna Julia Cooper. Angelina Weld Grimké participated in these events and wrote articles advocating feminist ideals.[32]

MISS ANGELINA GRIMKÉ

Figure 2.2. Angelina Weld Grimké was a suffragist and activist fighting for racial and gender equality. Angelina Weld Grimké. In *Negro Poets and Their Poems*, edited by Robert Thomas Kerlin. Washington, DC: Associated Publishers, 1923. Schomburg Center for Research in Black Culture, Jean Blackwell Hutson Research and Reference Division, New York Public Library Digital Collections.

Grimké's life challenged the notion that heteronormative domestic arrangements fulfilled a woman's natural purpose. In her later life, she lived as a lodger in a family home in Washington, DC before moving by herself to New York City. She flourished as a writer during the 1920s. Her poetry and writings about racial and gender equality later became symbolic of the great works created by a generation of literary geniuses during the era known as the Harlem Renaissance.[33]

Itinerant Domesticities

The variety of temporary living situations that suffragists experienced during their activist careers opened a range of queer possibilities. Alma Benecke Sasse's and Hazel Hunkins's work as itinerant suffrage speakers highlights the homosocial domestic arrangements experienced by many suffragists. Sasse and Hunkins met while attending Vassar College, an all-women university in Poughkeepsie, New York. The queer space of the university bonded them closer together and fueled their feminist sentiments. In 1913, they continued their education at the co-ed University of Missouri, where they socialized with and dated men. But, they both frequently expressed their preference for the homosocial environment of Vassar College.[34]

Sasse and Hunkins referred to their living quarters at the University of Missouri as their bachelor apartments. It was not uncommon during this era for women to share the same bed. The ubiquitousness of this practice was clear in the casual manner in which Hunkins writes about their sleeping arrangements to her mother: "I sleep as well with Alma as I do alone and I think it's better sleeping out doors to-gether than separately in the house, and Alma's rest is as good as mine. We don't wake up from the time we strike the bed until 7 a.m."[35] It appears from this excerpt that Hunkins may have been attempting to address her mother's concerns about the pair sleeping together. Bed sharing was common in Hunkins's generation and before. But, there was growing concern about the potential that such close contact would lead to homosexual activity.

By the 1910s, medical professionals increasingly cautioned parents and students about crushes and bed-sharing. In his 1914 book, *Ten Sex Talks to Girls*, David Irving Steinhardt explicitly warned his readers to "avoid girls who are too affectionate" or girls who "admire your figure and breast development" or invite you "to remain at their homes all night, and to occupy the same bed they do." Steinhardt warned about the dangers of sharing a bed with another girl, and he condemned snuggling: "Avoid the touching of sexual parts, including the breasts, and, in fact, I might say avoid contact of any parts of the body at all . . . and let your conversation be of other topics than sexuality." He insisted that beds are for sleeping, "do not lie in each other's arms when awake or falling asleep . . . When you go to bed, go to sleep just as quickly as you can. If possible, avoid sleeping with anyone else." In Steinhardt's description, certain girls were portrayed as predatory, homosexual aggressors.[36]

Despite all the sensationalistic hysteria in the warnings, fears about homosexuality were not entirely unfounded. Studies confirmed that sexual relationships between college women were indeed quite common. Katharine Bement Davis's study of women's sexuality conducted in the 1920s revealed the extent of sexual activity and especially homosexual activity among "good girls" of the middle and upper classes. Davis was a graduate of Vassar College who went on to earn a PhD from the University of Chicago and became director of the Bureau of Social Hygiene. Because previous studies had pathologized sexuality by focusing solely on the sexuality of criminal women, Davis chose to survey educated, middle-class women in an effort to reveal the sexual habits of so-called normal women.[37] Many of the 2,200 women who responded had attended college during the 1900s and 1910s. The published results revealed that these women engaged in much more heterosexual and homosexual activity than anyone had previously acknowledged. Davis found that more than 50 percent of the women reported having had intense emotional relationships with other women, and in 26 percent of these cases the feelings were accompanied by overt sexual practices. Davis's research also shattered the idea that women's institutions fostered an environment that led to homosexuality since most of the respondents attended coeducational institutions. Nor could universities be blamed for homosexuality, as Davis found that more than 43 percent of the respondents reported having intense emotional relations with other women even before college.[38]

Hunkins's mother may have been worried about the physicality of the relationship when she wrote expressing concern about the sleeping arrangements. However, if concerns about bed sharing and homosexuality were expressed to them, Hunkins and Sasse did not seem phased. Although many young women in their era did engage in lesbian sex, I do not know if Hunkins and Sasse did. On the surface, their relationship appeared similar to other crushes and romantic friendships of the era. What I do know is that while society laid out clear heteronormative expectations for their lives, Sasse and Hunkins dreamed of continuing their homosocial domestic bliss beyond their college years.

After graduation, Sasse and Hunkins lived apart while working as suffrage organizers and itinerant speakers. In 1916, Sasse moved to New York and later to Oklahoma and Missouri to work on state suffrage campaigns. Throughout 1916, Hunkins was an organizer for the National Woman's Party (NWP), traveling around Colorado and California. Their lives as suffrage lecturers deviated substantially from the lives of most women. Rather than committing themselves to family and home, they immersed themselves in a homosocial environment with other like-minded activists. As they traveled from city to city, they lived in hotels, often rooming with other suffragists.[39]

Although their travel and work schedule was intense, they enjoyed a sense of liberation through life on the road. Hunkins wrote to her mother that her suffrage work had awakened in her "a love of adventure" and had "opened the portals to many things."[40] In a later letter, she wrote to assure her mother that she was making the right life decisions: "I am going places and meeting people, and doing things that make life interesting and I think that what I am gaining is so much more than I could any other way."[41] These liminal queer spaces, far removed from the world of heteronormative domesticity, allowed suffragists to imagine new possibilities.

Even as they were apart, Sasse and Hunkins continued to write to one another, expressing their hopes for the future. They created a joint savings account to fulfill their dream of traveling abroad together. Sasse wrote Hunkins: "Oh the wanderlust I feel in my heart—just you and the Sea! Oh Honey, soon—soon—soon."[42] They hoped to live and work at Constantinople College for girls. When Hunkins learned that there was a position for her but not for Sasse at the college, she told her mother in a letter that she absolutely would not go without Sasse.[43] With all the sentiment of a romantic friendship, Sasse wrote a heartfelt poem to Hunkins, who she had nicknamed Herzblatt (German for "sweetness"):

INCOMPLETE SPRING
The feet o' me pass thru the forests—all cool,
And stray o'er the sun-flooded hill–
The eyes o' me dance in the moss-circled pool
But the heart o' me's—longin' ye still.

The mind o' me strives in the world of men
As I seek but to do—and—to will!
And Victory waits for the pluckin'—but then–
Oh, the heart o' me's longin' ye still.

Oh, say ye'll come back with the dawnin' o' Spring—?
To the place which ye only can fill–
Sure, a bird cannot fly, when he's lost of a wing!
And the heart o' me's longin' ye still."[44]

In 1917 and 1918, Hunkins was more or less permanently in Washington, DC, living at the NWP headquarters. Sasse was in New York working with NAWSA organizations. While rooming at the Hotel Martha Washington, the first hotel in the city built exclusively for women, Sasse sent a letter and poem to Hunkins. The poem revealed her longing for their college days when they were constantly together.

> *To Herzblatt [sweetness]—some two years ago.*
>
> COMPENSATION
>
> We hear in this restless world of ours,
> An endless, common plea–
> That the future grant again,
> To man
> The joys of the used-to be.
>
> Men sigh for former wealth, for
> Fame–
> For love—and fancies free,
> And curse the Fates, who
> Close the gates–
> On the world of the used-to be–
>
> Yet I treasure close within my heart
> Memories so dear to me–
> That I hold all present pain
> For naught
> To the joys of the used to be.
>
> And still my altar fires burn
> As alone—on bended knee.
> I bless those gods who gave me
> You–
> Once—in the used to be.[45]

Though they were often apart, their mutual devotion to suffrage bonded them in common cause. But, Sasse worried about Hunkins's increasing participation in "militant actions." In 1917, Hunkins answered the NWP's call to picket the White House. Her decision to participate in these protests upset her family and friends, who warned her that she was endangering her good reputation. When she was arrested in July 1917, her mother was horrified. News of the arrest also hit Sasse hard. Writing from Westport, New York to her "Darling, darling mine," Sasse expressed her concern to Hunkins:

> when I read things like that about you—I simply can't stand it! I simply want to wilt up and die before you plunge into any more horrible notoriety . . . the Buffalo paper says you are to have a trial (ye gods!) on Saturday and I wonder?? Honey—Honey—does my love for you and the big things that we have longed for and planned for count for absolutely nothing? You are absolutely ruining your chances for every opportunity that will come to you. How could we ever get a job in Constantinople or anywhere—when your name is being heralded so unpleasantly all over the U.S.? Oh—I am so worried and so sick at heart.[46]

Sasse pleaded with Hunkins to stop while simultaneously offering to help: "Do you need anything? You know that everything I have in the world is yours . . . Oh sweetheart—come to me somewhere some quiet place for some week end where our tongues may rest and our very tired hearts may talk."[47]

This disagreement about appropriate tactics offers us a glimpse into the depth of affection that Sasse had for Hunkins. Their friendship endured through this incident. In the winter of 1917–1918, Sasse and Hunkins lived together as Sasse continued organizing work for NAWSA and Hunkins for the NWP. When Hunkins contracted the measles, she wrote to her mother about how wonderful Alma had been in caring for her. Once the quarantine lifted, Hunkins wrote: "Alma went to Michigan and I am alone and I am darn lonesome. There is no other person, I know who so completely satisfies all companionship longings as she does. She was wonderful to me when I was sick."[48]

Hunkins's commitment to suffrage and to her idealized future with Sasse sometimes waivered under the pressure exerted by societal expectations. Her mother disapproved of her continued participation in the suffrage movement. Hunkins begged her to try to understand. In a

July 1917 letter, Hunkins wrote to tell her that she did not want to come home: "But if you want me to come home and be, from now on and forever a school teacher . . . and marry some dub for money or so that I won't be an old maid . . . why I would do it."[49] Hunkins's plea reveals the gendered expectations she knew she was failing to live up to. Her mother wanted her to come home, take a respectable job, marry, and aspire to a higher social status. Hunkins was aware that the worst possible thing she could become in the eyes of society was "an old maid." Still, she imagined other options for her life and insisted: "I'll die if I ever have to 'settle down.'"[50]

The liminal queer domesticities created in the context of suffrage activism influenced suffragists' visions of what was possible for their futures. But, heteronormative expectations tugged on them. Hunkins's and Sasse's lofty plans and dreams of a life replete with travel and adventure together never quite materialized. After the ratification of the Nineteenth Amendment, they continued to pursue full lives as career women, but they drifted apart from each other as their paths increasingly diverged. Their vision of an alternate future faded. They married men, had children, and largely acquiesced to familial demands. But for a short time at least, the temporary queer domesticities they created in their suffrage activism allowed them to experience a different kind of liberation.

Other suffragists, especially those who experienced less familial pressure than Hunkins, fully enjoyed the freedom of their queer domestic arrangements. Margaret Foley was a prominent suffrage activist from a working-class Irish American family in Boston, Massachusetts. She worked as a hatter in the Guyer Hat factory in Boston before becoming a labor organizer with the Boston Women's Trade Union League. From 1906 to 1915, Foley traveled throughout the country as an organizer for the Massachusetts Woman Suffrage Association.[51]

As a suffrage celebrity, Foley had many male suitors. In a September 1911 letter from Nellie Green, a friend who traveled with her across the Atlantic, Green recalled Foley's charms with the British men aboard the ship:

I can see you so plainly sitting or rather reclining in the deck chair using the artillery of your expressive eyes at every poor unfortunate male who passed you, or rather who did not pass you, for that is what they did—just sat down & capitulated—worshipping at the shrine of Venus . . . Do you remember the fellow of the brown eyes . . . who used to pursue you & I am sure had designs on you, especially at the dinner-table! I suspect the poor fellow felt like eating you instead of his dinner.[52]

The following year, another friend, Ettie Lowell, tried to play matchmaker and arrange for Foley to meet a man who was interested in marrying her.[53] But Foley generally refused to marry since marriage was much too restrictive.

Foley's itinerant suffrage life and single status allowed her the option to engage in romantic and sexual relationships of her own choosing. Ben Reitman, an anarchist and birth control activist, carried on a heavy flirtation with Foley. Reitman told Foley, "if you suffragettes don't stand behind the Birth Controllers, I don't see what good your emancipation is doing. After all, it isn't the vote you want, it is the right to be free, economically, spiritually and sexually."[54] Reitman was in a relationship with Emma Goldman at the time. As "free lovers," however, Reitman and Goldman maintained an open, non-monogamous relationship. Reitman regularly pursued other lovers.[55] Foley corresponded with Reitman and met up with him when their paths crossed. These meetings were apparently very infrequent since Foley was traveling the country extensively and Reitman was often in and out of jail for his activism. Reitman called himself her "Anarchist Sweetheart." In one letter, Reitman looked forward to the day they could meet again:

Wish we could take a long walk in the park and talk about life and work, then we could go to a comfortable home and I could put my head on your beautiful breast and weep for joy. Write me. Love me. Want me. Ben.[56]

They continued a flirty correspondence. Eight months later, Reitman suggested they meet up in New York:

I expect to be in New York early in October, and I do want to see you. You are such a terribly busy, popular woman that you never give your honest admirers the chance to seriously flirt with you. You know, I can do most everything else in twenty minutes except make successful love to a woman of your type, so some day, after you have visited all your friends and told them about all your wonderful successes, and you are in a playful mood, I hope we will be able to visit.[57]

It is unclear whether or not they ever actually engaged in any type of sexual relationship. Reitman was definitely sexually pursuing Foley but was frustrated by his inability to "seriously flirt" with her. Despite her multiple suitors, Foley was never engaged to, nor did she marry, any man. In addition to her ideological opposition to marriage, it is possible that Foley was more interested in women than men.

Foley met fellow suffragist Helen Elizabeth Goodnow while campaigning for suffrage. Goodnow, who became the central figure in Foley's life from 1916 onward, had been working as a suffrage speaker for the Massachusetts Woman Suffrage Association. Goodnow volunteered to serve as Foley's secretary on a lecture tour. She was soon enamored with Foley and wrote to her grandmother: "I really think Foley likes me better than most any other of her friends. Funny isn't it."[58] Toward the end of the tour, Foley and Goodnow took a week to rest at a mineral springs in Mt. Clements, Michigan. Goodnow gushed over their "perfectly glorious week alone together." She wrote her grandmother:

> I wish I could possibly be able to tell you what a wonderful trip this is and how happy I have been . . . [Margaret] and I have had a perfectly glorious week alone together. Think of the hundreds of people who would give anything to be with her for a week. We read together, walked together, got up and went to bed when we felt like it. And she really loves me. Think of Margaret Foley liking little me.[59]

Goodnow ended the letter reminding her family: "Again I repeat I can't tell you how happy I am with Margaret."

Eventually, Goodnow and Foley decided to make their itinerant queer domestic arrangement permanent. Sometime before 1920, Goodnow moved in with Foley in Boston. They lived together for nearly forty years until Foley passed away in 1957.[60]

Presumptive Heterosexuality

Some queer suffragists relied on the appearance of heteronormative domesticity and assumptions of heterosexuality to allow them to freely live their queer life. Alice Dunbar Nelson married Paul Laurence Dunbar, a prominent Black poet, in 1898. This marriage ended in separation four years later due to Dunbar's alcoholism and abuse. As a suffragist, Dunbar Nelson was well aware of the necessity of countering images of gender and sexual deviancy. As a Black woman, she was also aware of the importance of combatting racist stereotypes regarding Black criminality and sexual immorality. Her public presentation as a respectable heterosexual married woman protected her reputation and the reputation of all Black suffragists. However, her private life was infinitely more rich and complicated than the public image suggested.

Dunbar Nelson served as president of the Wilmington Suffrage Club and was a member of the Delaware Republican State Committee. In the 1910s, the Congressional Union of the NAWSA recruited her as an organizer. She toured throughout Pennsylvania and Delaware speaking alongside well-known suffragists like Mary Church Terrell. In her suffrage speeches, she often employed the rhetoric of municipal housekeeping to argue that women's suffrage and participation in the public sphere was a natural extension of her role as mother and wife in the domestic sphere.[61] Dunbar Nelson's frequent references to heterosexual domesticity were a consciously strategic maneuver.

White suffragists chose to focus solely on the goal of winning the vote, regardless of whether this would include suffrage for Black women. In the process, white suffrage organizations reinforced racial hierarchies and perpetuated racist rhetoric. Black suffragists were simultaneously appealed to, patronized, and marginalized by mainstream suffrage organizations. Even as she resented having to constantly perform middle-class respectability, Dunbar Nelson leveraged her status to challenge racism from her marginalized position within mainstream suffrage organizations. She called attention to issues that impacted the Black community such as overcrowded housing, domestic violence, segregation, and racialized violence. Early in her career, Dunbar Nelson embraced racial uplift ideology. This strategy proved expedient in the moment, but over time Dunbar Nelson grew weary of uplift rhetoric and assimilationist tactics and adopted a more militant consciousness.[62] She also began to push back against anti-suffrage arguments that relied on the separate spheres doctrine or middle-class notions of normative domesticity. She noted that the Black woman "since emancipation has never been able to remain at home. She has been compelled to go out and do all kinds of manual labor. Her toil and endeavor has enabled the race to make wonderful progress which it has made in the last fifty years."[63] She insisted that they needed the ballot to fight against the discrimination that Black people faced.[64]

In an effort to promote herself, Dunbar Nelson emphasized her prior married status and heteronormative domesticity. When her ex-husband passed away in 1906, Dunbar Nelson told Paul Dunbar's biographer Linda Keck Wiggins that their married life had been far from happy as she suffered from his abuse. Wiggins chose to keep this information out of the official biography in order to preserve Paul Dunbar's reputation. Despite her private revelations, Dunbar Nelson also chose to present an alternate narrative of their life together in public. She presented herself as: "Mrs. Paul Laurence Dunbar, widow of the famous poet." Her speeches typically began with a reading of one of Dunbar's poems. She also referenced his support for suffrage in her speeches. In recounting her married life, she told audiences that her years with Dunbar were the happiest years of her life. She believed that this public performance of domestic bliss was essential to combatting narratives of suffragists as sexually abnormal women. Equally important, Dunbar Nelson was acutely aware of the necessity of resisting racial stereotypes of Black men as animalistic and prone to violence. Thus, long after her marriage had ended and Dunbar had passed away, she cultivated a public persona as a heterosexual, grieving widow.[65]

Privately, however, Dunbar Nelson's queer relationships and domesticities deviated substantially from this image. When she was single she lived in multiple locations, sometimes with her family and at other times in boarding houses. She had a number of sexual relationships with both men and women throughout her life. One of her most significant queer relationships was with Edwina B. Kruse, who served as the principal at the high school where Kruse worked in Wilmington, Delaware. The intensity of the relationship between Kruse and Dunbar Nelson is evident throughout their correspondence. Kruse frequently began her letters by

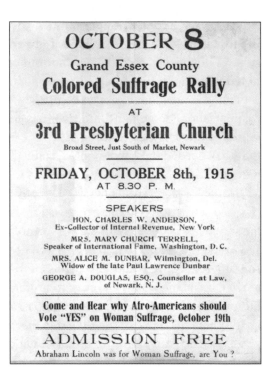

Figure 2.3. Alice Dunbar Nelson emphasized her heterosexual respectability by using her former married name in her public appearances. "Colored Suffrage Rally." Scrapbook 3. Alice Dunbar Nelson papers, University of Delaware Library, Newark, Delaware.

addressing Dunbar Nelson with terms of endearment such as "Dearest little sweetheart" or "Sweet, my only Heart." She always signed her letters as "Your own Ned." The relationship was also physical. On November 4, 1907 Kruse wrote:

> How your pen picture of a Sunday together drove me wild! To have you snuggle up in my arms would be bliss indescribable and when you do come back I'll take you up in my arms and never let you go . . . I love you, I love you, oh! how I love you and I love no one else, think of no one else.[66]

The longing and tension in these letters was heightened by their separation. Dunbar Nelson was away studying at Cornell University in Ithaca, NY. Kruse expressed fear and jealousy over Dunbar Nelson's new friends and flirtations: "I want you to know dear, that every thought of my life is for you, every throb of my heart is yours and yours alone. I just cannot ever let anyone else have you."[67] Kruse's feelings did not subside. A few weeks later, on October 18, 1907, she wrote:

Alice, Alice, can you hear me calling through the distance—oh! I want you Alice, I want you—Do you love me or do you just write me those sweet things? I hope your heart is so full of love for [me] that you won't want to love those people up there.[68]

Dunbar Nelson's queer domestic arrangements allowed her to pursue multiple romantic relationships. A jealous Kruse discouraged her from taking a roommate: "I would not want you to have a roommate! I could not bear to know that any one roomed with you or were close to you in any way. I should never want to be again!"[69] Kruse also complained about Dunbar Nelson staying up too late and allowing other women into her room. Although she framed it all out of concern for her health and academic success, the comments were clearly tinged with jealousy.[70]

But Kruse was most concerned about Dunbar Nelson's relationship with Professor Lane Cooper at Cornell. She warned that Cooper was no good because he was a white man and because he had a bad temper:

No matter how jealous I am you must tell me every little thing, because you are mine! With me you have been comparatively happy with him—you would have, after awhile—hades—you thought you had it with Paul Laurence Dunbar—it would be worse . . . Alice—my arms are empty, my life is empty—I feel as if I cannot, cannot live the year out without you. Come to me in spirit—I try very hard to make you come—darling.[71]

Dunbar Nelson attempted to assuage Kruse's fears by writing: "I am very careful to be as true to you in word, thought and deed as woman can be." She assured Kruse, "I don't care enough about any of them, or all of them put together to do one single thing that you wouldn't approve of, or that I wouldn't have you do."[72] She also complained about feeling blue, declaring to Kruse, "I miss you more each day. I laugh and joke sometimes, etc. etc. and end by saying I want to be home! I want my Ned!"[73]

Despite these reassurances, Kruse continued to accuse Dunbar Nelson of cheating on her. After a reunion at Christmas in 1907, Kruse worried that she would return to Cornell and resume an affair with Cooper:

Do you want to kiss me? Do you kiss those old white things? I hope not—I would not kiss any one at all. Your kisses pressed on my lips—

just before the train left are still there and will be until you take them off with others.[74]

Dunbar Nelson expressed her affection to Kruse, writing about her intense desire to cuddle up to her "Nedkins."[75] But she minimized their relationship to outsiders. Kruse angrily resented it when Dunbar Nelson described their relationship to someone else as akin to sisters: "that generally means that any close relationship has ceased and that some other fellow holds the closer relationship. If I am to be a sister or you are to be my sister I'll be nothing."[76]

Kruse's anger and jealousy were not without foundation. Dunbar Nelson had apparently been unfaithful to Kruse multiple times over the years. Her 1906 to 1907 diary details a torrid year-long sexual affair that she deliberately sought to hide from Kruse. Writing in the style of a romantic novel, Dunbar Nelson described the dilemma: "A long talk, all about this new phase of the affair. Two people wishing to be loyal he to Minnie, she to Ned, yet loving, drawn into that love by fate."[77] The multiple references to hiding the affair from Ned and the need to be loyal suggest that she viewed her relationship with Kruse on par with her man lover. Dunbar Nelson's infidelity combined with Kruse's jealousy continued to chip away at their relationship. They gradually grew apart even as they continued to love each other in their own ways.

Dunbar Nelson eventually married again, twice. But these marriages did not hinder her romantic interest in and pursuit of women. She wrote details about these relationships in her diary, revealing a thriving lesbian and bisexual subculture among Black clubwomen in the 1920s and 1930s.[78] Dunbar Nelson's private sexual life demonstrates the ways that some suffragists relied on presumptive heterosexuality and the appearance of heteronormative domesticity while freely living private queer lives.

Boston Marriages

Perhaps the queerest of all the queer domestic arrangements was the ubiquitous Boston marriage. These partnerships represented the most common and, in some ways, the most radical challenge to heteronormative domesticity. Boston marriages stood as a direct affront to the patriarchy because these women not only refused to marry but rejected men altogether by choosing to commit their lives to other women. Yet, ironically, suffragists in Boston marriages also sometimes reinforced systems of oppression by denying the sexual dimensions of their relationships and by modeling white, middle-class notions of proper femininity, gender conformity, and domesticity.[79] Anti-suffragists insisted that heterosexual marriage was the only acceptable role for women. Any deviation was used as evidence of the abnormality of suffragists and the dangers of the enfranchisement of women. Therefore, although suffragists in Boston marriages were quite open about their relationships with other suffragists, what they were willing to reveal publicly about their intimate lives varied substantially. Each couple adopted their own strategy for navigating their personal and professional lives.

Mary Askew Mather and Alice P. Smyth formed a very public Boston marriage in Wilmington, Delaware that they framed as a deep friendship, and therefore an implied asexual relationship. This framing was no doubt a conscious decision influenced by Mather's experience with suppressing her queer desire in her youth. Mather's Smith College diary reveals the intensity of her feelings for classmate Frona Brooks.[80] Parents and educators during this period generally viewed crushes as mostly innocent but worried that so-called exclusive friendships posed a problem. They warned girls against developing these overly intimate friendships with other girls.[81] This may account for the tension in Mather's writings between her longing to have Brooks all to herself and the insistence of her friends that the couple avoid such exclusivity. This social policing of the boundaries of the relationship is perhaps what led to its demise over the following year.

Mather learned a valuable lesson that remained with her into her adult relationships. After graduating and moving back home to Wilmington, she met her life partner, Alice P. Smyth. They were frequently seen together working for social causes. They served as the founders of the Wilmington New Century Club, members of the Young Women's Christian Temperance Union, and suffragists with the NAWSA. In 1911, both women served on a suffrage delegation to the Delaware legislature. Mather made a conscious decision to keep her relationship with Smyth very public, taking to heart the experiences of her youth. Smyth accompanied Mather to her fortieth college reunion in 1923. There, Mather reunited with old friends, including Frona Brooks. Smyth posed in the reunion photos as a special guest behind her partner.[82] They never hid the fact that they were "devoted companions," but their conformity to gendered expectations of femininity and the implied asexuality of such relationships added an aura of respectability that somewhat deflected suggestions of sexual abnormality. Mather's and Smyth's devotion and commitment to each other was so public that it was, therefore, above reproach.

The whiteness and class status of suffragists like Mather and Smyth also shielded them from scrutiny of their queer domestic arrangements. Their commitment to reform work and suffrage activism added to their respectability as long as it operated within existing gender and racial hierarchies. White women embraced a racial hierarchy backed by social evolutionary theory that positioned white people as the most civilized and therefore the most evolved of all the races. They relied on these evolutionist discourses to justify their reform work, believing that their advocacy of suffrage was essential to uplifting and protecting women of "less-civilized" races and classes from oppression and abuse. This was also rooted in notions of binary biological differences between men and women that relied on a belief in women's so-called natural role as caretakers. By framing their work in this way, white women's public activism posed less of a threat to gendered expectations and was permitted as an extension of their civilizing mission. Although women were still expected to marry and rear children, some women's queer domestic arrangements and decision not to marry could be justified as a necessary sacrifice if they turned their maternal impulses outward in their commitment to public service. By the early twentieth century, queer suffrage couples deployed this strategy to shield their relationships from attack.[83]

Virginia suffragists Nora Houston and Adele Goodman Clark similarly used their privileged positions as wealthy white women to justify their involvement in the suffrage cause and deflect criticism from their queer domesticity. They both enjoyed the benefits of growing up in wealthy families, and their profession as artists also vaulted them into the upper echelons of society. Neither ever married. Instead, they bought a home and lived together as a couple.

Houston and Clark were both active in the local and state Equal Suffrage League lending their artistic talents to help design flyers, posters, and other suffrage art. But the local Richmond press attacked the women of the newly formed Equal Suffrage League, labeling them as radical "suffragettes." When Houston gave a suffrage speech in a park, an angry crowd threw rocks at her. Fellow members of the Art Club of Richmond objected to their association with suffrage, and several individuals resigned from the club over the issue. Still, Houston and Clark remained undeterred and continued their suffrage work. They lobbied the Virginia state legislature, organized suffrage rallies, and delivered street speeches. They leveraged their social status and careers as "eccentric artists" to push the bounds of acceptable behavior.[84]

But Houston and Clark admitted that this strategy was only partially effective. Although most suffragists were generally quite accepting of the queer living arrangements in suffrage circles, some objected to the perception generated by the "bachelor women" in the movement. Clark recalled that there was a "terrific lot of talking about the childless woman [in the suffrage movement], which was exceptionally cruel."[85] Especially in conservative southern regions, these rumors proved devastating to the reputations of some suffragists who were accused of destroying the so-called traditional family through their formation of queer domesticities, their advocacy of free love, or their use of birth control.

Although Houston and Clark fought against sexism and homophobia, queer white suffragists like them also helped maintain a system of white supremacy by policing access to the vote. Major suffrage organizations courted the support of white southern voters by conceding to demands for segregated organizations and abetting disenfranchisement tactics. After the ratification of the Nineteenth Amendment, white suffragists of the NAWSA and NWP rejected the requests of Black suffragists for assistance in fighting disenfranchisement and stood back as the NACW alone fought racist efforts to prevent Black women from voting.[86]

Houston and Clark were among a small minority of white suffragists who joined Black suffragists in the fight against disenfranchisement. In an effort to dissuade Black women from voting, Richmond opened a segregated registration area in the basement of city hall and reduced its hours of operation. Houston and Clark allied with Black suffragists to fight the electoral board and insist on the same registration hours for white and Black women. Clark admitted, however, that white suffragists did not dare to invite Black suffragists to the Equal Suffrage League to discuss these problems out of fear of being "accused of trying to get the

Negro vote out." Instead, Houston and Clark relied on their whiteness, class status, and reputation as eccentric artists to host a private meeting in their studio with Black suffrage leaders. Together the two groups developed a strategy to prevent voter intimidation by creating patrols of white allies to police the polling stations and report incidents of harassment and violence against Black voters on Election Day. Although Clark noted the importance of this secret alliance, she later expressed regret over her personal failure to do more to publicly fight segregation.[87]

Houston and Clark's queer domesticity nurtured them in their fight for gender equality. They used their race and class privilege to challenge disenfranchisement but ultimately failed to effectively confront the racism within the suffrage movement. Historian Rosalyn Terborg-Penn has argued that, although perhaps not overt in their racism, southern white wealthy suffragists "came into being because of white hegemony" and thus consciously or unconsciously helped preserve white supremacy.[88] Therefore, even well-intentioned white suffragists like Houston and Clark, who themselves had faced marginalization in the suffrage movement for their queer domesticities, helped uphold white supremacy and perpetuate a system of racism and inequality.

Conclusion

The examples in this chapter illustrate the range of queer domesticities among suffragists. Although these living arrangements clearly transgressed expected norms in multiple ways, most felt that they had to operate within the confines of the heteropatriarchy and to conform at least outwardly to white, middle-class notions of proper domesticity. The reluctance of some suffragists to commit to traditional heterosexual matrimony generally unsettled the public, as evidenced by attacks on unmarried women. Spinsters justified their choice not to marry by insisting that their commitment to reform work and suffrage activism represented a form of self-sacrifice and dedication to the common good that transcended the benefits of heterosexual marriage. Queer suffragists who did marry concealed their queerness and lesbian love affairs through the front of marriage or presumptive heterosexuality.

Other queer suffragists relied on presumptive asexuality to deflect suspicion from their private queer relationships. Whiteness, class, or professional status could also protect queer suffragists from criticism. Although association with powerful spouses and families often put them more directly in the leering public eye, their status could also sometimes protect them from social ostracization or persecution. Women who lived with other women could avoid scrutiny if they exhibited outward signs of femininity and gender conformity. Lesbian couples often publicly insisted that their relationships merely represented close friendships. As long as they did not deviate radically from white, middle-class norms, these relationships were tolerated. Thus, these queer domestic arrangements could be both entirely transgressive in their challenge to traditional heterosexual marriage and simultaneously conservative, largely conforming to accepted heteronormative standards.[89]

3

Queering Family

When suffragists Dr. Sara Josephine Baker, Ida Wylie, and Dr. Louise Pearce moved in together on a farm in Skillman, New Jersey, they admitted that their queer suffrage family must have seemed odd to the neighbors. Pearce and Baker had worked with the suffrage movement in the United States, while Wylie was active in the militant suffragette campaign in the United Kingdom. Before meeting Baker, Wylie had a romantic relationship with a Welsh suffragette named Rachel Barrett who worked as an organizer for the Women's Social and Political Union (WSPU) and edited their newspaper, *The Suffragette*. They relocated to the United States together. After Wylie's romance with Barrett fizzled, she moved to New York City and took up residence with Baker, with whom she apparently developed a romantic relationship. Baker and Wylie later moved out of the city and retired to the farm in Skillman in the 1930s. Their friend, Dr. Louise Pearce, moved in with them shortly thereafter.[1] Wylie described their unique family arrangement in her autobiography:

> I know I can count on . . . them to the death. In every day life and in their different ways they look after me and see that I don't go out with my hat back to front, and when I fall over my own feet they pick me up and dust me off. On my side I am secretly convinced that I manage both of them. So we are all three quite reasonably happy.[2]

Wylie noted that their chosen family and queer domestic arrangement was unusual: "I don't know what Princeton thinks about us . . . Three professional women . . . living amicably and even gaily together is an odd phenomenon."[3] They cared for and supported each other until their deaths.

In the last chapter, I examined how suffragists formed a variety of queer domesticities. In this chapter, I will continue that theme and also explore how suffragists created queer chosen families and extended communities. Chosen families represented a group of individuals who, though not usually biologically related, formed close emotional ties with one another. These families often consisted of multiple adults providing emotional, financial, and/or medical support for each other. Some queer suffrage couples who lived in Boston marriages adopted and raised children together. Other chosen family arrangements emerged when young adult suffragists found mentors and "adopted" mothers in older suffragists. The bonds that they built with each other in the suffrage movement helped connect them. Queer communities, consisting of an eclectic mix of professional colleagues, friends, family, lovers, and former lovers, also provided mutual friendship, support, love, and protection. Couples and families in these networks frequently corresponded, socialized, and vacationed together. Chosen families challenged the white, heteronormative, middle-class family ideal by allowing suffragists to freely live in queer relationships, adopt children, and build community beyond their biological families. These emotional connections were especially important since some suffragists found themselves ostracized by their biological families for their "radical" feminist views or norm-defying behavior and relationships.[4]

The creation of chosen families both replicated and disrupted traditional notions of domesticity. Anthropologist Kath Weston has argued that queer chosen families simultaneously challenge the hegemony of biological families while also ironically assimilating to heterosexist society by attempting to live up to standards of respectability. Weston used examples from the 1980s to show that this accommodationist tactic earned queer families some acceptance in mainstream society.[5] Although the historic context is not the same, there is a somewhat similar pattern with queer suffragists in the early twentieth century. In the last chapter, I mentioned that suffrage couples in Boston marriages found a surprising degree of tolerance because they largely conformed to societal notions of acceptability. These couples outwardly highlighted their gender conformity and femininity, downplayed their queerness, and contributed to their local community. Other than the queer relationship, Boston marriages did not radically deviate from respectable white, middle-class norms of domesticity. Despite the surprising range of queer chosen families, suffragists attempted, at least publicly, to justify or normalize their relationships within these heteronormative constructs.

Chosen Families

Chosen families provided essential support networks for queer suffragists who felt disconnected or rejected by their biological families. Although some individuals retained strong emotional ties to their kin, others described a feeling of not belonging. This sometimes led to estrangement and a severing of ties from their biological families in their youth or young adult life. As a young child, Gail Laughlin defied gender norms and expectations. She preferred to spend time outdoors with her brothers rather than playing inside with dolls or other so-called feminine activities designed to prepare young women for their future roles as wives and mothers. Laughlin enjoyed activities that had been defined by society as traditionally masculine hobbies such as fishing and golfing. She greatly upset her mother by rejecting marriage and motherhood, declaring that she desired to pursue a career instead. Laughlin was determined to earn a degree, but the family could not afford to send both her and her brothers to college. She spent years defying the wishes of her mother and working as a bookkeeper in order to save up the money to go to Wellesley College. In her professional life, she adopted masculine fashions and mannerisms that earned her the designation of a mannish woman. Although she went on to become a successful lawyer and suffragist, her family objected to her rejection of traditional gender norms and embrace of a queer gender identity.[6]

Suffragist Anne Martin's reflections on the pain of losing her mother to death highlighted the larger sense of disconnection she felt from her family throughout her life. In a poem titled "Transition," Martin mourned both the loss of her mother, Louise Martin, and their inability to understand each other. She noted that as a child she "only cared for books and sport" while her mother wanted her to "learn to sew." She loved reading, daydreaming, and playing outdoors. But her mother preferred that she focus on domestic tasks:

> Her age believed the outside world
> Belonged to men and boys;
> To womenkind and girls belonged
> All inside household joys.[7]

Martin described herself as the "black lamb in the fold" for her gender-transgressing life. She concluded that because of this her mother "could not love me as she loved my sisters and my brothers."[8] Anne Martin fulfilled the obligation of caring for her mother as she aged even though Martin felt isolated at times from her family.[9]

The disconnection that queer suffragists felt was more than compensated for by the connections they created with fellow suffragists. Laughlin formed a chosen family and made a home with suffragist Dr. Mary Austin Sperry. Martin never married, formed intimate relationships with women, and lived in a variety of queer domestic arrangements. She created a chosen family with suffragists who supported her not only through her career as a suffragist in Nevada but in her campaign as a candidate for the US Senate. Her close friendship with Mabel Vernon, one of the leaders of the Congressional Union, reveals how suffragists viewed each other as surrogate family. Vernon had worked alongside Martin in the 1914 Nevada suffrage campaign. They both participated in and were arrested in the 1917 Washington, DC pickets (see chapter 5). Vernon served as Martin's campaign manager in her 1918 and 1920 runs for the US Senate. Vernon temporarily stayed in the Martin family home and they roomed together as they traveled throughout the state. Vernon's letters indicate she provided much needed emotional support for Martin as well. In April 1918, Vernon telegrammed Martin, who was on the campaign trail:

MISS YOU INEXPRESSABLY HAVE SPENT EVENING SORTING YOUR CORRESPONDENCE . . . WILL BE THINKING OF YOU CONSTANTLY MUCH LOVE TO YOU B L V D.[10]

I am not sure what the relationship was between Vernon and Martin in 1918. Neither ever married, and both later had romantic relationships with other women. Dr. Margaret Long, who volunteered as their driver during the campaign, also had a close relationship with Martin, and some historians have speculated that they were later lovers. In the 1930s, Vernon coupled up with Consuelo Reyes-Calderon, a Costa Rican immigrant and international women's rights activist.[11] At the very least, the letters between Vernon and Martin in 1918 reveal the close familial relationships that suffragists formed on the campaign trail.

Adopted Children

Queer suffrage couples also formed chosen families by knitting together relationships between their biological kin and their non-biologically related friends, lovers, and adopted children. Leona Huntzinger and Elizabeth Hopkinson met while working in the lace mills in Philadelphia. They became close friends, possibly lovers, and Huntzinger moved in as a boarder in the Hopkinson home where she essentially became a member of the family. They worked in the mills for more than fifteen years before becoming suffrage activists. In 1915, the Pennsylvania Woman Suffrage Organization temporarily hired Huntzinger as a suffrage organizer representing working women.[12]

In May 1916, the two pals, as they publicly referred to each other, determined to travel across the country, supporting themselves by working odd jobs along the way. In Chicago, they found temporary employment as housekeepers and lived in a boarding house with other domestic service workers. Rather than continuing west, Huntzinger and Hopkinson made the decision to head back east when offered a new job opportunity as suffrage speakers with the New York State Suffrage Association. They decided that if they purchased a Ford, they could save money by living out of the car as they continued their travels. In June 1917, they embarked on a six-month tour of New York State. During the day, they delivered suffrage speeches to crowds of onlookers from the back seat of the car. At night, they folded the car seat down to create a bed where they slept. They ignored taunts from young boys and men who sang out "We should worry! We should fret! We will marry a suffragette." This common refrain not only reflected the heteronormative expectation of marriage but also repeated the proposition that suffrage and equal rights made women unmarriageable. But to Huntzinger and Hopkinson, suffrage and their itinerant life provided a sense of exuberance. They enjoyed living and traveling together, free from the expectations and constraints of heteronormative society.[13]

In the years after their suffrage campaigning, Huntzinger and Hopkinson settled down to create their own unique form of chosen family. They purchased Three Springs Farm where they lived in Bacton, Pennsylvania. By 1930, they had adopted four young boys (aged 7 to 13) who lived and worked with them on the farm. The children were likely part of a program such as the Children's Aid Society (CAS). Founded in 1853 in New York City and organized in Pennsylvania in 1884, the CAS sought to find homes for abandoned or destitute children. The CAS often placed children on farms to assist in agricultural work. This chosen family, consisting of two suffragists turned farmers with their "adopted" children, represented a very queer family formation.[14]

The notion of unmarried women taking in and raising children was a simultaneously conservative and radical concept. Though rare, Huntzinger and Hopkinson were not the only suffragists who settled down together on a farm and built their own family. Mary S. Malone and Anna Woods Bird were both active suffragists in Delaware. Malone was also a reformer who worked as a factory inspector in Wilmington, enforcing the state's ten-hour work law which was intended to protect working women. Malone and Bird purchased the Beaver Brook Farm in Chadds Ford, Pennsylvania around 1915 and lived there together until 1956. They also adopted a child and created an extended community that included other suffragist couples.[15]

Suffragists and reformers who chose not to marry and instead devoted their lives to altruistic causes gained some respectability by emphasizing their role as mothers to all of society's children. Claudia Nelson, a historian of family childhood history, has noted that because spinsters were criticized for their rejection of marriage and motherhood, their choice to adopt children was sometimes viewed as a way of fulfilling their duties as women. But Nelson also argued that "nontraditional adoption could challenge both the patriarchal family and heterosexist reproductive norms."[16] From this framework then, two unmarried women raising adopted children entirely without men was especially radical. Over time, some institutions grew more reluctant to place children in such households, especially as Boston marriages came under increasing suspicion as likely abnormal (lesbian) relationships between women.[17]

Suffragists Elisabeth Irwin and Katharine Anthony also created a chosen family by adopting children. Irwin was a psychologist and educator who opened her own school in New York City. Anthony was a writer who wrote feminist biographies of important historical women like Catherine the Great, Queen Elizabeth, and Susan B. Anthony. When Anthony and Irwin met, sometime around 1910, Irwin was living in Greenwich Village with fellow Smith College graduate Elizabeth Howard Westwood. Irwin and Westwood apparently were lovers. At some point, Anthony moved in with them in their flat in the Village. When Westwood passed away, Irwin and Anthony continued living together at various locations in the city. They also purchased a summer home in Gaylordsville, Connecticut and referred to themselves as the Gay Ladies of Gaylordsville. Although their use of the term did not correspond to our modern usage, it does indicate their identification as a happily coupled pair.[18]

The choice of suffragists like Irwin and Anthony not to marry men or have their own biological children, subjected them to criticism about their inability to form a "proper" family life. Anti-suffragists suggested that they were abnormal women. A Texas woman named Mrs. George F. Arnold wrote a letter to the *Houston Post* dismissing Anthony and other suffragists for their lack of knowledge of family life. She directly attacked Anthony's book on feminism for claiming that boys and girls were born the same and develop gendered characteristics largely as a result of social influence. Arnold wrote that just like other suffragists this "shows that she [Anthony] too has no personal knowledge of the babe in the cradle."[19] These attacks on suffragists' personal lives not only reflected heteronormative bias but also failed to recognize suffragists' chosen families. Anthony did have children. When Irwin and Anthony met, Irwin had already adopted a boy named Luigi Balestro. After Elizabeth Westwood died in 1915, Irwin legally adopted a nine-year-old girl whom she named Elizabeth Westwood Jr. in her former partner's honor. The next year Irwin informally adopted a four-year-old girl. Irwin and Anthony raised all three of these children as their own.[20]

Although Irwin was technically the legal guardian of the children, Irwin and Anthony named their youngest daughter after both of them by combining their names. By naming their child, Katharine Irwin, they affirmed their parental status in a way that social norms or the law would not allow them to do. Naming methods was one of the creative ways that suffragists queered traditional notions of family. In heteronormative families, boys were often named after biological fathers and grandfathers and assigned the designation of junior. Similarly, Irwin queered heteronormative family practices by naming her first adopted daughter, Elizabeth Westwood Jr. Thus, Irwin not only memorialized her deceased lover but also used the designation "junior" to usurp this male privilege.[21]

Irwin and Anthony's chosen family expanded over time. Even after their adopted children had grown and formed families of their own, Irwin and Anthony continued to care for their extended family. They were in their sixties when they adopted their grandsons since their daughter Katharine was no longer able to care for them. Irwin and Anthony's chosen family remained an important part of their lives up until their dying days.[22]

Adopted Mothers

Younger queer suffragists sometimes formed chosen families by "adopting" parents from suffragist elders. These were especially significant relationships as chosen parents could provide support and acceptance that young queer suffragists had been denied by their own biological families. Albert Eugene De Forrest's close relationship with his adopted suffragist mother through his gender transition demonstrates the importance of queer chosen families in the suffrage movement.

De Forrest was assigned female at birth, named Mary Jane Bradley, and raised as a girl by his parents. Throughout his childhood, youth, and young adult life, De Forrest explained that he was a boy but was ignored by others who insisted that he publicly present and identify as a girl. While attending Vassar College in 1867, De Forrest met Dr. Alida Cornelia Avery, a suffragist and the resident physician at the university. De Forrest consulted Avery on a variety of issues, including his concern about being forced to wear women's clothing. Avery apparently listened with a sympathetic ear and provided advice and guidance in his college days and throughout his life. De Forrest described Dr. Avery as a mentor and adopted mother. The two no doubt found common ground in their objection to societal norms that confined individuals to cisheteronormative boxes. As a young woman, Avery resented the notion that women should focus on a future as wives and mothers and chose instead to become a doctor. Avery was an ardent advocate for the rights of girls and women. She waged a persistent battle against sexism and gender discrimination in her personal and professional lives.[23]

Avery and De Forrest parted ways for a time after Avery retired from Vassar and moved to Denver to establish a private medical practice. She helped lead the fight for a woman's suffrage referendum as the founder and first president of the Colorado Territorial Woman Suffrage Society (later the Colorado Woman Suffrage Society). During the period that Avery resided in Colorado, De Forrest remained on the East Coast developing a career on the stage. De Forrest agreed to a non-sexual, marriage of convenience with the Reverend John Milton Hart, a graduate of Yale University and the Union Theological Seminary in New York.[24]

De Forrest and Avery reunited in California in the 1880s. Avery established a medical practice in San Jose and became very active in the California suffrage campaign.[25] De Forrest relocated to California with Hart and taught elocution and oratory classes in the San Francisco Bay area as Mrs. Mary J. Bradley with the stage name "Eugenie De Forrest." When Hart passed away in 1893, De Forrest recalled the marriage of more than eighteen years as a pleasant one where they lived together as "married chums." De Forrest explained that Hart was supportive when he had confessed despair and discomfort at wearing women's clothing. It is not surprising therefore that shortly after Hart's death, De Forrest announced his decision to exclusively wear men's clothes. In 1893, he declared that he would only play male roles on stage from that time forward. He continued to use the name Eugenia.[26]

The newspaper writers who reported on De Forrest's life story appeared to be mostly sympathetic, portraying him simply as an eccentric actor. But the San Francisco Board of Supervisors had passed a city ordinance in 1863 making it illegal to dress in the clothing of the opposite sex. Violators were subject to fine, arrest, and up to six months' imprisonment. By the late nineteenth century, the police often used the ordinance as a justification to harass people who transgressed gender norms and to institutionalize gender non-conforming offenders. De Forrest, with the help of Avery, obtained letters from medical doctors and sought permission from the San Francisco and San Jose Police Departments to wear men's clothing as an exception to the city ordinance against cross-dressing.[27]

Although De Forrest had formal authorization to dress as he pleased, he was not completely shielded from negative comments or criticisms. A writer for the *Wasp*, a weekly San Francisco satire magazine, poked fun at the situation by announcing:

> A certain Eugenia de Forest, actress, proudly flanks the walks of San Jose in full masculine attire. She says it gives her freedom. She longs for the free and easy life of the lords of creation. Wonder if she shaves? And does she swear? Eugenia did you ever have a jag? Eugenia, there is a world of experience before you.[28]

The writer implied that adopting so-called male behaviors such as swearing, shaving, and drinking would be a step too far. Wearing men's clothing thus subjected De Forrest to continued public ridicule.

Despite this negative commentary, De Forrest asserted his right to live as his true self. Two years later, De Forrest made a public announcement in the *Berkeley Advocate*. On December 14, 1895, he wrote a notice that was published in the newspaper:

> To the Public: Some years since I assumed male attire by advice of the highest medical authority. Albert Eugene De Forest[29]

De Forrest also publicly changed his first name. An accompanying ad announced oratory and acting classes by "Eugene De Forest" rather than Eugenie. An article in the same issue of the paper announced the arrival of "Mr. Eugene De Forest" to Berkeley. The article lauded his credentials as an actor, noting that "he has led with the great stars" of the stage and that critics "speak of his work in terms of highest praise." The article concluded by announcing that "he is a Christian gentleman of birth and breeding and commands the respect of all who know him."[30] The exclusive use of male pronouns throughout the article signaled De Forrest's full social gender transition.

Other newspapers quickly picked up the story, some more respectfully than others. The Grass Valley *Daily Morning Union* reprinted the article under the headline "De Forest Is a Man." The writer used she/her pronouns when referencing De Forrest's prior life and then switched to he/him pronouns when referring to his new life. The writer told the audience that: "De Forest has known his real sex for some years and today published an advertisement announcing he was a man, that he might retain self respect."[31] In a less respectful article that frequently used she/her pronouns, the *Los Angeles Times* noted that after a life-long search "she had discovered herself" and wished to be known hereafter as "Mr. Eugene" rather than as "Miss Eugenie." At one point the writer offensively referred to De Forrest as "she, he or it."[32] Both papers attempted to understand the situation by describing Eugenia De Forrest as a woman of the "Dr. Mary Walker type," referencing the well-known gender nonconforming woman suffragist.

It is important to note the difference between Walker and De Forrest. Feminists like Dr. Mary Walker wore men's clothing as a statement of their right as women to wear the clothing of their choice and to freely express themselves as women. They discarded restrictive clothing and claimed male privilege by dressing practically and comfortably. But they were women and wanted to be acknowledged as women. Whereas individuals like De Forrest wore men's clothing, not for the express purpose of furthering the women's rights movement, but instead as an outward indicator of their gender. De Forrest was a man and wanted the public to acknowledge him as a man. Contemporary comparisons between De Forrest and Walker were therefore not accurate representations of the situation.[33]

After the formal public announcement, De Forrest continued to live and work in the San Francisco Bay Area, sometimes going by the name "Eugene De Forest (Forrest)" or by the full name "Albert Eugene De Forest (Forrest)." He thus socially transitioned very openly and publicly with apparently very little opposition in 1895.[34] Historian Emily Skidmore has argued that "it is perhaps a testament to the open community of 1890s San Francisco that De Forrest made this transition without leaving the city."[35] An alternate reading offers an equally plausible interpretation. Historian Amy Sueyoshi has argued that stories of transgressions of gender, sexual, and racial boundaries in early San Francisco generated limited controversy because they were largely interpreted as "entertaining anecdotes" that posed little "threat to the existing social order."[36]

The reaction of his adoptive mother and the community of suffragists that De Forrest chose as his family was also complicated. Avery had maintained a mothering relationship with De Forrest since they met at Vassar. When they reunited in San Jose they resumed that relationship. Press reports that appeared shortly after De Forrest's 1895 announcement suggested that Avery might not have been initially supportive of his public transition. Surprised by the news, she reportedly questioned his sanity. In an interview with the San Jose *Evening News*, Avery insisted that De Forrest was a widowed woman who chose to wear men's clothing for hygiene reasons. Avery was an advocate of dress reform and had argued in the past that women should be freed from the dictates of fashion for health purposes.[37] It seems that Avery fully supported De Forrest's decision to wear men's attire as long as it was framed as a commitment to women's rights and as long as De Forrest identified as a woman. I do not know if Avery ever came to fully accept his transition but years later, after Avery's death, De Forrest told reporters that Avery was his "friend" and "confidante" who took him in as her "adopted son." De Forrest praised his adopted mother, insisting that she was the only family that truly cared for him. "She understood my nature and agreed with me that it was the only possible life I could live."[38]

With the love and support of his adoptive mother and her suffrage friends, De Forrest became a dedicated reformer. De Forrest lived with Avery in the years after his transition. They were active in reform efforts together, including the temperance and suffrage movements. The temperance movement was a conservative Christian movement that became closely associated with the suffrage movement when Frances Willard and the Women's Christian Temperance Union (WCTU) became vocal activists for women's suffrage, believing that women were uniquely positioned to exercise their moral influence over society. With the power of the vote, they hoped to pass temperance legislation to protect women and children from neglectful, abusive, and violent alcoholic husbands and fathers. The California branch of the WCTU was created in 1879. A coalition of temperance women and suffragists lobbied the California state legislature for a suffrage bill in 1889. De Forrest delivered public lectures on temperance at St. George's Hall in San Francisco and at the United Presbyterian Church in San Jose. Avery and De Forrest built an extended community of temperance and suffrage friends. Although Avery's death in September 1908 was shocking to De Forrest, who found himself suddenly deprived of the love of his adoptive mother, he continued to rely on his suffragist chosen family for support.[39]

The press continued to depict De Forrest's transition as an entertaining novelty until he attempted to exercise the full rights and privileges enjoyed by cisgender men. Shortly after Avery's death, De Forrest moved to southern California to begin his life anew in a community that was not aware of his gender history. On November 17, 1911, De Forrest married Margaret Barton Hawley in the First Methodist Church in Santa Barbara. Although De Forrest revealed his gender history to Hawley, this marriage apparently did not last long. The two divorced shortly thereafter.[40] Reports of gender non-conforming individuals appeared in the newspapers from time to time. But individuals like De Forrest faced significant risks, especially when they moved to new locales. The threat of persecution, arrest, imprisonment, and punishment were ever present.[41] De Forrest's engagement to another woman in Los Angeles in 1915 ended in his arrest. De Forrest informed his fiancée of his gender history and expressed his desire for a marriage of companionship. She apparently agreed, but someone reported De Forrest to the police. After De Forrest's arrest and the extensive press coverage his story received, his fiancée denounced the pending marriage and claimed not to have known about his assigned sex at birth.[42]

During this difficult time, De Forrest once again relied on his suffrage chosen family for support. In interviews with the press, he insisted that he did not want to harm anyone but only to live freely. In one particularly painful interview, he recounted the entire story of his life for a curious and prying reporter. The reporter recalled that De Forrest's eyes filled with tears as he explained that: "I want the world to know my story."[43] Suffragist Clara Shortridge Foltz, who was a part of De Forrest's queer chosen suffrage family, volunteered as his lawyer to defend him against criminal charges. Upon the advice of Foltz and medical doctors who examined De Forrest and declared him "mentally normal," the Los Angeles Police Department dropped the charges against him and allowed him to dress as he pleased. Emily Skidmore has argued that De Forrest's race and class status afforded him some privilege by shielding him somewhat from public derision and criminal prosecution. As a white, middle-class individual, he was depicted not as a criminal or sexual deviant but at first as an eccentric actor and later as an unfortunate individual "handicapped by his constitution." Thus, he was allowed to explain himself to the press and negotiate with the police.[44]

Has
Body
of
Woman
and
Mind
of
Man

Two Views
of
Prof. Eugene
De Forest
in
Male Attire,
and Mrs.
Clara
Shortridge
Foltz,
'Man'-Woman's
Attorney

Elocutionist
Tells
of
Her
Dual
Personality

Renounced by the woman who had
been asked to become the wife, in
a third marriage, Professor Eugene
De Forest, who last night was arrested on the charge of having mas-
queraded for twenty-five years as a
man, when in realty the professor is
a woman, today became the storm
center of the agencies of science and
the law to determine whether the professor should be known as a man or
a woman.
    The woman to whom Professor De
Forest claimed she was engaged was
found today by Evening Herald reporters. She is Mrs. B. Durrea, who
lives in a handsome home at 1307
West Eleventh street.
    RENOUNCES DE FOREST

Figure 3.1. Eugene De Forrest created a chosen family among suffragists. "Woman's Story of Life as Man." *Los Angeles Evening Herald.* September 1, 1915, 1.

After his arrest and subsequent release, De Forrest remained in Los Angeles and continued teaching courses in oratory, singing, dancing, and acting until his death on October 8, 1917. He contracted pneumonia in September 1917 and went to the County Hospital for treatment. He insisted on his right to be housed in the men's ward, but hospital officials refused to comply with his request. De Forrest once again sought legal aid, most likely from Foltz. Concluding that he was mentally competent, they admitted him to the men's ward in accordance with his request.

After he passed away from pneumonia, the physician at the County Hospital who completed the death certificate listed De Forrest's sex as "female?"[45] His death certificate and burial record, however, officially recorded his name: "Albert E. De Forrest."[46] Chosen suffrage family was thus crucial to queer individuals like De Forrest who were marginalized in mainstream society.

Chosen families were also important to queer suffragists of color who experienced marginalization not only because of their gender or sexuality but because of their race. As a Chinese American doctor who transgressed normative racial and gender boundaries, Margaret Chung relied on various chosen families throughout her life and became an adoptive mother to others. Chung was the daughter of Chinese immigrants and the oldest of seven children. She bore heavy responsibilities in her family after her parents' death, providing emotional and financial support and serving as the primary mother figure to her siblings.[47]

Chung also created chosen family in her professional life among her medical colleagues and suffragist allies. Bertha Van Hoosen served as the head physician at the Mary Thompson Hospital in Chicago where Chung interned. Van Hoosen described the group of nurses and interns as family and Chung as especially popular. Van Hoosen even noted years later that because of Chung's popularity, they had to institute a rule banning the sharing of beds. Van Hoosen no doubt made this remark only to show how well-liked Chung was, but the creation of rules against bed-sharing during this era reflected larger concerns about the potential of all women's environments to foster lesbianism.[48]

Chung was a vocal proponent of women's rights from her early college days. She viewed her pursuit of a medical degree as a significant part of a larger battle against restrictive gender norms. In 1912, while studying at the University of Southern California, Chung insisted on women's equal rights in China and the United States. The issue of enfranchisement was especially complex for Chung. Chinese immigrants were barred from naturalization and were therefore denied the right to vote under the United States' Naturalization Act of 1870. Anti-Chinese sentiment further led to the passage of discriminatory immigration laws such as the 1882 Chinese Exclusion Act that banned the entry of Chinese laborers. Merchants were exempt from the ban but they still encountered segregation when they arrived in the United States, including xenophobic naturalization policies that denied both Chinese men and women the right to vote. As an American citizen by birth, Chung did not face the same issues that her immigrant parents did. She won the right to vote in 1911 when California enfranchised women voters. But Chung was keenly aware of the persistence of racism and segregation. In Los Angeles, Chung served as the secretary of the Woman's Auxiliary of the Chinese American League of Justice. She was also a member of the Chinese Protective Association and the Chinese Women's Reform Club. Chung and her suffragist family not only advocated for the voting rights of American and Chinese women but also banded together to resist the United States' racist and discriminatory policies against Chinese immigrants and Chinese Americans.[49]

Chosen family and extended community were especially important to Chinese American suffragists in their efforts to fight gender and racial oppression. Despite their native-born status, Chinese American women, like Chung, faced blatant discrimination on account of both their sex and their race. White Americans alternately demonized and exoticized Chinese women. Working class Chinese immigrants were seen as economic threats to the livelihood of white Americans. Middle-class white Americans stereotyped working-class Chinese women as prostitutes. They viewed actual Chinese sex workers as victims in need of saving both for their own sake and for the supposed threat they posed to middle-class morality. Middle-class Chinese American women were also particular objects of fascination as they were often depicted as quaint, beautiful, and passive models of domesticity and femininity. A journalist writing for the *Los Angeles Herald* described Chung as having a "flower-like" and "ivory tinted face" with "almond eyes." Reporters focused on Chung as a novelty and an outsider due to her Chinese heritage. The writer, for example, described Chung as "oddly attractive in her American clothes" and speaking "in perfect English," implying that she was somehow not from the United States although she was American born.[50] This "othering" of Chinese American women perpetuated the myth of the "perpetual foreigner."[51]

Chung's status as a single woman further subjected her to scrutiny about her "abnormal" family life. Chung never married and there is some evidence that she engaged in erotically charged relationships with other women.[52] Her blatant defiance of gender norms cast suspicion on her private life. Chung not only pursued a career as a doctor and fought for women's equality but she queered the norm through her gender expression. In her early career, she adopted a masculine appearance that included slicked-back hair, black tailored suits, sailor hats, and a cane. Chung also participated in behaviors typically associated with men—such as drinking, gambling, and swearing. Among friends, she referred to herself as "Mike." Like other suffragists, Chung's advocacy of women's rights and association with progressive thinkers fostered her gender rebellion.[53]

Chung's chosen family insulated her somewhat from charges of abnormality. The efforts of writers to reinterpret and soften Chung's mannish gender presentation by emphasizing her role as an adopted mother reflect the degree of anxiety generated over transgressions of gender. Gerald J. O'Gara's article in the December 1924 issue of *Sunset Magazine* described Chung as "professionally mannish" in her "silk shirtwaist, soft collar and bow tie." O'Gara reassured the readership, however, that Chung was a womanly woman who embodied "a woman's tenderness and a mother's love" that she "showered on a growing family" that included the six siblings that she helped support.[54] This affirmation of Chung's feminine and motherly attributes thus sought to assuage fears that her outward mannishness reflected an inward gender or sexual abnormality.

Chung served as a mother figure to her siblings and continued to build an extended chosen family. During the 1930s and 1940s, Chung was active in Red Cross work and lobbied Congress for the creation of the WAVES (Women Accepted for Volunteer Emergency Service) so that women could support the war effort by serving in the Naval Reserve. Chung became the informal adopted mother for the naval pilots who came to her for medical treatment. She hosted weekly family meals and offered emotional support. They called her Mom Chung and viewed her as a surrogate mother. Since she joked that she could not be their mother because she was unmarried and most of the men were white, they nicknamed themselves "Mom Chung's Fair-Haired Bastard Sons." She was so popular that the Chinese government relied on her to recruit American pilots for the Flying Tigers. Although they eventually numbered in the hundreds, Chung's sons kept in touch with her and often visited her home. She cultivated her new motherly role and image as she continued her work as a physician during World War II.[55]

Chung's creation of a chosen family and the cultivation of her image as the motherly "Mom Chung" helped create a professional aura of middle-class respectability. Her decision to adopt a more feminine style of clothing in later life may have emanated from similar concerns about presenting an outward appearance of respectable heterosexuality or asexuality. But Chung's cultivation of her image as "Mom Chung" was also a genuine effort to create a chosen family. Chung's biological family remained an important part of her life. As a queer woman of color actively trying to resist and survive in a sexist, racist, and xenophobic society, Chung relied on community for support and nurturance. Throughout her education, career, and suffrage activism, she created a queer chosen family. In her later life, Chung's numerous pilot "sons" served as another chosen family that provided her with a sense of purpose and belonging.

Queer Community

In addition to chosen families, queer suffragists also built extended queer communities that supported and nurtured them personally and professionally. Katharine Anthony and Elisabeth Irwin for example built a queer community with other feminist and professional women in New York City. By the 1910s, Greenwich Village had already become a popular site for writers, artists, and reformers. Anthony and Irwin's home, "Number One Patchin Place," became a community gathering place. Suffragists, artists, and writers dined together at their home and engaged in lively discussion and debate. The relationships they formed and the community they built provided professional and personal support for suffragists.[56]

Lucy Diggs Slowe and Mary Powell Burrill also built an extended community of family, friends, and allies in their Washington, DC home. This network not only fueled their activism for racial and gender justice but provided them with an important support network to rely on in difficult times. Burrill met Slowe in 1912 when they were both teaching high school in their respective cities of Washington, DC and Baltimore, Maryland. A few years later, Slowe moved to Washington, DC with Burrill. They later purchased a home and remained together for the rest of their lives. Beginning in 1922, Slowe served as Dean of Women at Howard University. Burrill was not only a teacher at Dunbar High School and Armstrong High School, but was also a playwright who tackled issues of racism and gender inequality.[57]

In their professional lives as educators and suffragists, Slowe and Burrill built a queer community of friends, colleagues, and students working together for racial and gender justice. Burrill was active in the Black literary and artistic community in Washington, DC. She interacted with prominent writers, artists, and poets famous for their roles in the cultural renaissance of the New Negro Movement (later known as the Harlem Renaissance). As a student at Howard University, Slowe had forged deep friendships with her sorority sisters in Alpha Kappa Alpha and faculty such as George William Cook and Coralie Cook. George was active in the NAACP and Coralie was a suffragist and co-founder of the National Association of Colored Women (NACW). Slowe's activism in the NAACP and the suffrage movement was greatly influenced by these mentors. As assistant secretary of the Baltimore NAACP, Slowe advocated for women's right to vote. She expressed the hope that with the franchise, Black women and men would work together for racial justice. In 1919, Slowe was elected president of the College Alumnae Club, an association of college-educated Black women where she worked with notable suffragists such as Mary Church Terrell. As founders of the National Council for Negro Women in 1935, Slowe and Burrill also worked closely with suffragist Mary McLeod Bethune, who had previously served as president of the NACW.[58]

Together with their queer community, Slowe and Burrill directly challenged racism and sexism in society. Chosen family, extended kin, and allies were especially crucial to the survival of Black women who faced oppression and violence from a hostile society. Black communities frequently organized around a sense of collective responsibility where they emphasized the responsibility of every individual in caring for others in the community. Slowe and Burrill especially relied on their queer extended community in their later lives as they faced racist, sexist, and homophobic attacks.[59]

White sexologists typically constructed Black women's sexuality as deviant.[60] This, coupled with the suggestion that suffragists in general were sexually abnormal, led Black suffrage leaders to respond defensively by elevating the image of the respectable married middle-class

Figure 3.2. Lucy Diggs Slowe and Mary Powell Burrill created an extended network of friends and allies who supported their suffrage activism. Lucy Diggs Slowe, right, with her partner, Mary Burrill. Moorland-Spingarn Research Center, Howard University Archives, Howard University, Washington, DC.

Black suffragist. School administrators concerned with the lesbian threat on campuses discouraged single-sex education, encouraged more co-educational extracurricular activities, and sought to hire married women or male faculty members as models of "normal" relationships. Throughout the 1910s and 1920s, during the height of their suffrage and anti-racist activism, Slowe's and Burrill's social position and standing in the community insulated them somewhat from attacks against their personal lives.[61]

But, in the increasingly oppressive era of the 1930s, homosexual relationships between women were more frequently depicted as abnormal affronts to respectable domesticity. There was also growing backlash against feminism. Educators, and especially black feminist educators, found their lives under increasing scrutiny. Mordecai Johnson, president of Howard University, constantly clashed with Slowe over a range of issues. His sexist views of women as leaders infuriated Slowe, who continuously pushed back against his efforts to strip her of her power and authority on campus. At one point, Johnson vigorously opposed Slowe's living situation and insisted that she move out of the home that she had purchased with Burrill and live on-campus, closer to the students. Slowe wrote a letter of protest to Abraham Flexner and the Board of Trustees that revealed the depth of her attachment to her home:

> I do not want to sell my home . . . every year groups of students meet with
> me around my open fire or under the trees on the lawn . . . for ten years I
> have built up this home and shared it, at no expense to the University, with
> the students. Naturally I am attached to it and do not wish to leave it.[62]

Although Slowe framed the significance of the home in reference to
her work with students at Howard, the house was a symbol of her life
with Burrill and the community they had built together. It had become
a gathering place for their activist and educator friends. Slowe believed
that this attempt by Johnson to dictate her housing arrangement was a
deliberate effort to demote her to the status of house matron. Scholars
have also speculated that it was an attempt to separate her from her
queer relationship with Burrill.

With the support of their suffrage extended family, Slowe resisted
Johnson and fought back. Coralie Cook and Mary McLeod Bethune, for
example, wrote letters to the administration and directly intervened on
Slowe's behalf. They praised Slowe for her dedication and commitment
to the women of Howard University and urged the administration to
treat her with the respect she was due. With their friends and allies ral-
lying around them, Slowe and Burrill ultimately won the right to remain
in their home off-campus.[63]

Just as Slowe and Burrill relied on their extended network for support, the queer community also proved important to suffragists whose
views of sex and marriage radically departed from the mainstream. During the suffrage era, new ideas about free love challenged traditional
family structures and emphasized the importance of queer community.
Free lovers insisted that individuals should be free to enter and leave
sexual relationships without the regulation of the state. Thus, unmarried
couples and individuals who left one relationship for another would not
be judged for engaging in sexual relationships outside of marriage. Con-
trary to the attacks levied by their critics, most free lovers of the suffrage
era did not advocate polygamy or simultaneous sexual relationships
with multiple partners (although some did). Instead, free lovers typically
engaged in and advocated for long-term monogamous relationships free
from regulation by government or church authorities. These ideas were
radical for the time in part because they allowed women greater freedom over their bodies and the power to leave unsatisfactory relation-

ships without seeking permission from the state. They envisioned free love as a blow to the patriarchy that had trapped them in loveless or abusive marriages. Thus, most feminists of the period agreed with these ideas in principle even as they personally disassociated themselves from the negative connotations of the term "free love." Others, like Victoria Woodhull, more openly embraced the label. Individual suffragists found ways to navigate the complexities of their personal and professional positions on the issue.[64]

Frances Maule was a suffragist who embraced the idea of free love and broadened the notion of queer chosen family and community. Maule was an active advocate of women's rights working on the New York state suffrage campaign. She met Edwin Bjorkman in New York City. Bjorkman was a Swedish writer, socialist, and free lover who believed in social cooperation as a means to improving society's problems. The two married in January 1906.[65]

Maule and Bjorkman created a queer chosen family and community when they joined an experimental cooperative community known as Helicon Home Colony in 1906. Author and suffragist Upton Sinclair founded the colony in Englewood, New Jersey. Inspired by progressive ideals, Sinclair hoped to create an efficient environment for creative types that simplified daily living by minimizing the drudgery of housework and childcare, especially for women who bore the brunt of domestic tasks. He purchased the campus of a former boys' school and invited writers, artists, musicians, and professionals to apply. About seventy individuals eventually lived at the colony, paying a weekly rent that included the services of a cook, a domestic, a gardener, and a nursemaid. The children enjoyed relative freedom to play and socialize with each other housed in their own separate quarters. This allowed the adults to work and live unencumbered by the demands of parenting and housework. The colonists likened themselves to a family and, in many ways these like-minded writers and artists did function as a family unit. They divided up tasks and gathered together for meals. They enjoyed philosophical discussions about a range of radical topics around the dinner table and fireplace. Individuals formed intimate friendships and sometimes fell in love.[66]

The public was generally suspicious of the colony in part because the press dubbed Helicon Colony a hedonistic haven for sex-crazed anarchists and free lovers. One newspaper went so far as to report that police had raided Helicon Hall to stop "free love" activities. Sinclair fought back and demanded a retraction of the false story. He continuously sought to create a positive public image of the colony. Although it was not at all what the press envisioned, the colonists of Helicon did embrace non-traditional views of marriage and love. Sinclair was married to Meta Fuller. They both were advocates of free love and publicly insisted they were monogamists. But both were rumored to have had extramarital affairs during their marriage that led to a much publicized divorce in 1911. Sinclair apparently had at least one affair with a married woman at Helicon. Maule and Bjorkman were also advocates of free love and declared monogamists. Bjorkman translated and produced Swedish plays for audiences in Greenwich Village that espoused his free love principles and the radical idea for the era that marriage should not confine love.[67] Their experience at the colony came to an end when the dormitory caught fire and burned to the ground in March 1907.

But, the queer community they formed at Helicon Hall endured. The Sinclairs and the Bjorkmans remained close. In a May 1907 letter, Maule wrote to Meta Sinclair, sending their love to both her and Upton. Maule expressed deep concern over Meta's well-being as she apparently struggled with serious health and marital issues. Maule wrote:

> a great wave of love and tenderness swept over me and I wish that I might take you in my arms and kiss you and tell you how much I love you. I have seldom felt so strong and active an affection for anyone as I have for you, dear girl, and it has been a real deprivation to me not to be able to see you.[68]

Maule offered friendly advice encouraging her to "look for the joy" in life and focus on exploring the "heights and depths and lengths and breadths" of her present experiences. The importance of their supportive and loving relationship is clear when Maule encourages Meta to "make use of me in the old way—as a sort of sympathetic bucket into which you could pour all your thoughts." In reference to Meta's earlier letter, Maule notes, "the fact that you have my old chain touched me very deeply. If you really care to keep it as a memento of me, I shall be touched more deeply still."[69] A few months later, Maule learned that Meta sought treatment at the sanitarium at Battle Creek, Michigan to recuperate from a breakdown. Maule wrote a letter full of concern addressed to "Darling Meta" and noted that "you are the only person I ever address as 'darling' in a letter. I guess it is because with you, I mean it. Some way or other you always seem to me such a darling. The word fits you."[70] The care and sentiments expressed in these letters reflect the blurred lines of the queer relationships that developed between couples at Helicon Hall and the community they created that provided support long after the experimental colony ended.

Maule's suffrage chosen family played a significant role in her life as well. In the years immediately following the Helicon fire, Bjorkman and Maule moved back to New York City and Maule turned her attention more fully to her suffrage work. She was at first employed by NAWSA to lead the publicity department. The New York State Woman Suffrage Party later hired Maule to work as a speaker and field organizer under the direction of Carrie Chapman Catt. She also wrote extensively for the cause and traveled throughout the state delivering street speeches and raising money for suffrage.

Maule was acutely aware that her queer beliefs about family and marriage were altogether too radical for the mainstream suffrage movement. She frequently held her tongue in public "for the good of the cause" but vented to Bjorkman in her private letters. She complained about the "average wife & mother woman'" that she met in her travels. She described them as entitled and incapable of real suffrage work. Maule criticized their maternalist thinking: "they all devoutly believe all the gruff about the spiritual superiority etc. of woman—and . . . really do think that they can uplift politically merely by casting the light of their countenances upon it."[71] She complained about the conservativeness of the women in the movement for embracing middle-class, heteronormative views of marriage and family:

> I cannot speak freely for fear that what I say may . . . "hurt the cause." . . .
> I feel that I have silenced my utterances . . . to the point of absolute innocuousness. I must have done so, since I seem to leave behind me nothing but praise! Now when you've got to the point where you say nothing to give offense to anybody, you must have produced as nearly nothing as anything can be . . . all the leaders in whose districts I speak plead for me to come back—on the grounds that "Mrs. Bj. is just the type that this

district needs." Ain't it a scream? I really do seem to have "taken well"—as they say—up in these parts—from which I gather that I give them the impression of being a conventionally correct lady of conservative views and gentle manners who dresses nicely and agrees with everybody. When you come home Edwin, we will have to go off on a dreadful disreputable bat![72]

Maule recognized the necessity of presenting herself as a respectable married woman who conformed to traditional gender norms in order to win the support of the general public. This included playing down her beliefs about free love and marriage.

Maule's letters reveal that she believed in the right of women to take lovers outside the bounds of traditional marriage. Referring to a lonely widow she met on the suffrage campaign trail, Maule expressed her thoughts on free love: "I suspect that what she wants more than anything else in life is a really big, absorbing, passionate love . . . she married at twenty-one, and apparently cherished only a mild regard for her husband. He has now been dead some years . . . now isn't it a shame that she hasn't a right to go and find herself a lover?"[73] Maule railed against societal expectations that condemned women for engaging in sexual relationships outside of marriage.

Maule and Bjorkman's relationship was loving and supportive. Bjorkman traveled frequently for his work and when he was not traveling, he lived in their apartment in the city. They wrote to each other extensively when apart. Maule's letters to Bjorkman were full of affirmation and affection. She frequently began with salutations like "my precious Boydie and ended with "a tender, fond goodnight kiss and my heart's love . . . I love you, my own. Your girl."[74] She reminded him often how much she loved him. Bjorkman reciprocated with equally loving and affectionate letters to his wife.

Yet, Maule and Bjorkman's marriage was also characterized by tension and strife partially as a result of her devotion to her suffrage chosen family and her queer living arrangements. She traveled from city to city, boarding with other suffragists as she moved. Bjorkman, not quite as progressive as he perhaps imagined himself to be, at times grew annoyed with her constant travel and her inability to come home as frequently as he liked. Maule responded by suggesting he travel to meet her. Bjorkman sent her an angry letter and Maule shot back in a reply letter:

It was very thoughtful of you to send that bitter letter of yours by special delivery in order that I might have Sunday to get over it and be fresh for my Convention on Monday! Suppose next time you go yourself one better in the way of consideration, and, having relieved your mind of a similar burst, you deposit it in small fragments in the waste paper basket, and then write a bright and cheery letter instead.[75]

Asserting the equal importance of their work, Maule clearly laid out the options for him:

1. I cannot count on getting home during the rest of the campaign except at rare intervals, for very short periods, and at very great expense.

2. You have landed a job which you can do anywhere—given a reasonable amount of quiet, privacy and comfort.

Now if you want me, come where I am—and put up as best you can with possible shifts & readjustments. If you want the comfort and security of home, stay home and make up your mind to very rare and fleeting glimpses of me.[76]

Putting into practice their ideas about free love, Bjorkman and Maule separated in 1918 due to "temperamental incompatibility."[77]

Before and especially after her divorce, Maule increasingly turned to her suffrage chosen family for support. She moved into an apartment building in Greenwich Village with other suffragists. Maule forged intimate relationships with radical women who embraced a diverse set of political and social beliefs, from anarchy and socialism to birth control and free love. Queer relationships were also common among this group of Village suffragists. Anecdotal evidence suggests that Maule and fellow suffragist Kathleen De Vere Taylor eventually became lovers. The 1930 and 1940 censuses show Maule and Taylor living together until Taylor passed away in 1949.[78]

Conclusion

The stories highlighted in this chapter demonstrate the ways that suffragists queered notions of family and community. Chosen families allowed suffragists to pool their economic resources to provide financially for each other. This was especially important for queer suffragists who were thereby freed from the necessity of marrying for economic security. Chosen families also provided the emotional support and love that queer suffragists had been denied from their biological families. Together they developed strategies for protecting and nurturing their most marginalized members, allowing each other the freedom to live as their true selves. They comforted each other through personal triumph and tragedy and cared for each other throughout their lives.

The suffrage movement's focus on projecting a public front of heteronormative respectability made the creation of extended queer communities among suffragists especially important. These networks provided queer suffragists with the support they needed to live fulfilling private and professional lives while deflecting public scrutiny. Queer suffragists especially depended on this community not only in their struggle for women's right to vote but in their battles against the barriers imposed by a cisheterosexist society. These relationships ultimately proved crucial to the success of the suffrage movement as they nurtured, maintained, and motivated queer suffragists to carry on the fight for the vote.

4

Queering Transatlantic Alliances

In 1908, an American student in London named Alice Paul was converted to the cause of women's suffrage after hearing a rousing speech by Christabel Pankhurst of the Women's Social and Political Union. Paul soon forged a friendship with British suffragette Rachel Barrett, who asked her to help sell the suffragette newspaper *Votes for Women*. Paul was in awe of Barrett's boldness and commitment to the cause. Barrett was a queer woman and the editor of the WSPU newspaper. She endured multiple arrests, imprisonments, hunger strikes, and forcible feedings. She evaded rearrest by donning disguises. Barrett was protected by a community of sympathetic suffragettes, including her lover Ida Wylie, who nursed her back to health after her hunger strikes and hid the fugitive Barrett in their homes. Paul followed the example of her friend Barrett and other British suffragette sisters and was arrested in London for damaging property. She also went on hunger strike in prison. Paul met another American student named Lucy Burns in a London police station. Armed with the queer tactics they learned from British suffragettes and inspired by the queer alliances they created, these two spinster women returned to the United States, where they launched the militant wing of the American suffrage movement through the Congressional Union (CU) and later the National Woman's Party (NWP).[1]

No examination of the queer history of the American suffrage movement would be complete without looking at the ways in which queer transatlantic connections fueled the cause. Queer friendships and romantic relationships cemented ties between suffragists. Paul was not the only American suffragist who found inspiration across the Atlantic. Others carefully studied the tactics of British suffragettes, hoping to apply the strategies they learned to the suffrage campaign in the United States. They gained inspiration from charismatic suffragette leaders and they forged alliances between suffrage organizations. The relationships they formed often transcended the norm as suffragists developed deeply professional and personal connections. These queer transatlantic alliances proved crucial to the success of the campaign for the vote in both the United Kingdom and the United States.[2]

Queer Tactics

American suffragists queered the norm by studying and adapting the tactics of British militant suffragettes. Margaret Foley's experiences in Britain, though brief, had a significant impact on her suffrage campaign strategy. Foley was a working-class, queer, Irish American woman who became active in the labor and suffrage movements during her time working in a hat factory in Boston. In April 1911, Foley traveled to Europe with Florence Luscomb under the auspices of the Boston Equal Suffrage Association for Good Government and the Massachusetts Woman Suffrage Association. Their main intent was to serve as delegates to the International Woman Suffrage Convention in Stockholm, Sweden. However, their secondary goal was to study the methods of the various suffrage organizations in Britain. They told reporters before they left that they were in sympathy with the militant British suffragettes because: "they seem to be the only ones who are accomplishing anything over there . . . [The Englishman] never gave the women anything until they showed they could fight."[3] Foley and Luscomb hoped to study some of these fighting techniques and were even willing to face arrest and imprisonment if necessary, though they assured the reporters that such extreme tactics most likely would never be necessary in the United States.

Foley and Luscomb spent two months participating in suffrage meetings, rallies, and processions in England. They visited the headquarters and attended the events hosted by suffrage organizations such as the Women's Freedom League, the Actresses Franchise League, the Men's League for Women's Suffrage, the National Union of Women's Suffrage Societies, the Men's Political Union, the Artists' Franchise League, and the Women's Labor League. However, they were most impressed by the Women's Social and Political Union (WSPU). Emmeline Pankhurst founded the WSPU in 1903 and ran the organization with the help of her daughters, Christabel and Sylvia. Since its inception, the WSPU had peacefully petitioned Parliament to pass a bill for women's suffrage, to no avail. Pankhurst gradually decided that they had to switch tactics if they were going to win the vote. Luscomb especially expressed approval of the WSPU's policy of opposing the party in power until they passed women's suffrage (a tactic that would later be used by the NWP in the United States). The WSPU became known as the militant branch when they began to take bolder actions such as heckling politicians, organizing marches and demonstrations, and destroying public property in order to draw attention to their cause. During the period of time that Foley and Luscomb were in England, the WSPU had declared a truce and temporary ceasefire while the Parliament debated the Second Conciliation Bill. This bill would have given the vote to property-owning women. Foley and Luscomb arranged personal meetings with the officers of the WSPU, including the Pankhursts and Emmeline Pethick Lawrence. They attended lectures and participated in demonstrations and marches. Foley sold "Votes for Women" papers in Trafalgar Square.[4]

Inspired by what they saw in England, Foley and Luscomb returned to the United States to resume their suffrage work with renewed vigor. Other American suffragists, including Harriot Stanton Blatch, had previously visited Britain and also gained a new perspective on suffrage tactics. The result in the United States was a gradual shift from more private actions such as lobbying and petitioning politicians to more public actions such as open-air speeches, parades, and demonstrations directly appealing to the people. As early as the summer of 1909, Massachusetts suffragists launched a campaign of extemporaneous open-air speeches. After her return from Britain in 1911, Foley was even more committed to this strategy and began an intense speaking schedule. She also adopted a new tactic, common among the suffragettes of Britain, of publicly challenging politicians with anti-suffrage views. These tactics, which transgressed norms of respectable feminine behavior, earned Foley the nickname the "famous heckler" and made her a popular figure with the American press.[5]

As a queer woman, Foley defied expectations through her rejection of matrimony and her itinerant life as a suffrage organizer (see chapter 2). She lived a life outside the boundaries of normative femininity. Other suffragist women, however, worried about using the radical tactics of the British suffragettes out of concern that it would compromise their reputation as respectable women and for fear of offending or isolating the men in their lives. Margaret Foley, however, was not concerned about her feminine reputation, nor did she particularly care if men were offended by her tactics. Her working-class background likewise freed her from some of the constraints imposed on middle-class women who were expected to perform gentility and meekness. Foley fearlessly confronted male politicians. In September 1911, she interrupted a speech by James H. McInerney, who was running as a candidate to the Massachusetts state legislature. She demanded that he explain why he would not support women's suffrage. Rather than respond to her question, McInerney told her: "You had better go home and mend your husband's stockings." In a bold challenge to the heterosexist statement, Foley matter-of-factly informed him that she did not have a husband. Undeterred, Foley interrupted him again during a speech a few days later. He told the crowd: "I told Maggie the other night to go home and mend her husband's stockings. Since then I have learned she has no husband, but when I get elected to the house next year I will do my best to get a husband for her."[6] Foley again was not phased and instead demanded three minutes at the end of his speech to state the case for women's suffrage. But McInerney did not concede and quickly fled after he concluded his talk.

A few days later, Foley once again used the queer tactics she had learned in Britain to confront McInerney. As she approached a rally he had organized, a police officer told her, "If you open your mouth tonight I will split your head open and run you into the station."[7] McInerney, spotting her in the crowd, began to ridicule her and attempted to turn the crowd against her. But instead, a few men in the crowd encouraged her to speak. Just as she moved to do so, the police officer stepped forward, punching and kneeing her in the back. She called out to a sergeant to complain that the officer who struck her was not fit to be a police officer. She then raised her hand to try once again to speak to McInerney. The offending police officer stepped forward, elbowing her in an effort to silence her. The other officers intervened and forcibly escorted her to the police station. They chastised her and then released her. In defiance of both McInerney and the police, Foley walked outside the station and organized her own impromptu rally. She stood in the back of her car and gave a lively suffrage speech to the captivated audience of two thousand people.[8]

Foley's tactics so queered gender expectations that critics assailed her for her "unwomanly" behavior. Massachusetts politician Albert Langtry, who himself had been heckled by Foley, declared that Foley and her suffragist hecklers were "no ladies." He attacked her as a "brazen woman" for interrupting him while he spoke. Although he insisted he was a suffrage supporter, Langtry declared that Foley "makes all decent women who believe in suffrage ashamed."[9] He argued that Foley's unconventional tactics defied the norms of ladylike behavior and therefore threatened the success of the entire suffrage movement.

This confrontational British strategy of interrupting politicians and challenging them to state a position on woman's suffrage, however, proved effective in applying pressure on lawmakers. It was also quite popular with the public and the press. The Boston *Transcript* declared that Foley had returned from Britain a militant suffragist.[10] Although she had contended that more extreme militant tactics, like the destruction of public property, were not necessary in the United States, she told a *Boston Globe* reporter that "the militants have not only awakened England, but have stirred the whole world." Foley insisted that her goal was to "educate" American politicians: "Those who are just ignorant or just prejudiced—well, we shall simply hound them into knowledge."[11] Foley's fame as a militant suffragist spread and she earned the respect and admiration of many ardent fans.

The queer alliances that Foley had created during her time in Britain proved important in her efforts to further the cause of women's rights. In 1916, while on a suffrage campaign tour with her future partner Helen Elizabeth Goodnow, Foley reunited with Emmeline Pankhurst in Chattanooga, Tennessee. Pankhurst was traveling on a lecture tour throughout the United States. Foley and Pankhurst spoke at the same event and together advocated for women's rights around the world. Pankhurst also used her American lecture tour to counter common stereotypes about suffragists. Goodnow described in her letters how shocked everyone was upon learning that the demure woman was the same "militant suffragist" described in the newspapers. Goodnow noted that Pankhurst "is the quietest and most ladylike person you would ever see."[12] The British suffragette leader seemed to defy categorization. On the one hand, Pankhurst cultivated a feminine appearance and demeanor that stood in stark contrast to the negative press depictions of mannish suffragettes. On the other hand, she engaged in militant methods that stretched the boundaries of femininity. Foley, and other American suffragists, recognized the importance of this balance and especially the power that a transgression of norms could have on liberating women from gender oppression. In her own queer way, Foley adapted the strategies to the American environment.

Nevada suffragist Anne Martin also applied what she had learned in Britain to the American suffrage campaign (see chapter 3). In 1909, Martin was living in Britain when she was recruited as a speaker for the WSPU. She enrolled in an intensive suffrage speaker training course to learn how to successfully engage audiences, and she quickly graduated to street speaker and organizer status. The WSPU repeatedly organized large deputations of suffragettes who marched to Parliament en masse, insisting on their right to speak to the prime minister and present him with petitions to demand the vote. When these efforts failed, the women would rush the House of Commons where they were met by lines of police officers waiting to arrest them.[13]

Martin participated in several of these deputations, but the most notable one occurred on November 18, 1910 in an event that became known as Black Friday. Suffragists demonstrating in Parliament Square were attacked by police officers who physically and sexually assaulted women, hurling them back into an angry crowd to face further violence. The incident lasted for more than six hours as hundreds of women suffered injuries such as black eyes, bleeding noses, and dislocated joints. Martin recalled the brutality the suffragettes endured that day as police used their "bodies, elbows, and fists with great effect," they "hurled, kicked, and knocked" the suffragettes to the ground.[14] More than one hundred women were arrested and imprisoned. Martin herself was arrested and charged with obstructing the police but was quickly bailed out by Frederick Pethick Lawrence, treasurer of the WSPU.

The story of Martin's arrest made the news in her home state of Nevada.[15] Family and friends wrote to express their surprise. Martin's friend, Joseph C. Hopper, sat down to read the newspaper and was shocked to by the story about her role in the fight with the police. He immediately wrote to Martin:

> It was a struggle between tears and laughter, with lapses during the day toward weepiness . . . I don't believe that the "Bishop's girl" would scratch even a Bobby—and with 800 American Jackies looking-on and cheering.[16]

Martin, however, was not dissuaded by the comments of family and friends. She continued to participate in the increasingly militant actions of the WSPU suffragettes.

The following year, in November 1911, Emmeline Pethick Lawrence sent a letter to the members of WSPU calling for another deputation of women. She wrote:

> The time has come when for once family relationships, personal interests and even ordinary duties must be laid aside in obedience to a supreme call of public honor and of public duty.[17]

This sense of duty motivated many women to answer the call. What they sacrificed in family relationships they gained in the new bonds that they formed with each other. Martin became good friends with several WSPU suffragette leaders, including Emmeline Pethick Lawrence, Evelina Haverfield, and Annie Kenney. Martin may have felt a special affinity for these particular women in part because they also led unconventional lives. Scholars have debated about the queer personal lives of many of these famous suffragettes. Pethick Lawrence attracted a number of infatuated admirers. Kenney may have had multiple sexual relationships with women, but the evidence is not conclusive.[18] Haverfield was in a romantic relationship with Vera "Jack" Holme, a fellow WSPU member who defied gender norms with her masculine fashion and behavior. Haverfield and Holme moved in together in 1911. Upon Haverfield's death in 1920, Holme inventoried their shared property, including a bed that was carved with their initials.[19]

These queer relationships among the women encouraged a strong sense of devotion to each other. This devotion, coupled with the emphasis on honor and duty to the cause, compelled them to carry on the fight. Martin's suffragette friends wrote to her personally about their pride in belonging to a "great and glorious movement" and their willingness to give their body "for the uplifting of Womenhood."[20] Martin answered Pethick Lawrence's letter and joined the deputation on November 21, 1911 in Trafalgar Square.

According to her own account of the day, which she gladly shared with the press, the WSPU's tactics had changed since Black Friday. Martin explained that women began carrying bags of stones because they preferred "to break a window and be promptly arrested to having our bodies broken by the police."[21] Martin wore fencing armor to protect herself against the assaults of the police. They also determined to fight back if necessary. When a police officer grabbed a suffragette by the throat, Emmeline Pethick Lawrence asked him to let her go. When he refused, Pethick Lawrence slapped him in the face. Pethick Lawrence, Martin, and Haverfield were all arrested that day.

After her release, Martin returned to Nevada. Before she left, Haverfield wrote to bid her goodbye and remind her of the many friends she left behind in Britain. She told Martin that all her "work and self-sacrifice here will not be in vain."[22] Their friendship was clear in Haverfield's sadness over her departure and in a postscript she added to let her know that she would cherish the coral pin Martin had given her.

Martin returned home a believer in the importance of queer alliances and in the effectiveness of militancy. She told reporters that despite ridicule, the suffragettes of Britain have adopted tactics that proved effective and "are now understood as a serious deliberate political policy designed to embarrass a government which otherwise would not listen to them. As a result of these tactics suffrage has become a question of practical politics."[23] Martin would also assure her American audience that the style of suffrage militancy deployed in Britain was not necessary in the United States. But, she incorporated some of the British tactics into her own suffrage activism.

In 1912, Martin was elected president of the Nevada Equal Franchise League and immediately organized the campaign for a state suffrage amendment. Martin launched an aggressive statewide speaking campaign. Margaret Foley even traveled to Nevada to work with Martin and stump for suffrage. Martin also relied on her transatlantic connections to help with the campaign. Emmeline Pankhurst offered to deliver a series of lectures in Nevada in February 1912, but apparently was unable to follow through since duty called her back to England.[24] Christabel Pankhurst wrote in February wishing them great success and noting that a victory in Nevada would help further their cause in Britain. Nearly two years later, in October 1914, Annie Kenney, who was speaking in North Dakota and Montana, wrote to Martin offering to travel to Nevada to assist in the campaign there.[25] Kenney referred to Martin as an "old friend," recalling their shared experiences in England. Kenney delivered a series of pro-suffrage speeches in Nevada in the final weeks before the election. Their campaign was ultimately successful in November 1914 when Nevada men voted to enfranchise women.[26]

Martin turned her attention to the fight for a federal suffrage amendment. She especially approved of the new tactics by CU leaders Alice Paul and Lucy Burns. They adopted the WSPU strategy of opposing the party in power, regardless of the stand of individual politicians on the issue of suffrage. The goal was to pressure President Wilson and the Democrat Party into supporting a federal suffrage amendment. Martin was one of the first to put this technique into practice. She mobilized suffragists in Nevada to work against a pro-suffrage Democrat candidate. The strategy was a controversial move that distanced them from NAWSA and marked them as militants in the eyes of more conservative suffragists.[27]

Martin continued to embrace British tactics of suffrage militancy when she was elected as the first national chairman of the NWP in 1916. She joined the NWP pickets in their campaign to picket the White House. She immediately organized and led a large WSPU-style deputation of suffragists in Washington, DC, on March 4, 1917 to march around the White House, demanding their right to directly speak with the president (see chapter 5). The incident was successful in garnering media attention. Martin was among the first NWP suffragists arrested later that summer in the picketing campaign. In 1918, she returned to Nevada to run for the US Senate. The NWP endorsed her through her 1918 and 1920 campaigns. Although ultimately unsuccessful, Martin was the first woman ever to run for the US Senate.

Queer Inspiration

Other American suffragists gained more than just tactical inspiration from the charismatic leaders of the British suffrage movement. Alice Morgan Wright was a young American suffragist whose experiences with the suffragettes of Britain, and especially her queer adoration of Emmeline Pankhurst, transformed her into a lifelong activist. Shortly after graduating from Smith College in 1904, Wright left her family in Albany and moved to New York City, where she attended the Art Student League to study sculpture. During this period of time, she was active in the suffrage movement as a member of the Collegiate Equal Suffrage League. In 1909, Wright went to Paris to study art at the Academie des Beaux-Arts and the Academie Colarossi.[28]

Wright's embrace of militant activism began shortly after she boarded a ship bound for Europe and met Emmeline Pankhurst. The now internationally famous British militant suffragette leader was returning home from a speaking tour in the United States. Wright, who was well-acquainted with Pankhurst's suffrage work and had heard her speak, was enamored upon meeting her heroine and endeavored to socialize with the WSPU leader at every opportunity during the voyage. Writing to her friend Edith Shepard back home in New York, Wright recalled her feelings upon sighting Pankhurst for the first time:

> I started out with the sentiments of one who might have [illegible] by the stirrup of Joan of Arc, touching the "hem of her garment" you know, feeling the warmth of her halo and the breath of her wings.[29]

Wright was captivated by Pankhurst's charm and charisma, noting how easily the older woman was able to bridge the gap between their ages by moving seamlessly from adult-like serious introspection to child-like playful gregariousness:

> You should have seen her at one moment huddled up in her deck chair with the sorrows of the universe marked out all over her face, and the next, with tremendously high color, arm in arm, the four of us hoppity skipping up and down the soaking deck at top speed.[30]

Pankhurst was angst-ridden over the serious illness of her son, who had been paralyzed by polio, and by news of setbacks in the fight for the vote in London. Wright empathized with Pankhurst's situation, recognizing the issues weighing her down and attempted to entertain her in an effort to alleviate her distress. Pankhurst seemed to enjoy the company of the young artist and easily connected with the young woman on a personal level. Pankhurst's ability to make Wright feel important inspired intense devotion and loyalty. Wright confessed her feelings of love and admiration for Pankhurst to Shepard:

Well, of course you want to know all that I can tell you about her ladyship and glad am I to be at it, though I don't want you to read this to the others because she has somehow grown so precious to me that I can't talk about her to anyone but you, comprendo-tu?[31]

Bidding farewell to Pankhurst in London, Wright noted that she was "sick for the sight of her [Pankhurst] even more" but she nevertheless continued on to Paris to begin her studies at the American Art Student's Club.[32]

Even as she pursued a career as an artist, Wright remained a committed suffragist. Inspired by Pankhurst, she devoted herself more ardently to the cause. She avidly read *Votes for Women* and multiple American and European newspapers to remain up to date on suffrage news both back home in New York and in Europe. Whenever possible she participated in suffrage activities in the city, including distributing WSPU educational literature on the subject. Wright also maintained frequent correspondence with Shepard in New York, sharing suffrage news and information. She often asked Shepard to send along clippings and photographs of Pankhurst. Wright also helped organize several suffrage meetings in Paris, inviting Pankhurst to speak at the events.[33]

Wright had met Pankhurst during a period of increasing militancy in the British suffrage movement that culminated in frequent clashes with the police. Black Friday had resulted in the death of Emmeline Pankhurst's younger sister, Mary Clarke, who died from injuries sustained as a result of police violence. As the police condoned campaigns of violence against British suffragettes, Pankhurst insisted on the necessity of further militant action. During this period of rising tension within the British suffrage movement, Wright maintained a direct correspondence with Pankhurst. In March 1911, Wright wrote to Pankhurst that she would travel to London to take part in a gathering at Albert Hall where Pankhurst was scheduled speak in support of the Second Conciliation Bill. Wright apparently stayed until June, participating in suffrage actions.[34]

Pankhurst's and Wright's queer connection helped forge partnerships across the Atlantic. Wright returned home to visit her parents in the United States in the fall of 1911. Shortly thereafter, Pankhurst traveled to the United States with Emmeline Pethick Lawrence to begin a suffrage speaking tour. Wright offered to meet Pankhurst and Pethick Lawrence at the dock in New York in October 1911. Pankhurst gratefully wrote to Wright: "I shall be very glad to see your welcoming face when we land."[35] Wright later wrote to Edith Shepard describing the reunion: "Mrs. Pankhurst was looking particularly beautiful and made a great speech at the Brooklyn Academy of Music."[36] Although Pankhurst's schedule was busy, Wright helped organize a speaking engagement for Pankhurst in December in her hometown of Albany, New York. Pankhurst stayed as a guest in the family home, where she met and became friends with Alice's parents, Henry and Emma Morgan Wright. Pankhurst continued her tour, giving speeches in Boston and New York. Wright reunited with them in New York City and arranged to accompany them on the steamer back to Europe. Wright, Pankhurst, and Pethick Lawrence sailed together across the Atlantic in January 1912.[37]

Wright returned to Paris but continued to correspond with Pankhurst in England. Pankhurst's frustration and increasing belief in militancy was clear in her letters to Wright. The government appeared to be making no concession to women's demand for suffrage. On February 11, 1912, Pankhurst wrote to Wright: "Here all our minds are full of what will be in the King's speech. We are preparing for action so expect to hear of broken windows ere long." Pankhurst also lauded the sacrifice of the suffragist prisoners and the stories of their exciting "exploits both in & out of prison."[38] Wright was anxious to be more directly involved in the action but she hesitated, recalling Pankhurst's advice to her on the steamer that she stick to "sculpting and stay out of causes."[39]

As expected, the King's speech was so vague on the issue of women's suffrage that the infuriated suffragettes mobilized for action. On February 16, 1912, Pankhurst spoke before a mass meeting of suffragettes, including newly freed suffrage prisoners:

> Why should women go to Parliament Square and be battered about and insulted, and most important of all, produce less effect than when we throw stones? We tried it long enough. We submitted for years patiently to insult and assault. Women had their health injured. Women lost their lives. We should not have minded if that had succeeded, but that did not succeed, and we have made more progress with less hurt to ourselves by breaking glass than ever we made when we allowed them to break our bodies.[40]

The WSPU organized a demonstration. On March 1, 1912, Pankhurst kicked off a window-breaking campaign by smashing the windows at the Premier's house. She was arrested the next day and sent to Holloway Prison.

Inspired by the news of Pankhurst's speech and arrest, Wright heeded the general call for militant action and quickly traveled to London to participate in the demonstration. She could no longer suppress her burning desire to be a part of the historic moment. On the night of March 4, 1912, Wright joined a group of suffragettes who spread out throughout the city in small teams and initiated a pre-arranged window-smashing protest. Armed with hammers and stones, Wright, along with Lily Lindsay and Enid Renny, walked to the Young Street Post Office. Lindsay struck a window with the hammer to no avail. Wright stood by nervously holding a stone wrapped with a suffragette pamphlet and a note that read: "Taxation without representation is tyranny." She hesitated to throw the stone because she did not want to damage English property. Finally, Renny hurled a rock at the window, breaking the glass. They were among more than two hundred other suffragettes who were arrested in the protests during that first week in March. Wright was sentenced to serve two months' hard labor in Holloway Prison. The police raided the WSPU headquarters and took Emmeline Pethick Lawrence and her husband Frederick into custody. They were imprisoned on the charge of "conspiracy and inciting to commit malicious damage to property." Christabel Pankhurst eluded arrest and went into hiding in Paris.[41]

Upon news of Wright's sentencing, a shock wave rippled across Albany society. Major American newspapers including the *Washington Post*, the *New York Times*, the *Boston Globe*, the *Chicago Tribune*, and the *San Francisco Call* reported the story that an "American girl" had been arrested in London. Journalists conveyed surprise at Wright's arrest, noting that she was "a highly educated young woman, of advanced ideas."[42] Leaders of the Albany Equal Suffrage Club expressed distaste over the news and declared that they disapproved of militant actions. Reporters hounded the Wright family, asking what they intended to do to help free their daughter. Henry Wright made inquiries with lawyers and government officials. Emma Morgan Wright made immediate plans to sail for England in an attempt to free her daughter from prison.[43]

Demanding that the government recognize them as political prisoners, the imprisoned suffragettes launched a hunger strike. They had first utilized the tactic of hunger striking in 1909 and discovered that it was particularly effective for attracting media attention to their cause. But, the government's implementation of the brutal practice of force-feeding quickly followed. Nurses held the women down while doctors shoved plastic tubes down their throats or through their nostrils. Concoctions of milk and eggs were then poured into their stomachs. Suffragists described the vomiting, bleeding, and pain they endured during and after such violent procedures. Alice Morgan Wright participated in the hunger strike and was scheduled for a force-feeding. She noted in her recollections that the suffragette prisoners were so weakened that they fainted during prison church services. Wright was thankfully spared the horror of force-feeding when the strike was called off after the government agreed to recognize their status as political prisoners and restore some of their privileges.[44]

Behind the bars of Holloway, Wright bided her time by documenting her queer love and admiration for Pankhurst. She paid tribute to her heroine by sculpting a bust with a tiny bit of plastoline she had smuggled in for the purpose. Wright worried about Pankhurst, who was hunger-striking and struggling to overcome an acute bout of bronchitis. Pankhurst had also been denied exercise privileges to prevent her from communicating with the other women. The imprisoned suffragettes tried to cheer her up by breaking the windows of their cells in protest. In a show of solidarity, they sang the *March of the Women*—a song composed by fellow imprisoned suffragette Ethel Smyth that called for a women's revolution.[45] Wright, longing to see her heroine, drafted poems on prison paper declaring her commitment to the cause and devotion to the now mythical leader:

> Four walls go round my prison floor
> Somewhere beyond there your cell is
> I look at them and think of this
> Till they grow beautiful all four.
>
> Can prison walls put out the stars
> Or take my love for you away?

Wide as is night, wide as is day
Still wider are these iron bars.

That let both night and day come through,
My little bench can lift me high
Enough to feel the friendly sky
Draw near me, nearer still are you!

Whatever out of depth or height
This silly door locked up so tight
such curious things as men contrive!
Or times or seasons may arrive
How good it is to be alive
In this same world with you tonight![46]

Wright's prison poems openly and fervently expressed her love for
Pankhurst as she ached to comfort the suffrage leader in her time of need:

What if today and yesterday
Have given me no sight of you
It is enough the whole night through
To think perhaps tomorrow may.

My thoughts all fly to you so fast
Perhaps the beating of their wings
Will warm your cell and drive the things
That bother you away at last.

I think—although you do not know—
Your heart must be a little gay
Because of me, since day by day
And hour by hour, I love you so.

I ache to have the strong sun beat
My hot heart to a shaft of light
And through your bars guide its swift flight
In sunny squares to kiss your feet.[47]

While Wright willingly waited in prison for the opportunity to be nearer to Pankhurst, Emma Morgan Wright anxiously worked to secure her daughter's release. She arrived in London and made direct appeals to the American embassy. She requested permission to see her in prison but was told she could only do so on the condition that Wright promised not to participate in future actions. Wright refused to agree to the terms. The embassy therefore denied the release request. Emma Morgan Wright appealed to the British home office and was finally granted the right to visit her daughter. The government once again offered to release her if she agreed to cause no more damage. She again refused, insisting that she had not committed any crime. After more than six weeks of imprisonment, Wright was finally released and returned to her studio in Paris.[48]

Wright's commitment to the cause remained as fervent as ever, but she never again participated in direct militant action. This decision was no doubt partially because of the response of her parents and friends in New York who strenuously objected to her embrace of militant tactics. Wright's ties to the WSPU remained strong because of her personal relationship with Pankhurst and fellow suffragettes. Emmeline Pethick Lawrence penned a personal letter to Wright following her release to thank her for her service to the cause. The suffragette leaders understood the significance of these personal ties in retaining the devotion of their rank-and-file members.[49]

After her return to Paris, Wright attempted to drum up support for the WSPU and strengthen transatlantic alliances by defending militant methods. She wrote letters to the American press, sharing the story of her unjust imprisonment and condemning the British government for imposing harsh sentences on suffragettes simply for holding "certain political views."[50] Wright also continued to worry about Pankhurst and the Pethick Lawrences, who had been rearrested and sentenced to nine months in prison for their role in instigating the mass window-breaking campaign. From Paris, Wright helped gather signatures and letters of protest in an ultimately successful attempt to secure their transfer from the 2nd to the 1st division in a formal recognition of their status as political prisoners. After realizing that the same privileges would not be extended to other suffrage prisoners, however, Pankhurst resumed a hunger strike. More than eighty suffrage prisoners eventually joined the protest. Forcible feedings soon followed. Emmeline Pethick Lawrence eventually collapsed from the strain of force-feeding. When the doctor and wardresses attempted to enter Pankhurst's cell, she threatened to fight back. Prison officials finally conceded and left her alone.[51]

Pankhurst was released from prison in July, greatly weakened by the hunger strike. She recuperated in France with Christabel, who was still hiding from police. Wright and her friends met up with them briefly before Emmeline returned to London in September. Christabel remained to organize suffrage activities from Paris. Wright was still devoted to the organization and worked closely with Christabel as the secretary of the newly formed Paris branch of the WSPU. She wrote to Emmeline Pankhurst frequently to keep her informed about the group's activities. Pankhurst replied with words of encouragement to Wright and the young suffragists she recruited, recommending they help raise funds for the imprisoned suffragists by participating in the suffrage self-denial drive and donating the collected funds to the WSPU.[52] The queer relationships that the suffragettes forged in their fight for the vote were only further solidified by their shared traumatic experiences in prison. Their devotion to each other grew as they severed old ties to family and friends and forged new bonds.

The militant zeal Pankhurst cultivated in Wright followed her back to the United States. In April 1914, Wright returned to New York and set up a studio in Greenwich Village. Using the organizational skills she learned from the Pankhursts, Wright helped plan the hugely successful October 1917 New York suffrage parade, where she participated as one of 20,000 marchers leading a division of 2,500 women carrying signatures of women desiring the vote.[53]

Wright's queer suffrage relationships continued to inspire her politically and personally. In the second half of her life, Wright's most intimate relationship was with her college friend Edith Goode. While Wright was in Europe studying art and working with the WSPU, Goode was fighting for suffrage through the CU and later the NWP. She served as the chairman of the District of Columbia Branch of the CU and performed in several suffrage plays (see chapter 5). In the spring of 1916, she traveled around the country on a speaking tour with the "Suffrage Special." Goode was one of twenty-four suffragist envoys sent by the CU to enlist the support of western women in the campaign for the federal amend-

Figure 4.1. Alice Morgan Wright liked this image of herself best because "it is not sissy and might get a laugh." Alice Morgan Wright in Studio Sculpting. Series VI: Photographs. Alice Morgan Wright Papers, Sophia Smith Collection, Smith College Libraries, Northampton, Massachusetts.

ment. In 1917, she helped organize the NWP's Silent Sentinel protests at the White House demanding Woodrow Wilson's support of the Nineteenth Amendment. After Goode and Wright reunited in the 1920s, they became life partners.[54]

Wright's transatlantic connections remained important well beyond the passage of the Nineteenth Amendment. In the 1920s and 1930s, Wright and Goode worked together with the NWP to fight for passage of the Equal Rights Amendment. They also tapped into Wright's transatlantic alliances to organize women's rights at the global level as members of the Women's International League for Peace and Freedom and the World Woman's Party (WWP). Wright maintained her friendship with Emmeline Pethick Lawrence, who had assumed leadership of the WWP. In the 1940s, Wright and Goode worked with a delegation of women from around the world, many of whom were former suffragists, to demand that the United Nations adopt a declaration of full equality for women and a Commission on the Status of Women.[55]

Queer Devotion

There was a clear exchange of ideas and tactics as prominent suffrage leaders crisscrossed the Atlantic. As we have seen, queer connections between American and British suffragettes helped cement these alliances. The story of American suffragist, Zelie Emerson, also illustrates these transatlantic ties. Emerson, an upper-class society girl turned reformer from Michigan, was working at Chicago's Hull House in 1912 when Sylvia Pankhurst stopped in the city on a speaking tour. Emerson had served as the treasurer of the Women's Trade Union League (WTUL) in Chicago and was advocating on behalf of the rights of women workers. She believed the vote was crucial to improving the conditions of laborers. Sylvia Pankhurst was aligned with the interests of the labor movement and formed the East London Federation of Suffragettes (ELFS) to advocate for the rights of working women. Her 1912 American tour was intended to raise money for the WSPU and gain support for women's suffrage.[56]

After watching Pankhurst speak in Chicago, Emerson felt inspired, believing that if British women could win the vote then the momentum would spread around the world. She befriended Pankhurst and decided to travel back to London with her to join the militant movement. Emerson jumped straight into the fray. She was arrested multiple times for breaking windows and had multiple violent confrontations with the police. While imprisoned at Holloway, Emerson joined with other suffragettes in hunger, thirst, and sleep strikes. These severely damaged her health.[57]

Emerson's zeal for the cause was further fueled by her zeal for Sylvia Pankhurst. On February 14, 1913, Emerson and Pankhurst were arrested for breaking windows. When a police officer handled Emerson roughly and pinched her, she decided to physically fight back by kicking him in the shin and punching him in the face. As a result, she was sentenced to six weeks' imprisonment. Pankhurst faced a two-month sentence. Once in prison, they immediately launched another hunger strike. In a letter written to Keir Hardie describing their efforts to conceal the fact that they were not eating from prison officials, Emerson's affection for Pankhurst is clear. Emerson expressed her deep concern about Pankhurst's condition since she had neither seen nor heard from her. Emerson was determined to outwit her captors and bravely carry on with the hunger strike even as her own health rapidly deteriorated. She lost nine pounds in two weeks. When Pankhurst finally saw Emerson in the yard, she was shocked by how ill she looked.[58]

Prison doctors force-fed Emerson and officers punished her with solitary confinement. The daily forcible feedings proved a horrific ordeal. After the procedure, Emerson attempted to vomit up the food in further protest. Sylvia Pankhurst resisted force-feeding as well. In a letter written to her mother for publication, Pankhurst assured her readers that they were doing all they could to fight the doctors. Emerson's friend and fellow American, Lillian Scott-Troy, led a delegation to serenade the hunger strikers outside the jail. They sang "The Star-Spangled Banner" and "The Battle Hymn of the Republic" in honor of Emerson. Scott-Troy and the WSPU wanted to draw media attention to Emerson's case in hopes of highlighting the brutality of the British government's methods of forcible feeding. Emerson's mother arrived in London to try to plead with the embassy for her daughter's early release. On April 8, 1913, after a five-week thirst and hunger strike, Emerson was released from Holloway. She was hospitalized shortly thereafter and underwent surgery for appendicitis.[59]

Emerson's queer devotion to Sylvia Pankhurst kept her committed to the cause. She was not dissuaded by her prison and hospital experiences. She continued to agitate for suffrage and soon led rallies urging supporters to amplify their militant methods. In October 1913, Emerson participated in a rally alongside Sylvia Pankhurst in the East End of London. The event erupted in violence when the police marched onto the stage to arrest Pankhurst. The suffragettes fought back, throwing chairs at the police. Using their clubs to subdue the fighting suffragettes, the police knocked Emerson unconscious, fracturing her skull. A month later, the police again fractured Emerson's skull by beating her over the head with their batons when she attempted to protect Pankhurst from arrest.[60]

Emerson's story had been closely chronicled in the American press. The coverage of Emerson's experiences in England revealed the increasingly polarized debate in America between the critics and the defenders of militant tactics. The American magazine *The Forum* did not hold back in condemning Emerson's actions as "bad taste and bad manners" in "interfering in the affairs of another country." The author further condemned the militant suffragettes as "a group of hysterical women" who have damaged the cause.[61] An editorial in *Life Magazine* also expressed disdain for Emerson: "She went to England to raise hob, butted into a British difficulty that was no concern of hers, destroyed property, was justly punished, refused to accept the punishment, and set her mother and her American friends to shrieking for help."[62] Yet, most sympathized with Emerson and the fight for women's suffrage. Emerson's story led the Chicago Women's Trade Union League to pass a resolution declaring the "cause of democracy and humanity is one in all countries" and expressing their sympathy with "the long struggle of our British sisters to gain the vote." They further decried "the cruel and degrading practice of forcible feeding," calling for its immediate end.[63]

Emmeline Pankhurst recognized an opportunity to strengthen transatlantic connections through Emerson's story. Pankhurst was in the United States in October 1913 when Emerson's second assault by police and subsequent concussion became front-page news in the nation's top newspapers. She used the occasion to make her point to the American public. She told reporters in Detroit: "This incident will cause some American people to realize the desperate battle which we women are fighting in London."[64] Emerson's mother stepped out of the crowd in Detroit, introduced herself to Pankhurst, and asked what had happened to her daughter. Pankhurst, moved with emotion, invited her to speak in private where the two women bonded and wept over the news of Emerson's condition and their mutual concern for their daughters' safety.

Emmeline Pankhurst, always recognizing the value of publicity, believed that the compelling story of Emerson would evoke the sympathy of the American public and could help win international support for women's suffrage. The WSPU wrote detailed accounts of Emerson's imprisonment and made sure that the story spread widely. After her release, Emerson herself wrote descriptions of her arrest, imprisonment, and hunger strike for newspapers and magazines. She justified her actions to the public, explaining: "It is because I believe that women who are voteless and are allowed no part in the making of the law should refuse to submit to the law. Because women are denied votes, I broke the window; because women are denied votes I think it right to protest against my sentence by every means in my power."[65] Emerson's story did generate international support for the cause.

Emerson's deep and growing affection for Sylvia Pankhurst pulled her even deeper into radical activism. Emerson worked with Pankhurst to create the East End People's Army. Emerson told reporters that the purpose of the People's Army was "to protect militants from the brutality of the police, who during the last month were ordered by the authorities to make no arrests, but to inflict as many bodily injuries as possible." Emerson noted that all members of the People's Army would be drilled "in the use of clubs, fists, and jiu-jitsu."[66] She testified at one of her trials that she had decided to carry a "Saturday night club," a rope dipped in tar and weighted with lead, to defend herself against the police. When attorneys suggested that this was a "formidable weapon," Emerson shot back, "Not so formidable as a policeman's truncheon."[67] Experiences with police brutality convinced suffragettes like Emerson that men would not protect them; they needed to empower themselves politically and physically in order to be truly free. The following month, Emerson was once again arrested in a suffrage protest. The officer painfully twisted her arm and she resisted arrest by using the pole of the suffrage banner she was carrying to smash in a policeman's helmet.[68]

Emerson's conflicts with British authorities ultimately led to the government's efforts to deport her in 1914. Following additional arrests in the winter and spring, the government decided to expel her from the country. She threatened to legally fight any attempt at deportation and continued to risk arrest through violent encounters with the police. Sylvia Pankhurst, apparently concerned about Emerson's health, convinced her to return home to the United States to recuperate. Emerson left England in May 1914.[69]

A letter written at some point when Emerson was still in London suggested a larger source of tension between the two women that may have led to Emerson's decision to leave. Sylvia Pankhurst was embroiled in arguments with her mother and sister over her association with the labor movement and her prior romantic relationship with Labour Party politician Keir Hardie. Emmeline and Christabel expelled Sylvia and the ELFS from the WSPU. In response, the ELFS formed an independent organization under Sylvia Pankhurst in January 1914. At the same time, British and American newspapers and magazines reported every detail of Emerson's deportation story, some deriding Emerson as a villain. Concerned about the negative publicity over Emerson's deportation proceedings, Sylvia Pankhurst and Zelie Emerson's relationship apparently buckled under these larger pressures. In a letter written around this time, Emerson asked why Pankhurst did not want to her to speak for the WSPU or the ELFS anymore and why Sylvia would not see her.[70]

Another possible explanation for the schism between Emerson and Pankhurst is that their personal relationship was becoming too intense. The depth of Emerson's feelings for Pankhurst were revealed in the 1914 letter: "you know that nothing that has happened or may happen between us can ever alter my feeling toward you." Emerson noted that she hoped in the future that "I can be of some service to you and the cause for that is, after all, the only thing that matters." A poem at the bottom of the page from Emerson to Pankhurst suggests a possible romantic relationship between the two.

> You did not understand, & in your eyes
> I saw a vague surprise,
> As if my voice came from some distant Sphere
> Too far for you to hear;
> Alas! In other days it was not so
> Those days of long ago.
>
> II.
> Time was when all my being was thrown wide.
> All veils were drawn aside
> That you might enter anywhere at will.
> Now all is hushed & still
> Save for a sound recurring more & more
> The shutting of a door.[71]

Emerson concluded the letter by thanking Pankhurst "for the hair"— perhaps a lock of hair as a memento. Emerson's intense letter and poem suggest that she had romantic feelings for Pankhurst. Barbara Winslow, Pankhurst's biographer, has speculated a sexual relationship between the two women.[72]

The intense connection between Zelie Emerson and Sylvia Pankhurst demonstrates the significance of queer alliances between American and British suffragists. American women like Emerson were motivated to engage in militancy not only because of their commitment to the cause of suffrage but also because of their queer devotion to British suffragettes. Likewise, British suffrage leaders recognized the importance of these relationships. These personal entanglements brought their interests intimately together in common cause.

Conclusion

The queer transatlantic alliances formed between American suffragists and British suffragettes were not only political but also deeply personal. Margaret Foley and Anne Martin used the tactics they learned in the United Kingdom to transform their suffrage campaigning. The friendships and tactical relationships they created with suffragists endured beyond her time in Europe. Alice Morgan Wright's affection for Emmeline Pankhurst inspired her feminist activism in both the United Kingdom and the United States. The friendships Wright made participating in the British campaign would prove especially useful in the long term through her work as a global women's rights activist. Zelie Emerson's romantic relationship with Sylvia Pankhurst helped bridge the gap between nations. Emerson's embrace of British militancy to the extent of risking arrest and physical abuse proved a powerful public relations tool that the Pankhursts were able to use to garner international support for their cause.

These queer transatlantic ties, though unconventional, strengthened the bonds between the continents. Queer suffragists already lived on the margins, often operating outside the mainstream of convention in their daily lives. In some ways, this allowed them greater freedom to transgress barriers by embracing militant tactics. They facilitated the movement of people and ideas across the Atlantic. They created new possibilities for connection as suffragists began to see the ways in which their lives and their movements intersected. These unconventional relationships helped tear down the walls that divided women. They helped forge global connections and inspire an international women's rights movement. Born of personal friendships and romantic sentiments, these queer ties proved essential not only to the furtherance of the fight for the vote, but to the larger campaign for women's rights around the globe.

5

Queering Space

Heads definitely turned when Annie Tinker led a cavalry of suffragists on horseback in the 1913 New York City suffrage parade. She was
dressed in masculine breeches, coat, boots, and a men's silk top hat with
lines of suffragists trailing behind her in pseudo-military style fashion.
Tinker, or "Dan," as she preferred to be called, lived an unconventional
life. She defied notions of respectable femininity by drinking, smoking,
and engaging in rough sports. She fell in love with women and they
loved her in return. When Tinker first formed her suffrage cavalry, a
reporter for the *Washington Post* expressed surprise, noting that suffragists planned to "ride like men" in suffrage parades.[1] The press largely
portrayed Tinker's cavalry as an entertaining novelty: an odd but amus-
ing sight to behold. The *New York Times* posted a photograph of Tinker
riding in the parade and referred to her "mannish garb" as "distinctive."[2]

Yet, Tinker's unapologetic queerness made a bold statement. She
helped push the boundaries of respectability by defying the expectations not only of the general public but of the leaders of mainstream suffrage organizations. Her participation in the parade symbolized a larger
struggle. For gender-transgressing suffragists like Tinker, the fight for
enfranchisement symbolized liberation from societal restrictions that
limited their ability to fully express their true selves to the world. Tinker's presence in the suffrage parade signified a claiming of public space
that, at least temporarily, turned the city streets into a queer space.

The concept of queer space as articulated by scholars in the mid-
1990s imagined it in opposition to hegemonic heterosexual spaces. They
argued that LGBTQ individuals created their own spaces to resist the
dominant culture. Later scholars challenged the notion of queer space as
always necessarily transgressive or liberatory and/or narrowly limited to
gay and lesbian spaces. Broader definitions of queer space reimagined it
as a site where individuals challenged sexual, gender, class, and racial hierarchies. In this chapter, I borrow the concept of queer space not just to

refer to sites occupied by queer suffragists but also to refer to sites where suffragists flouted sexual, gender, class, and racial norms. This included private spaces like women's clubs and public spaces like the stage and the street, where suffragists deconstructed white, middle-class, cisheteronormative assumptions. Their norm-defying gender expressions and behaviors turned public spaces into sites of queer resistance.[3]

Queering the Club

Suffragists transformed women's clubs into revolutionary queer spaces that fostered radical thought and inspired militant activism. Club women met in the physical space of churches, community centers, restaurants, or private homes. Within these homosocial spaces, suffragists interacted with individuals representing a range of genders and sexualities and developed intimate bonds with each other. They engaged in vigorous political discussions and debates. In the sheltered space of the club, suffragists felt temporarily freed from the societal restraints that limited their thoughts and behavior. Because these clubs were by their nature transgressive, they often gathered outside the auspices of formal suffrage organizations.[4]

Heterodoxy, an exclusive feminist discussion club operated by suffragists in New York City's Greenwich Village, serves as an illustrative example of a queer feminist space. Marie Jenney Howe, one of the founders of the New York State Suffrage League and the New York City Woman Suffrage Party, created Heterodoxy in 1912. The name of the club reflected the intent that membership be limited only to women who held unorthodox opinions about the issues of the day. The club members consisted primarily of reform-minded and politically engaged upper- and middle-class professional white women. Membership was limited and required a process of approval. In keeping with their norm-defying philosophy, the club was not restricted only to white women. Grace Nail Johnson, a suffragist and Black civil rights activist, was a member of Heterodoxy, and the club invited Black guests and speakers to participate.[5]

The suffragists of Heterodoxy met every other week for lunch, discussion, and debate either at the Greenwich Village Inn or Polly Halliday's Bohemian café. The privacy of the meetings allowed Heterodoxy members to broach controversial topics. Since their discussions were "often personal and intimate," the bylaws of the organization required confidentiality of all members and forbade any publicity or communication with the press. Topics of discussion included suffrage, feminism, socialism, anarchy, Black civil rights, birth control, free love, and homosexuality. Most Heterodites were also active rebels who organized labor union strikes, socialist rallies, and suffrage demonstrations. Several Heterodites, such as Doris Stevens, Paula Jakobi, Alice Kimball, Mary Ware Dennett, Dr. Sara Josephine "Jo" Baker, and Alison Turnbull Hopkins, were jailed for picketing with the National Woman's Party (NWP).[6]

The queer suffragists of Heterodoxy facilitated discussions that challenged accepted notions of love, sex, and marriage. Edith (Lees) Ellis, suffragist and wife of the famous English sexologist Havelock Ellis, was one of the speakers who frequently visited Heterodoxy in the early years. Havelock Ellis was well-known for his research on human sexuality, and homosexuality in particular. He also linked lesbianism to the women's suffrage movement in a way that led to the implication that both were abnormal. Edith Ellis identified as a "sexual invert" or lesbian and was one of the subjects of his research. They maintained an open marriage and Edith had affairs with women. Havelock Ellis later described his wife's lesbianism, their unique relationship, and their love for each other in his autobiography. Edith traveled to the United States on a speaking tour in 1914. In New York City, she spoke on "Love" at a spring meeting of Heterodoxy. Although we do not know if she spoke about lesbianism at that meeting, Ellis did articulate a radical view of marriage that was more akin to notions of free love with her argument that marital relations should be free from government interference. She emphasized the need for women to be economically independent and for husband and wife to live apart if necessary. Edith and Havelock Ellis maintained separate residences throughout their marriage.[7]

Heterodoxy thus became a liberating place where suffragists felt free to express their diverse genders and sexualities. In 1919, Heterodite Florence Guy Woolston wrote a satirical article describing the characteristics of the women of Heterodoxy. Woolston began with a description of the members' clothing, noting that some wear "male attire for the upper story and would go further were it not forbidden by law."[8] A 1920 Heterodoxy scrapbook provides visual evidence of the variety of gender presentations of the Heterodites. Photographs of Dr. Josephine "Jo" Baker and Myran

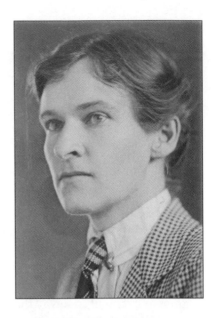

Figure 5.1. Kathleen De Vere Taylor was gender non-conforming in all aspects of her life. Miss Kathleen Taylor, of New York. Speaker and organizer for the Woman's Party in Kansas. ca. 1916. Harris & Ewing. Records of the National Woman's Party, Manuscript Division, Library of Congress, Washington, DC.

Figure 5.2. Dr. Josephine Baker went by the name "Jo" and lived in a queer chosen family with two other suffragists. Dr. Josephine Baker, 1917. Heterodoxy to Marie, [1920]. Papers of Inez Haynes Gillmore, 1872–1945, Schlesinger Library on the History of Women in America, Radcliffe Institute for Advanced Study, Harvard University, Cambridge, Massachusetts.

Figure 5.3. Myran Louise Grant was one of the gender non-conformists of Heterodoxy. Myran Louise Grant, Heterodoxy to Marie, [1920]. Papers of Inez Haynes Gillmore, 1872–1945, Schlesinger Library on the History of Women in America, Radcliffe Institute for Advanced Study, Harvard University, Cambridge, Massachusetts.

Louise Grant show them wearing men's collared shirts and ties. Kathleen De Vere Taylor's three photographs reveal her preference for pants over skirts. In her official NWP promotional photograph, Taylor was dressed in a men's houndstooth-checked pattern jacket and plaid tie.[9]

Beyond their clothing, the queer suffragists of Heterodoxy challenged gendered conventions in a number of other aspects of their lives, including their adoption of male names and titles, their choice of careers, and their assumption of male privileges in their demand for equal rights. Kathleen De Vere Taylor's transgressive clothing style symbolized her boundary-transgressing life. She worked as an organizer for Harriot Stanton Blatch's New York's Women's Political Union (WPU). Taylor helped organize street-corner speeches and open-air meetings, sometimes directly in front of anti-suffrage headquarters. These bold strategies countered common assumptions that women were, and should be, naturally submissive and docile. Taylor broke barriers in other ways too. She became one of the first women to manage a brokerage firm in New York City and she catered to an exclusively female clientele.[10]

The suffragists of Heterodoxy also challenged norms through their choice of romantic partners and establishment of queer domestic arrangements. The members of the club included never-married women, women in traditional heterosexual marriages, women in open marriages, and women in relationships with other women. Florence Guy Woolston's 1919 satirical paper joked about the marriage customs of the group members:

> Marriage customs among the Heterodites are varied. Three types of sex relationships may be observed, practiced by those who call themselves *monotonists, varietists* and *resistants*. Most of the *monotonists* were mated young and by pressure of habit and circumstance have remained mated. The *varietists* have never been ceremonially mated but have preferred a succession of matings. The *resistants* have not mated at all. These classes are not at all arbitrary. Some monotonists have practiced variety secretly. Some varietists would like to become monotonists because the marriage union label is useful in some lines of professional work. Many of the monotonists wear rings to show that they have passed through the ceremonial and are nominally the exclusive possession of some male. The scientific observer, however, should not be led astray by outward totems because I have discovered several instances of ring wearing which are deceptive—rings not having been given by the ceremonial mate.[11]

Woolston's descriptions humorously reveal the variety of attitudes toward marriage and sexuality within the group. Since committed heterosexual marriages were the only socially acceptable relationships at the time, Heterodoxy suffragists were indeed queering the norm in their sexual lives. Their ideas broke down old taboos about sexuality, freeing it from its patriarchal association with marriage and reproduction. This allowed some of the queer women in the group the opportunity to be more open about their romantic relationships. Kathleen De Vere Taylor and Frances Maule, Mabel Louise Robinson and Helen Hull, Katharine Anthony and Elisabeth Irwin, Dr. Josephine Baker and Ida A. R. Wylie, lived together as couples in the city.

Heterodoxy was unique among women's clubs at the time in that it embraced, at least in theory, some degree of racial inclusivity. But most Black suffragists were largely excluded from white suffrage spaces by discriminatory policies. Black suffragists relied on the support of their own long-established groups, building community through their churches and social organizations. These groups provided services to the community while organizing to fight for political equality. Ida B. Wells-Barnett, along with white colleagues Viola Belle Squire and Virginia Brooks, queered the norm in the creation of the Alpha Suffrage Club in Chicago in 1913. Their goal was to work together to amplify the voices and concerns of Black women suffragists who had been excluded from white women's suffrage organizations. Illinois women had won the right to vote in 1910. At the local level, the Alpha Suffrage Club focused on registering Black voters, encouraging civic participation, organizing campaigns to elect Black representatives to office, and resisting efforts to disenfranchise Black voters. At the federal level, the club lobbied Congress and organized against segregation by fighting the Jim Crow car bills, anti-miscegenation laws, and African immigration exclusion.[12]

The Alpha Suffrage Club included among its leadership suffragists who queered the norm through their domestic arrangements and gender-defying behavior. Some members of the club, such as Viola Hill and Laura Beasley, consciously rejected matrimony, choosing instead to remain single. Beasley owned her own home and took in women boarders. Outsiders viewed the women of the Alpha Suffrage Club as exceptionally rebellious in their gender transgressions, especially in their public demands for political power. They met with opposition from individuals in their community who embraced patriarchal gender norms, believing that women's primary place was in the home, not in politics. As they canvassed their neighborhoods registering voters, they tried to win over resistant Black male voters by insisting that their goal was to ensure that more Black men be elected to office.[13]

Some queer Black suffragists directly fought the racism within national suffrage organizations by forcibly integrating white suffrage clubs and spaces. Inez and Vida Milholland, two prominent white suffragists, had long used their family home, Meadowmount in Lewis, New York, as a gathering site for suffragists to convene, organize, relax, and rejuvenate in intimate companionship with other women. Although Inez died while campaigning for suffrage in 1916, Vida Milholland and her partner Margaret "Peg" Hamilton carried on the tradition of gathering suffragists together at Meadowmount into the 1930s and 1940s. From the Milholland family home they organized for the Equal Rights Amendment and the international peace movement. Other queer suffragists, such as Mabel Vernon and Consuelo Reyes-Calderon, or Jeannette Marks and Mary Woolley, often stayed with Milholland and Hamilton at the estate. These couples created an extended community of support for each other. Meadowmount thus served as a queer space for their radical personal and political expressions.[14]

But Meadowmount also served as an example of how white suffragists policed the boundaries of queer suffrage spaces. In August 1924, Alice Paul of the NWP attempted to exclude Black suffragists from speaking at a commemoration of the 1916 death of suffragist Inez Milholland at Meadowmount. John Milholland, National Association for the Advancement of Colored People (NAACP) co-founder and Inez's father, had specifically invited prominent Black suffragists, including queer suffragist Lucy Diggs Slowe, to speak. Slowe was the Dean of Women at Howard University, where she lived with her partner Mary Powell Burrill (see chapter 3). But NWP leaders feared that the presence of Black suffragists would "mar the program."[15] Representatives of the NWP explained that the decision was a political one intended to retain the loyalty of Southern white supporters who they hoped would help elect their women candidates to Congress. They refused to acknowledge the ways in which their decision perpetuated a system of racism and inequality.

Slowe and her allies from the NAACP immediately called out the NWP for "cowardly capitulation to race prejudice . . . at the grave of Inez Milholland an active member of our association in her lifetime, who would have repudiated such a position as you have taken."[16] At the memorial service, John Milholland stepped forward to speak:

> Friends of Inez, I am her father. I feel it my duty to speak out against all injustice as she always did . . . I want to remind you that in the first suffrage parade Inez herself demanded that the colored women be allowed to march. And now to-day we were told that it would mar the program to have these guests of mine on the program. I have nothing to say except that Inez believed in equal rights for everybody.[17]

Milholland, defying the NWP's attempts to silence Black suffragists, invited Emmett J. Scott, the Secretary-Treasurer of Howard University, to step forward to speak. Scott gave a respectful speech paying tribute to Inez as a "friend of the friendless, and a defender of the weak." He especially praised her dedication to "making bondage more unholy and freedom more righteous." He insisted that Howard University held dear "the unflinching faith and courage of the woman who in the moment of her greatest triumph forgot not justice and fair play." Scott noted that Milholland had stood up for the rights of Howard students to participate equally in the suffrage parade. "She was unwilling to participate in a parade symbolizing a movement which was not big enough and broad enough to live up to the principles for which it was contending."[18]

Black suffragists like Slowe and Scott thus queered white suffrage spaces by forcibly breaking down barriers and integrating these spaces for suffragists of all races. Slowe was especially familiar with the impact of marginalization based on her experiences both inside and outside the suffrage movement. Throughout her life she confronted racism, homophobia, and sexism as she navigated her multiple intersecting identities as a Black queer woman. These demoralizing and dehumanizing experiences fueled her fight for justice. Slowe continued working for the equality of Black women throughout her career at Howard University.

Queering the Stage and Screen

Suffragists discovered the power of theatrical performances and motion pictures to launch direct assaults on the status quo. Gender-bending pro-suffrage performers pushed the boundaries of social acceptability through comedic acts that queered constructions of gender and sexuality. Suffragists also wrote their own plays and films, inverting cisheterosexist perspectives of home life and politics. At first glance, pro-suffrage plays and films appear rather conservative as they responded to anti-suffrage caricatures by perpetuating the image of suffragists as young, attractive, heterosexual women intent on becoming good wives and mothers. However, suffragists transformed the stage and screen into sites of queer resistance by promoting images of women as powerful and capable leaders, recasting unmarried women as heroines, and destigmatizing queer lives.[19]

Established star performers used their fame to simultaneously defy cisheterosexual norms and advocate for the women's right to vote. Trixie

Friganza was a Vaudeville comedic actress and well-known suffragist. Although forbidden by her employers to stump for suffrage on stage, she did garner an audience for suffrage off stage. Friganza delivered suffrage speeches for various organizations in New York and Chicago. Her feminism also included public advocacy for a fat-positive body image. Friganza insisted that women's obsession with thinness was unhealthy and argued that women should embrace a full figure as a sign of health and vigor.[20] She challenged heteronormativity on the stage by pushing back against the notion that a woman's natural state was matrimony. She sang: "the more I see of married life, the less I wish to see." Her performance of the song "No Wedding Bells for Me" articulated the sentiment that marriage was a dreary descent into poverty and domestic drudgery:

> No wedding bells for me,
> I'm happy as can be,
> She does up his shirts and collars,
> Runs the place on seven dollars,
> Gee whiz! I'm glad I'm free,
> No wedding bells for me.[21]

The lyrics depicted motherhood as equally onerous and challenged the sexual double standard that overlooked male infidelity in marital relations.

> You've children running all about,
> And tagging to your skirts,
> If one kid falls and gives a shout,
> You "kiss the place that hurts."
> You've dinner ready just at six,
> A message comes, "don't wait."
> That's hubby at his same old tricks,
> I guess he has a date.[22]

In a 1911 interview, Friganza expressed her views on marriage, insisting she would not marry because she enjoyed her economic independence: "if I married a man who could earn as much as I do, he would be insufferably bossy. If he didn't earn as much as I do, I wouldn't have any respect for him." She sympathized with what women "have to put up with because their men are the breadwinners." But she defensively noted that she was no man-hater, joking: "I do not entirely disapprove of men and sometimes believe they fill a small part in this world."[23] Despite her comedic disparagement of men and marriage, Friganza married multiple times. But her negative experiences with abusive and economically dependent husbands contributed to her disdain for marriage and belief in the necessity of women's rights.[24]

Vaudeville actor and suffrage supporter Julian Eltinge (William Julian Dalton) made a career transgressing gender norms. Eltinge's international reputation was built on his performance as a female impersonator. Awed audience members, entirely convinced by his portrayal, remained unaware of his identity until the very end of the performance, when he would reveal his "true sex" to them. Historian Daniel Hurewitz has argued that "Eltinge delighted audiences by offering the unbelievable possibility that womanhood, in specific, and gender roles in general were not truly fundamental or essential."[25]

Eltinge's public support for suffrage and women's equality helped further the cause. But his stage depictions of suffragists were more complex. In one performance he sang about the power of suffragettes:

> I am the leader of the Suffragettes,
> Quite the swiftest thing in cheviots.
> As a type of grace and symmetry,
> Not a girl has anything on me.
> Even the men my praises loudly sing;
> All I have to do is pull the string,
> And they all cavort like marionettes,
> 'Round the leader of the Suffragettes.[26]

This tongue-in-cheek comedic portrayal of a "suffragette" on stage relied on popular stereotypes of suffragists as attempting to seize power through manipulative means.

Yet, in his life off stage Eltinge was a vocal advocate for women's suffrage. Through his popular magazine, he advocated companionate marriages and declared that the ideal husband would be an advocate of women's suffrage and that the ideal wife would be a suffragist.[27] Although he was not a rank-and-file suffragist directly engaged in campaigning for the vote, his public support for women's suffrage carried weight because of his international fame and popularity.

Eltinge's support of suffrage and his career as a gender-bending performer demanded the invention of a carefully crafted public persona off stage to protect his personal privacy. Deflecting accusations of sexual abnormality, he dressed in male attire and portrayed himself as a "manly man" in press interviews. Journalists comforted readers by noting that in real life he was as "masculine as a prize-fighter." Eltinge attempted to further prove the point by announcing his future intent to marry and to "wear the trousers" at home. One reporter sought to assuage readers, noting that Eltinge was "thoroughly masculine" and "in every way normal, rational and serious minded."[28] Eltinge believed that emphasizing his cisheterosexuality was essential to countering the accusations of so-called sexual deviancy that plagued him as a result of his gender transgressive performances.

Eltinge continued his stage career as a female impersonator, advocated for suffrage, and never married. Although he identified as a heterosexual, cisgender man in interviews with the press, he kept his actual gender identity and sexuality private. After his death, friends suggested that Eltinge identified as a gay man but kept this hidden in order to protect his reputation. He sought to combat rumors of femininity and homosexuality by presenting a hyper-masculinized heterosexual and gender normative front in interviews. But his advocacy of women's rights and gender transgressive performances in the queer space of the stage helped deconstruct normative constructions of gender and sexuality.[29]

Eltinge's performance as a suffragist on stage relied in part on popular anti-suffrage tropes. Anti-suffragists had long used plays to poke fun at suffragists by resurrecting popular stereotypes of the suffragist as a mannish, man-hating spinster. This caricature was replicated in film as well. Charlie Chaplin's 1914 movie *The Militant Suffragette*, later renamed *A Busy Day*, depicted Chaplin dressed as a woman and exhibiting uncouth and rude mannerisms typically associated with men. Chaplin's suffragist ends up in several physical fights, dominating the men around her. In the 1912 film *A Cure for Suffragettes*, a group of women neglect their children to attend a suffrage meeting. These anti-suffrage films thus reiterated the alleged dangers of feminism in masculinizing women and making them unfit for marriage or motherhood. They emphasized that a real woman's place was in the home.[30]

Leaders of suffrage organizations, however, determined to counter these negative stereotypes by staging their own performances. The content of pro-suffrage plays generally highlighted the benefits of women voting as a means of protecting and preserving the family and the home. Still, these performances revealed some surprisingly queer themes that deviated from conventional notions of gender. In February 1914, the Congressional Union organized a Washington, DC performance of the British plays *Before Sunrise* and *How the Vote Was Won*. They recruited local suffragists to play the lead roles, including Smith College graduate and queer suffragist Edith Goode. Partly through the influence of her suffragist mother, Goode became active in the Congressional Union (and later the NWP). While attending Smith, Goode starred in several dramatic performances. Her brief stint as a suffrage performer in Washington, DC following graduation therefore seemed a logical merging of her theatrical and suffrage interests.[31]

The lives of the characters that Goode portrayed in the suffrage plays ironically mirrored her own life in many ways. As a young woman, Goode dated men but expressed anxiety over the prospect of marriage and a general desire to avoid matrimony. She felt constrained by commitments to family and dreamed of traveling. In letters to friends, she articulated a wish to be free from the limitations and expectations that society placed on women.[32] Goode's feelings as a young woman paralleled the character she portrayed in the suffrage play *Before Sunrise*. The story centered on the life of Caroline, a young woman coming of age in the 1860s. Caroline felt pressured by her family to marry a man she did not love. Her father expressed the belief that "a woman comes into the world to bring forth children, and to be man's comforter and help-mate."[33] Her mother warned her that she must marry by the age of 25 or risk becoming an old maid. Instead, Caroline desired to travel to Paris with her friend Mary. They hoped to live free lives as independent young women. Caroline's mother, however, objected, calling Mary "mannish" and insisting that it was not normal for two women to live together. The story ends with Caroline's ultimate concession to familial demands that she marry.

Although the play was set in the context of a prior era and before the idea of companionate marriage, the central message for contemporary audiences was clear: without political power, women lacked control over even the most basic decisions in their lives. Suffragists hoped that audiences would recognize that, like these outdated ideas about love and marriage, objections to women's suffrage were likewise archaic. Even more radical than their advocacy of suffrage, suffragists also used plays like this to challenge heteronormative constructions of gender, sexuality, and respectable domesticity. The choice not to marry had marked Mary as a different and dangerous manifestation of womanhood in the eyes of Caroline's mother. Although not specifically defined as a lesbian, the label of "mannish" served as code for Mary's alleged sexual and gender abnormality. But what was truly transgressive about the play is that rather than condemning Mary as the enemy, the playwright cast Mary as a heroine who offered Caroline salvation from the heteronormative prison that awaited her.

This challenge to heteronormativity was also a subtle theme in *How the Vote Was Won*, the second play performed by the Congressional Union in February 1914. Edith Goode again had a starring role in this performance through her portrayal of the character Molly. This light-hearted comedy told the story of a fictional women's strike organized by suffragettes in England. The women give up their work and sought the support and protection of their nearest male relative in order to prove the point that as self-supporting members of society, women were entitled to the vote. The central male character, Horace Cole, is distraught when his female relatives come to him seeking his support. Molly, an independent young woman living entirely on her own, also shows up at her Uncle Horace's doorstep seeking support. An enraged Horace tells her:

> You know perfectly well, Molly, that I disapprove of you in every way. I hear—I have never read it, of course—but I hear that you have written a most scandalous book. You live in lodgings by yourself.[34]

Molly counters by telling him to "cheer up, Uncle. Now's your chance of reforming me. I've come to live with you. You can support me and improve me at the same time."[35] Horace is aghast, insisting that he could not afford to do so and pointing out that Molly makes more money than he does. Molly reminds Horace that he had long disapproved of her independence and self-sufficiency. She recalled that he wanted her to marry and that when she had refused to marry and determined instead to support herself, he had called her "sexless." The story ends with Horace succumbing under pressure, conceding to the women's arguments, and marching off with them to demand women's right to vote.

Through their sympathetic depictions of Caroline and Mary in *Before Sunrise* and of Molly in *How the Vote Was Won*, the writers countered negative depictions of suffragists as old, selfish, dependent, mannish women. Instead, they constructed an image of suffragists as young, selfless, independent, feminine women desirous of a more modern and liberatory future for all women. In *Before Sunrise*, Mary tells Caroline that unmarried women in the future will know that "there is a full life of usefulness, and high endeavour and great happiness open to her, though she is mateless and alone."[36] Thus, even as suffragists affirmed the primacy of marriage and motherhood, they also pushed back against negative depictions of old maids and spinsters. From the queer space of the stage, they attempted to highlight and in some ways normalize spinsters and women living with other women. This was no doubt motivated in part by self-interest. The British suffragists and playwrights who composed the plays themselves lived unconventional queer lives. Bessie Hatton, author of *Before Sunrise*, and Cicely Hamilton, author of *How the Vote Was Won*, never married. Co-author Christopher St. John lived in a queer domestic arrangement with fellow suffragist Edith Craig and the artist Clare Atwood.[37]

Edith Goode's life also followed the liberatory path of the characters she portrayed on stage. She retained a sense of independence and freedom through her choice not to marry. Her life was rich and fulfilling not only because of her dedication to the causes of suffrage and later, animal rights, but because of the chosen family she created and the intimate relationships she developed with other women. From the 1920s until her death in 1970, Goode was the partner of suffragist Alice Morgan Wright (see chapter 6). These real-life queer relationships among suffragists paralleled the alternate homosocial futures alluded to by the characters in their plays.

In addition to theater, suffragists used film to simultaneously reinforce and challenge cisheteronormative depictions of women and family. In 1913, the Women's Political Union and Unique Film Company produced the film *80 Million Women Want—?*. The cameo performances of Harriot Stanton Blatch and Emmeline Pankhurst attracted a wider audience and added to the film's credibility. In many ways the film re-affirmed conservative notions of traditional family life, employing the increasingly common strategy of appealing to the masses by reflecting traditional values of heteronormative respectability to counter negative depictions of suffragists. The two love stories at the center of the film promise viewers that suffragists would not reject heterosexual love and marriage.[38] But, the film pushes back against gendered stereotypes in other ways. The women suffragists are all depicted as smart, capable, and powerful leaders rivaling and, in fact, outwitting the men. The alliances that the women in the film make to protect and advocate for each other stand as a clear testament to the significance of women's relationships. Women's power is the central theme of the film, often contrasted with the physical and moral weakness of the male characters. Actual footage of the 1913 New York suffrage parade reinforced this theme by highlighting not just women marchers but also Annie Tinker's suffrage cavalry. This powerful image of young, strong women dressed in masculine styles and riding on horseback in pseudo-military style down the street reinforced the message that women intended to claim the physical spaces and political power of men. The gender non-conforming presence of the suffrage cavalry queered the silver screen.

Queering the Streets

Suffragists increasingly claimed and queered public spaces through powerful visible displays such as suffrage parades. In 1908, New York suffragists, inspired by similar marches organized by suffragettes in Britain, proposed to hold a parade. But women parading in public was generally considered inappropriate at the time. Incredulous New York city officials denied them a permit. The suffragists marched anyway. They inverted gender norms by claiming the traditionally male spaces of the city as their own.[39]

Parade organizers recognized the power of these visible displays of women taking to the streets. Even through this radical act of seizing public space, however, suffrage leaders believed it was necessary to present a rather conservative image of cisheterosexual respectability. They asked marchers to adhere to specific gendered guidelines recommending fashionable feminine clothing and behavioral codes of conduct that projected an air of femininity and middle-class respectability. An organizer of the 1912 New York parade suggested that suffragists wear white dresses, tidy-looking small hats, and "neat gloves and shoes" so "that all may see how we take care of little things like this." She also recommended that they march in as dignified a manner as possible, being careful to avoid talking or laughing as they walk. Reminding them to be "attentive to keep in line," the organizer made it clear that the goal was to present a beautiful appearance of womanliness that did not step too far outside existing gender norms.[40] Though their participation in the parade alone marked a clear challenge to the patriarchy, women suffragists were ironically simultaneously propped up as objects marching for the viewers' pleasure. Their presence was intended to appease an apprehensive public by assuring them that granting women the vote would, for the most part, not disrupt the status quo.

Queer suffragists, however, defied these expectations through transgressive gender presentations that challenged preconceived notions of femininity and masculinity. Annie Tinker's suffrage cavalry rode in several New York City parades. Shortly after joining the Woman's Political Union, Tinker formed the cavalry as a means of attracting attention to the cause. Tinker's gender queer appearance definitely invited attention as the press flocked to interview the "mannishly" attired suffragist on horseback. A writer for the gossip magazine *Town Topics* described seeing Tinker at an event immediately following the May 1913 New York suffrage parade:

> Miss Annie Tinker, who delighted the marchers by her oddities, was easily found. Her silk hat had a fine polish and the satin bow in back of her head was big, new and crisp. It was bad for the cause, now that femininity is part of the plank . . . I disliked intensely the masculine fashion in which she handled her hat.[41]

The *Town Topics* writer, unnerved by Tinker's masculine dress and mannerisms, suggested that the trend of "femininity" in the suffrage movement had made gender non-conforming women like Tinker less acceptable than they would have been in prior years.

Mainstream suffragists, who were concerned about supporting a feminine image, tried to distance themselves from women like Tinker and dismiss her appearance as simply the choice of an eccentric wealthy woman. But the press was fascinated by Tinker. She leveraged her time in the spotlight to advocate for much more than the vote. She contested existing gender norms by insisting that women should be able to wear any clothes of their choosing. When a reporter who was curious about the cavalry's military-style attire asked whether she believed women should go to war, Tinker replied, "Goodness, yes, if they want to. Why not?"[42] Tinker's argument that women should be allowed to serve in the military deconstructed gendered notions of women as passive caregivers.

Women of color queered both gender and racial hierarchies through their appearance in public suffrage parades. Mabel Ping-Hua Lee rode with the suffrage cavalry in the 1912 New York suffrage parade. As a young Chinese American suffragist, Lee combatted restrictive gendered and racialized notions of acceptable feminine behavior. Her decision not to marry, along with her activism in the women's movement, defied normative expectations in both American and Chinese cultures. When she appeared in the 1912 parade, journalists focused on Lee's "foreign-ness" as a Chinese immigrant. They emphasized that her education in America had transformed her into an intelligent young woman while using her status as an immigrant to suggest that her "real home" was in China. The *Brooklyn Daily Eagle* reported that Lee "is preparing to go back to China and teach her sisters."[43] Reporters also highlighted Lee's "otherness" by focusing on her clothing, physical appearance, and language skills. A writer for the *New York Tribune* patronizingly noted that Lee, "a pretty little Chinese girl," had told white suffragists "in the best of college English how happy she was to live in this land of freedom."[44] Lee resisted these attempts to reduce her to the status of a "perpetual foreigner" or as a passive, demure object. Instead, she asserted her agency by declaring her thoughts on the necessity of women's suffrage. When confronted by American stereotypes of the conservativeness and alleged backwardness of Chinese culture, Lee praised Chinese students for leading the revolution in China and especially for the role of Chinese women in fighting for their enfranchisement. She criticized the United States, noting the "defect in the American Government" in "denying to women the right to vote."[45] Lee tackled the dual problem of sexism and racism while also pushing back against xenophobic representations of China and Chinese immigrants.[46]

Figure 5.4. Annie Tinker, or "Dan," as she preferred to be called, was known for her masculine fashion and unconventional life. Annie Tinker and unknown woman. Courtesy of the Incorporated Village of Port Jefferson Digital Archives, Port Jefferson, New York.

Indigenous women who participated in suffrage parades similarly faced and resisted attempts to "other" them. The fictional Dawn Mist (portrayed by Daisy Norris) is an example of the types of representations that were created about Indigenous women. The public relations department of the Great Northern Railway created Dawn Mist to enhance interest in Glacier National Park and increase ridership on the railway. They pitched stories to newspapers explaining that Dawn Mist was supposedly a member of the Blackfeet nation in Montana who had volunteered to join the 1913 suffrage parade in Washington, DC, leading a group of Indigenous girls on horseback.[47] Journalistic depictions of her life relied on various stereotypical depictions of Indigenous people alternately described as "bloodthirsty savages" or romanticized "noble savages." White writers also frequently imposed heteronormative and sexualized narratives on Native American women, Dawn Mist was referred to as a "dusky beauty," the "flower of her tribe," a "beautiful little savage," and an "Indian princess" wooed by male suitors representing "a hundred lovers" eager to marry her. Just as Asian women were depicted as passive and reserved, reporters described Dawn Mist as timid and fearful of white people. One writer described her as "shy as a wild deer," simultaneously both stereotyping her as passive and dehumanizing her.[48]

But Indigenous women could not be simply reduced to stereotypes, and they resented parade organizers' attempts to tokenize them. Although Dawn Mist was not real, other Indigenous women were real and did march in suffrage parades fighting for their rights as women and as Native people. Marie Bottineau Baldwin, a member of the Turtle Mountain (Ojibwe) Chippewa tribe, marched in the 1913 Washington, DC parade. Baldwin was an attorney who worked as a clerk for the Office of Indian Affairs. Although she was married, Baldwin deemphasized her marital status and attempts to portray her as a submissive wife in favor of her status as a professional, educated woman. Baldwin's presence in the parade disrupted stereotypes of Indigenous femininity and heterosexual availability. Despite parade organizers' expressed wishes, Baldwin did not dress in Native clothing. Instead, she wore her university regalia and marched as a representative of modern Native womanhood with the delegation of woman lawyers. Her physical presence and presentation as a modern Indigenous woman was a challenge to the myth that Native women were submissive objects and that Native people were an archaic, vanishing race. Indigenous women who advocated for suffrage were not only seeking their personal and political rights as women, they were also seeking their rights as native people. They resisted harmful stereotypes, sought acknowledgment as the original suffragists and occupants of the land, and insisted on recognition of tribal sovereignty.[49]

Black suffragists also boldly queered the suffrage movement by claiming their right to march. Despite the objections of Southern white suffragists, Howard University women expressed their intent to participate in the 1913 Washington, DC parade.[50] Marie I. Hardwick was a teacher and dorm matron at Howard University who chose not to marry. As an ardent suffragist, Hardwick actively recruited Howard students to march in the parade and wrote to Alice Paul, chairman of the procession committee, requesting permission to participate. Paul's response revealed the white supremacy inherent in the women's suffrage movement.

Southern white suffragists had threatened to withdraw their support if Black women and girls were allowed to participate in the parade. Paul feared that the participation of large numbers of Black suffragists, such as an entire contingent of marchers from Howard University, would lead to a total boycott by Southern white suffragists. In a letter to Alice Stone Blackwell, Paul expressed the hope that few Black women would participate in the procession. She insisted that the best approach was not to exclude them, but neither to encourage their participation. Paul decided to scatter those who did participate among the delegations of northern suffragists who expressed a willingness to march alongside them.[51] On January 28, 1913, Alice Paul replied to Hardwick, asking her to stop by headquarters to discuss the best place for their section in the parade.[52]

Other Howard students also directly wrote to Paul expressing a desire to march in the parade. Nellie Quander, another spinster woman, had served as the president of Howard University's Alpha Kappa Alpha sorority since 1910. On February 15, 1913, Quander wrote to Alice Paul noting that she also represented a group of college women who wanted to participate in the parade. But Quander objected to the discriminatory treatment they were facing from parade organizers and noted that "we do not wish to enter if we must meet with discrimination on account of race affiliation. Can you assign us to a desirable place in the college women's section?"[53] Quander sent a second letter two days later requesting an immediate reply. Paul replied on February 23, asking that

Quander stop by the headquarters to discuss the place for the Howard University women in the parade.[54] These stalling tactics, along with rumors that they would be segregated, upset Quander and other Black suffragists who complained about discriminatory treatment. Anna Howard Shaw, president of NAWSA at the time, intervened by directly telegramming Paul on February 28, 1913. Shaw objected to Paul's approach and ordered an end to discriminatory practices against Black marchers:

> Am informed that Parade committee has so strongly urged Colored women not to march that it amounts to official discrimination which is distinctly contrary to instructions from National headquarters. Please instruct all marshals to see that all colored women who wish to march shall be accorded every service given to other marchers.[55]

Howard University students refused to be segregated and marched in their caps and gowns along with a contingent of white college women. Mary Church Terrell, president of the National Association of Colored Women (NACW), and other alum of Howard University joined them. Ida Wells-Barnett integrated the parade by marching with white suffragists of the Illinois delegation. Virginia Brooks and Belle Squire marched by her side in a show of solidarity.[56]

In addition to Wells-Barnett and the Howard University students, several other Black suffragists defied segregation orders that day and marched with peers in various vocational sections of the parade. The NAACP, in their magazine *The Crisis*, congratulated Black women for sticking to "the courage of their convictions," making "an admirable showing at the first great national parade."[57] The Chicago *Broad Ax* celebrated them for breaking the color line by proudly marching with their white peers.[58]

Queering Washington

Suffragists also transformed physical sites originally built to exclude, restrain, and control them, into queer spaces of resilience and resistance. From 1915 to 1917, the Cameron House at 21 Madison Place near Lafayette Square in Washington, DC, served as the headquarters of the Congressional Union (renamed the NWP in June 1916). The house was built in 1828 by Benjamin Ogle Tayloe and subsequently was the home of several prominent politicians. It had become a gathering place for male political leaders. Since women had been denied the vote, they likewise were denied the opportunity to serve in elected office. Cameron House, located at the center of Washington, DC, in many ways symbolized the exclusion of women from political power. The Congressional Union chose the location for both practical and political reasons. The house's proximity to the White House and location next to the Belasco Theater with its large meeting space made it an ideal location. The transformation of the house from a site of men's privilege and political power into a site of women's resistance was especially significant. Suffragists recognized that their acquisition of the house with its history and location in the heart of Washington, DC, was a powerful symbol of women's ascension to political power.[59]

As the NWP headquarters, Cameron House served as a site for queer community building. The gender-segregated space facilitated the forging of powerful homosocial alliances and queer relationships. Suffragists organized luncheons, lectures, teas, and holiday socials in the Cameron House meeting rooms. They also sponsored larger meetings and conferences, including the first annual convention of the Congressional Union, which was held at Cameron House in December 1915. Ella Morton Dean served as the hostess of Cameron House, helping to arrange rooms for the various suffragists who stayed in the house when visiting the city to participate in meetings or engage in lobbying and protests. Women came together within the communal living spaces of the house, sharing meals, sleeping together, and forging intimate friendships and romantic relationships.[60]

Cameron House also served as a site of militant resistance as suffragists queered their protest tactics. From its doors, NWP suffragists launched their "silent sentinels" picketing campaign in January 1917. These militant protest methods radically deviated from the tactics employed by mainstream suffragists. On January 10, 1917, the first pickets stepped outside Cameron House with banners that read "Mr. President, How Long Must Women Wait for Liberty." They marched to the White House and stood there silently, demanding that Wilson support the federal women's suffrage amendment. Their picketing campaign lasted for nearly a year.

Queer suffragists like Mabel Vernon, Vida Milholland, and Anne Martin led these unconventional protests.[61] Mabel Vernon was credited as the first NWP suffragist to engage in direct militancy when in the summer of 1916 she interrupted President Wilson during a public speech to ask why if, as he claimed, he was interested in liberty and justice did he oppose the enfranchisement of women. When she repeated the question, she was removed from the event by the police. Vernon organized the NWP picketing of the White House which began shortly thereafter. On March 4, 1917, after months of picketing at the gates, suffragists insisted on their right to be heard. Vida Milholland led a march of 1,000 pickets and two bands around the White House. They marched in the pouring rain. Anne Martin acted as the spokesperson for the group, demanding a meeting with the president to present their resolutions. When denied entry, Martin told the guards defending the gates that it was imperative that the women speak with the president. The guards refused to grant access. Martin used the moment to highlight to the press the continued denial of democracy to women in the United States.[62]

The public and other suffrage organizations responded angrily to the tactics of the NWP. They received a flood of letters at Cameron House criticizing their actions. Mary Kimmell Plough wrote from Chambersburg, Pennsylvania expressing her disgust at the strategy and claiming it had only hurt their cause:

> If to secure a vote I must break the laws . . . why I shall make up my mind to do without a vote. If everybody acted as the Nationals do . . . why chaos would come again . . . Bad manners and bad tactics! You are queering the cause.[63]

Queering the cause was exactly what they were doing. The suffragists of the NWP were turning the traditional approach of advocating for women's suffrage upside down. They had decided that the days of petitioning, lobbying, and politely asking for the vote were behind them. The best way forward, in their opinion, was to invert gendered expectations about passive femininity by embracing a militant form of activism.

The government responded to these tactics by arresting and imprisoning the NWP suffragists in an attempt to suppress their protests. Arrests began to take place slowly in the summer of 1917, accelerating into the fall. Some women were hesitant to join the pickets, fearing judgment from their families or the men in their lives. Florence Whitehouse for example shied away from militant activism, writing to Alice Paul in 1917: "In regard to the picket line . . . I want to go and help so much, but Mr. Whitehouse is very much opposed to it and I could not go without deeply hurting him, so I must give it up."[64] Others were unable to picket because they bore primary childcare responsibilities. Suffragist Mary Johnson wrote to decline a request for help on the picket line, noting with regret that she could not be of service because "I have a family—of three children who need my presence in the home."[65] Divorced or unmarried women and those without children were often more willing to risk arrest.

Queer suffragists were among the first to be arrested. Mabel Vernon was in the first group of suffragists to serve a jail sentence for picketing in June 1917. Another suffragist sent a sympathetic letter to Vernon, applauding her for her pluck and fortitude in enduring prison but noting that her arrest must have been especially hard on Martin. The letter suggests the queer relationship that existed between Martin and Vernon: "I suppose it will be much worse for Miss Martin than for you. She will count the hours till you get out, I know."[66] Anne Martin and Vida Milholland were arrested in July.[67]

Another queer suffragist, Paula Jakobi, was one of the imprisoned suffragists who endured what became known as the "Night of Terror." On November 14, 1917, prison officials brutally beat the suffragists in their cells to try to force them to conform to prison policies. Jakobi tried to fight back as she was physically assaulted by guards: "so pulled and twisted that her hair was streaming in all directions."[68] Other suffragists endured assaults as they were beaten, slammed against cell walls, and chained to cell bars with their hands above their head. One woman suffered a heart attack as a result of the ordeal.

Suffragists went on hunger strikes to protest the conditions of their imprisonment. They were subject to force-feedings as a result. Elizabeth McShane lived in a queer domestic arrangement with fellow suffragist Mary Ingham, who was her primary contact and correspondent during her imprisonment.[69] McShane wrote to Ingham, but Ingham worried when she had not heard from McShane in a few days after learning that they were hunger-striking. She wrote letters and telegrams to Cameron

House asking for updates. In one desperate telegram Ingham asked, "HAS ANYONE SEEN HER" and "WOULD THEY LET ME GO."[70] After being moved from Occoquan Workhouse to the Washington, DC Jail, McShane wrote to Ingham to describe her brutal force-feeding:

> I have just been forcibly fed, and I feel that every atom of American self-respect within me has been outraged. I have been seven days without food, and today I fainted on the floor of my cell. Dr. Ladd came to see me . . . with a tube that looked like a hose, and a pint of milk in which two eggs had been stirred up . . . he put the tube in my mouth and told me to swallow it fast. I did it as fast as I could, but he pushed it down so fast that I gagged and choked terribly.[71]

These shared experiences bonded suffragists even more. McShane described how the imprisoned suffragists sought to comfort each other after the horrible experience of force-feeding:

> I went to Lucy Burns' cell and found her bent over a pail. Afterward I wept hysterically on her shoulder, and she, sweet thing, was most comforting. It was her fifth time. And think! I have twelve more before my term is up.[72]

Suffragists like McShane wrote letters to their loved ones not only to document their experiences but to seek support from their queer chosen families. McShane's chosen family was Ingham and she relied on this connection throughout her imprisonment. McShane described in her prison notes the importance of letters from loved ones: "I love these letters, but they make me feel so small & the prison bars so strong." Visits, when permitted, were especially treasured: "Miss Ingham came to see me . . . Wonderful to see her, only I wanted so much to go home with her."[73]

After serving out their sentence, the released suffragists returned to Cameron House for support and healing. Aleda Richberg-Hornsby, whom fellow imprisoned suffragist Elizabeth McShane described as "an interesting, boyish girl" for her gender non-conforming appearance and daring career as a pilot, suffered terribly from her treatment in confinement.[74] She had lost 15 pounds in less than two weeks. Due to her weakened state, government officials eventually ordered her release. The returning heroes were welcomed back to Cameron House, where they were fed and waited on by friends. Their suffragist sisters held jubilant celebrations in their honor. The house became a site of rest, recuperation, and community-building. Even in their weakened state, the NWP suffragists found strength at headquarters to carry on their radical protests.[75]

Cameron House itself also was the direct target of attacks. On August 14, 1917, an angry mob, enraged by the suffragists' banners, rioted and raged against NWP headquarters. An estimated 3,000–5,000 persons gathered around the suffrage picketers on Pennsylvania Avenue in front of the White House. The NWP banners called out President Wilson for his hypocrisy in advocating for democracy abroad while failing to support democracy for American women at home. Several members of the mob, including American sailors and soldiers in full uniform, approached the silent sentinels, grabbed their banners, and ripped them to shreds. They punched, kicked, choked, and shoved the suffragists. The crowd began to throw tomatoes and eggs at them. When the suffragists retreated to Cameron House, the crowd followed. A man tore down the American flag from the entrance of the headquarters. Another rioter fired a bullet through the window of the house, narrowly missing the heads of three suffragists inside, including Ella Morton Dean, the house matron. The defiant suffragists draped their Kaiser banners from the upstairs windows and balcony of the Cameron House, but these too were torn down by the mob. Similar attacks on the suffragists and the house continued over the next several days.[76] In a public statement to the press, Alice Paul declared: "We have no true democracy in this country, though we are fighting for democracy abroad. Twenty million American citizens are denied a voice in their own government."[77] The leaders of the NWP drafted a resolution demanding a congressional investigation into the actions of the men in uniform who led the attack.

Cameron House served as a symbol of suffrage activism long after it ceased to be the NWP headquarters. In 1937, Betty Gram Swing reflected on the significance of the house in a letter calling for a reunion of NWP picketers. She wrote that Cameron House symbolized "some of the great moments of our lives—our own realistic contribution in that long fight for woman's freedom." Her letter further reflected on the homosocial alliances they forged there: "We have a bond no years can break; we have a fire neither time nor tide can extinguish."[78]

Conclusion

Suffragists queered private and public spaces by transforming them into sites of radical activism and militant protest. From these spaces, they constructed new ideas and challenged mainstream notions of gender, sexuality, and race. But queer spaces were not always entirely transgressive spaces. Even as suffragists defied norms, they ironically reinforced hierarchical boundaries. They erected barriers based on citizenship, class, and race to regulate entry into these spaces. In their effort to maintain their place of privilege and power, white middle-class native-born suffragists built segregated spaces and policed their boundaries.

Black suffragists, Indigenous suffragists, and suffragists of color therefore further queered these spaces by calling out the hypocrisy of white middle-class suffragists. They denounced white suffragists for perpetuating exclusion through xenophobic and racist policies. They directly confronted and fought to dismantle racism and segregation in the white suffrage movement. They demanded an end to efforts to exclude them.

Queer suffragists adopted unconventional tactics in the fight for the vote that mirrored their unconventional lives. They often literally led the charge, marching the suffrage cavalry into battle. From the picket to the prison, they put their bodies on the line. Through multiple contested sites of queer resistance, they believed they could dismantle the racist cisheteropatriarchy.

6

Queering Death

When San Francisco suffragist Fidelia Jewett passed away, her partner Lillien Jane Martin donated a bench in her memory and had it placed in Union Square. Jewett and Martin met at the Girls High School where Jewett worked as a teacher and Martin as the school's vice principal. Martin studied psychology at the University of Gottingen in Germany and later returned to work as a professor of psychology at Stanford University. Jewett and Martin were both members of the National American Woman Suffrage Association (NAWSA) and leaders in the College Equal Suffrage League (CESL). They lived their queer lives in relative peace, establishing a home together where they lived for more than thirty years until Jewett's death in 1933. Martin hoped that the bench in Union Square would stand forever as a memorial to the life of an amazing educator. When Martin passed away ten years later, the bench itself came to symbolize their devotion to each other. A friend had Martin's name inscribed on the bench to honor the memory of both women who lived together as a couple.[1]

Queer suffragists lived and loved deeply. In life, they developed unique strategies that allowed them to navigate the confines of the gender and sexual norms of their day. In death, they queered traditional death rituals by enacting queer modes of grieving. Scholars interested in the field of queer death studies have suggested that queering death is a process and methodology that moves beyond an exclusive focus on gender and sexuality to "challenge understandings of death, dying and mourning anchored in and structured by the hegemony of heteronormative narratives."[2] Applying this lens can help us attain a better understanding of the death and mourning rituals of suffragists. Judith Butler's concept of ungrievable lives is also a helpful idea for this analysis. Butler defined an ungrievable life as "one that cannot be mourned because it has never lived, that is, it has never counted as a life at all."[3] The lives of suffragists often deviated from heteronormative and chrononormative

Figure 6.1. "Dr. Lillien J. Martin tells small Jacquelin Papert about Miss Fidelia Jewett, in whose memory Dr. Martin designed this bench on the Post Street side of Union Square and presented it to the city." "A Lasting Tribute to a Friend," *San Francisco Examiner*, October 18, 1934, 20.

expectations. Some women chose not to marry or have children. Instead, they pursued higher education, professional careers, established queer domestic arrangements, and created chosen families. Heteronormative society judged these non-traditional lives harshly, often labeling these suffragists as spinsters or abnormal women who failed to live up to their full potential as women by not fulfilling their roles as wives and mothers. In many ways, their lives never counted as full lives, as viewed from a narrow heteronormative perspective.

Death rituals not only function to allow the bereaved to move through the emotional process of grieving, but also, in some cases, they serve as important acts of resistance through their public declarations. Mourning and commemoration practices took on especially significant meanings for queer suffragists who lived non-normative lives. Some suffragists resisted societal norms at death by bypassing their biological families and willing their estates and their remains to their friends or partners. The deceased's posthumous declarations often revealed the extent of their devotion through their efforts to care for the loved ones they left behind. In coping with their sense of loss, surviving partners enacted grieving rituals that co-opted and queered death practices traditionally associated with heterosexual couples. Death also allowed them to memorialize their love for each other, finally somewhat freed from societal constraints. These memorials, some literally etched in stone, stand as powerful symbols of the enduring power of queer life and love.

Queering Dying

Suffragists queered notions of death by serving as chosen families who cared for each other in their final illness. Relationships forged during the fight for the vote often endured throughout their lives, far beyond the era of suffrage, and to their dying days. As Alice Morgan Wright and Edith Goode aged together, they continued to provide each other with love and care. Wright used her art and poetry to express her love for her partner. She sculpted a bust of Goode, and her notebooks contain several Valentine's Day poems that she wrote over the years. Each poem stood as a testament to her deep love for Goode.[4] As they both grew older, Wright reflected on their aging and on their life together:

> My hands are torn by the spokes I clutch
> as the wheeling years go by
> And the dust of their passing grays my head
> And my eyes are dim with the dust they shed;
> But it is gay and lovely
> To hear the dancing tread
> Of cooing pigeons on the roof
> Above my dusty head
>
> And think how year by year
> I love my lovely dear!
> She is my noonday bright
> She is my starry night
> She is my heart's delight
> My very dear
>
> At every setting of the sun
> A grisly shape presides
> O'er graying waves by the light outrun
> For another day is done, is done

And neither the foam nor the sand dune abides
But adventurous sandpipers
Invest a beach with cheer
Despite the twilight dear
Despite the ebbing tides

And year by year I love my dear
I love my lovely dear!
She is my noonday bright
She is my starry night
She is my heart's delight
My dearest dear.[5]

Wright and Goode both had their share of health problems, and they took turns caring for each other. In 1956, they ended up in the hospital at the same time. Wright wrote to a friend to describe how they stayed connected though separated in different wards:

> On the occurrence of E's operation I was relegated to the C. U. or Convalescent Unit from which every morning at 10.30 I hobble across the street and wave at her window from which at first her nurse and now she, waves back at me.[6]

A decade later, when Wright became very ill, Goode helped her write her obituary and a card to announce her passing. They discussed plans to distribute their estates after they were both gone.

Suffragists thus cared for each other in their darkest moments. Paula Jakobi was one of the suffragists of the National Woman's Party (NWP) who served as a Silent Sentinel during the pickets in front of the Wilson White House in 1917. When Jakobi lost her partner Anna Van Vechten sixteen years later, her suffragist family supported her through the illness and loss. Jakobi had been a member of Heterodoxy, the radical feminist club in New York City. Van Vechten was undergoing treatment for breast cancer in a hospital in Frankfort. Fellow suffragist and Heterodoxy member Rose Pastor Stokes offered Jakobi consolation, advice, and medical referrals.[7] Stokes had also been diagnosed with breast cancer and was receiving medical treatment in the same hospital in the room next to Van Vechten. Both women passed away in 1933 within a few weeks of each other. A devastated Jakobi, having lost both her lover and her friend, stayed with suffragist and Heterodoxy founder Marie Jenney Howe throughout the summer of 1933. In December, Howe wrote to share the news with suffragist Fola La Follette:

> [Jakobi] is all broken up and can't adjust to loneliness and old age. They lived together 14 years. It is not generally known, but I will tell you, that Ann committed suicide by throwing herself out the window. She had cancer and might have lived several months longer. This is what is so hard on Paula. The shock was too much for her.[8]

Well beyond their days working on the suffrage campaign, suffragists served as family and community for each other. They relied on each other for support, queering notions of love and family, until the very end.

Queering Grief

Queer suffragists co-opted traditional modes of grieving by adapting heteronormative methods of memorializing the deceased. Tasks such as making decisions about the interment of remains, organizing funeral arrangements, and writing the obituary traditionally fell to the spouse, children, or close family of the deceased. Just as husbands and wives memorialized their spouses through public rituals, queer suffragists chose to honor their partners by adopting similar rituals. Chosen families also often stepped up to perform mourning rituals that otherwise would be performed by biological family members.

Minnie Brown made the final arrangements and wrote the obituary for her beloved life partner, Daisy Tapley. The two women had met while working as singers with the Bert Williams and George Walker theatrical troupe. Tapley was married at the time to vaudeville actor Green Henri Tapley. Daisy and Green Henri Tapley separated after the Williams and Walker Company dissolved in 1910. Whether this had anything to do with the relationship between Tapley and Brown is unknown, but the two women moved in together shortly thereafter. They lived on West 136 Street in New York City. Brown began teaching piano, organ, and singing. Tapley's career continued to flourish. She became the first Black woman to record commercially in the United States when she recorded a duet with Carroll Clark for Columbia studios. Brown and Tapley performed together throughout the city in the 1910s and 1920s. They taught music and organized glee clubs of the YWCA in New York. They were both also active members of St. Mark's Methodist Episcopal Church and leaders of the National Association of Negro Musicians, founded in 1919.[9]

Tapley and Brown were committed to each other and to reforming society. As suffragists and civil rights activists, they fought together for gender and racial equality, insisting on their rights as Black women. They advocated for women's rights with the Empire State Federation of Women's Clubs, a branch of the NACW. They also publicly fought against racism and discrimination in 1918 when the YMCA refused to allow an integrated audience to attend a music recital they were organizing. They canceled the event rather than support such a stance. After that negative experience, they launched a series of educational recitals intended to cultivate an appreciation for the artistic talents of Black performers and prominent reformers. Tapley and Brown also participated in the 1917 Silent March in New York City. Nearly 10,000 people marched down Fifth Avenue in chilling silence. This powerful event, organized by the National Association for the Advancement of Colored People (NAACP), sought to call attention to the issues of segregation and lynching. The women dressed in white and the men in dark colors, carrying signs that read "Make America Safe for Democracy" and "Thou Shalt Not Kill." Tapley led the women's division of the march.[10]

Tapley and Brown lived together for nearly fifteen years before Tapley succumbed to ovarian cancer in 1925. Brown's grieving process demonstrates the ways that suffragists used public memorial practices to make queer lives visible. Tapley was interred at her home on Sag Harbor, Long Island, where she and Brown had spent summers together. Brown grieved the loss of her partner by donating flowers in remembrance of Tapley at St. Mark's Methodist Episcopal Church. This mourning ritual reflected Brown's commitment to Tapley before their religious community.[11] Brown also chose to publicly honor her partner's memory by taking out "In Memoriam" ads in the *New York Age*. The annual memorial read:

MISS MINNIE BROWN
NEW YORK
SOPRANO

MRS. DAISY TAPLEY
NEW YORK
CONTRALTO

Figure 6.2. Minnie Brown and Daisy Tapley lived together as a couple and after Tapley passed away, Brown published a memorial notice every year in the local newspaper on the anniversary of her partner's death. Elijah Chorus concert program, Jordan Hall, Boston. April 1915. E. Azalia Hackley Collection, Detroit Public Library, Detroit, Michigan.

In Memory of
Daisy Tapley
who Died, February 5, 1925
Minnie Brown[12]

Brown not only wrote and submitted the memorial for publication, but also continued to publish the notice every year on the anniversary of Tapley's death until she passed away herself in 1936. This public act of grieving, and the printing of their two names together, revealed the intensity of Brown's devotion to Tapley and exposed the extent of their intimacy in life. Through the mourning process, Brown insisted that Tapley's life was a life worthy of grieving.

For queer suffragists, the grieving process also often included erasing memories and creating new ones. Pennsylvania suffragists Edna Schoyer and Anne Shelton Richardson lived in a house that came to serve as an important symbol of their love for each other. The couple began living together in 1915 in a mansion that Richardson built on a 110-acre estate overlooking Mamanasco Lake in Ridgefield, Connecticut. Their house in Ridgefield not only served as the center of their personal life but also served as the hub of their social and political activism. The couple hosted suffrage meetings in their home and after 1920 helped organize the League of Women Voters.[13]

When Schoyer passed away in August 1946, a devastated Richardson continued to live in the house until her death nineteen years later. Richardson gave away her fortune, specifying a great number of charitable contributions in her will. But, Richardson made no such generous donation of the couple's home. Her attachment to the house as a testament to the life they built together was clear in her written intentions. She stated succinctly in her will: "it is my wish that the dwelling house constituting my residence in Ridgefield, Conn., which my beloved friend, the late Edna Schoyer and I occupied together for many years, be not occupied by others after my death."[14] She requested that the house be razed. The state of Connecticut, however, did not want to tear it down and tried to fight the stipulation in court. The court ultimately sided with Richardson and consented to demolishing it. Allowing the house to be occupied by others was perhaps too painful for Richardson to imagine. This symbol of their life together was thus erased upon her death. But, Richardson did not want her partner to be forgotten. In her will, she set aside money from her estate to donate flowers in memory of Edna Schoyer to St. Stephen's Episcopal Church. Richardson directed that flowers be placed on the altar on the anniversary of Schoyer's death and on Christmas each year. This tradition, symbolizing Richardson's love for Schoyer, continues to the present day.[15]

The unique nature of these queer relationships often necessitated a great deal of private grieving. Queer suffragists who lost their life partners were not always treated the same as heterosexual couples who had lost a spouse. This was particularly true for those suffragists who lived extremely private lives and had to keep their personal relationships secret. Alice Dunbar Nelson had a secret romantic relationship with Edwina

Kruse. When Kruse died years later, Nelson privately grieved the loss of her former lover. Reflecting on the death of Kruse in her diary she noted: "I loved her once. Twenty years ago, her death would have wrecked my life."[16] Dunbar Nelson chose to express her grief by paying tribute to her friend and lover through a poem and fictionalized novel based on Kruse's life. *This Lofty Oak* began with a loving poem declaring: "This lofty oak, that rooted deep, Bent yet its sheltering branches over all . . . drew life and happiness from out its heart. E'en though it fall, 't'will live as long as man."[17] Dunbar Nelson did not publicly identify Kruse as the subject of the novel. Instead, the story reflected her personal grief.

While some queer suffragists grieved the loss of their partner in private, others found a surprising amount of communal support in their grief. Elizabeth Cecilia Babcock and Hannah Keziah Clapp were educators who founded the Sierra Seminary, a private, co-educational school in Carson City, Nevada. Babcock and Clapp lived together for more than thirty-five years, fully committing themselves to each other. Clapp bought Babcock a diamond ring as a symbol of her devotion and Babcock wore the ring on her engagement finger for the rest of her life. They pooled their financial resources and built a large home with a beautifully landscaped garden in Carson City. In 1887, they relocated when the University of Reno hired Clapp to teach history and English. Babcock taught elementary school and helped to open the first kindergarten in the city. As suffragists, they participated in both state and national organizations. Clapp represented Nevada in the National Woman Suffrage Association and led the charge to introduce a suffrage bill to the Nevada state legislature. Clapp became vice president of the Nevada Equal Suffrage Association.[18]

Babcock suffered a debilitating stroke in 1896 and passed away in 1899. Clapp's sorrow over the loss of her partner reverberated throughout the community.[19] The Woman's Guild at Trinity Parish in Reno, of which they were both members, passed a resolution memorializing Babcock and expressing deep regret over the loss to "Miss Clapp, in particular."[20] The local community publicly mourned her passing and celebrated her life. Clapp received an outpouring of support from a number of individuals and organizations who expressed their condolences for her loss. Babcock's obituary in the *Reno Evening Gazette* revealed the depth of Clapp's pain:

> Miss Clapp has watched and nursed her with a devotion that but few couples possess, and now that a lifetime companion, friend, partner and more than sister has gone, Miss Clapp, with that devotion that has always been a characteristic part of her nature is nearly heart broken.[21]

Recognizing that the relationship was beyond that of "companion, friend, partner or sister," the writer acknowledged the significance of their loving relationship. This appears to be as close an acknowledgment of a lesbian relationship as it got in late nineteenth-century society. However, by lifting this friendship to a higher moral plane, the writer mythologized such relationships, placing them beyond the physical and into the spiritual realm. This suggests that outsiders generally viewed Boston marriages as asexual friendships and therefore as more socially acceptable than homosexual relationships.

While not acknowledging the full possible sexual extent of the relationship, in comparing the Clapp/Babcock relationship to that of a husband and a wife, the *Gazette* writer does acknowledge the grief Clapp must have felt over the loss of her companion:

> For over thirty-five years she has been a close companion of Miss Clapp and the two have shared each other's sorrows and joys during all these years . . . Miss Clapp is well nigh prostrated with grief over the loss of a companion that has been almost constantly at her side, both night and day, for three decades and a half.[22]

Five years after Babcock's death, the women's relationship was still remembered fondly in the local community. The *Reno Evening Gazette* recalled that Babcock's "devotion which she showed for the partner of her joys and sorrows, the friend for whom she left all others, as completely merging her life with that of Miss Clapp, she made with her a common home and a common purse, touched the hearts of all who knew them."[23] The collective condolences sent by suffragists and women reformers to Clapp following Babcock's death once again reveal the significance of support networks between women, and especially between suffragists, in this era.

Journalists helped share the story of their relationship. Miriam Michelson, a San Francisco suffragist, wrote to Clapp after Babcock's death seeking details about the couple's "very beautiful friendship" for an article in the San Francisco *Bulletin*. Michelson requested "details of your life together—when you [met], how long you have been together, the circumstances which bound you to each other." Michelson ended by noting that although they were strangers, even a "stranger can feel for so great a loss as this."[24] The resulting piece in the *Bulletin* demonstrated Michelson's affection for the two women and their love. The title of the article, "Nevada's Feminine David and Jonathan" alluded to the Biblical story of a homosocial and romantic friendship between two men.

Michelson's article and an accompanying poem by Kate Tupper ironically queered Babcock's and Clapp's relationship while simultaneously attempting to normalize the queer friendship for a heteronormative audience. The article began with a poem by suffragist and writer Kate Tupper (Galpin) insisting that the theme of the story was "not love of woman for man" but a "richer and rarer" story of "a woman's love for a woman." The full poem (written years earlier), while celebrating love between women, largely romanticized rather than pathologized their relationship as abnormal. In fact, as evidenced in this excerpt, Tupper seemed to justify this womanly love as merely an outlet for their unused maternal love:

> What will you say of a home
> To which two women's lives combine
> To make its shade a resting place,
> A heaven and a shrine?
>
> What will you say? Ask the weary man
> Who its rest ne'er sought in vain
> Though he came from the senate of miner's camp
> From the mountain or the plain.
>
> Ask the gray-haired mother of child bereft,
> Whose tears it has wiped away;
> Ask the motherless girl, who in its peace
> Has forgotten her loss for a day.

Ask the children sweet, or the children rough,
Who have nestled beneath its eaves,
And have felt the warmth of tender love
That for woes of childhood grieves.

And have felt the gentle brooding care
That all such woes could smother
Ah–Nature leaves some women childless
That all childhood may claim them mother.[25]

Excerpts of the Tupper poem served as an introduction to Miriam Michelson's article. Michelson similarly romanticized the love story of Babcock and Clapp, framing the relationship as a "friendship as pure, as loyal, as lasting as any masculine partnerships." She described this love between women as a rare and "quaint soul marriage." But, at the same time, Michelson described them as husband and wife. Michelson's use of heteronormative notions of domesticity normalized the women's relationship within the confines of accepted gender conventions. She described the relationship using binary notions of femininity and mas-culinity as she contrasted the physical appearance and behaviors of the two women. Michelson described Clapp as the "man" or "husband" with a "masculine mind," and "strong, almost rough-hewn features." She then positioned Babcock as the "woman" or "wife," a "delicate, dainty, short and slight, exquisitely feminine" woman. Michelson wrote that Clapp enjoyed "playing the man's part with hammer and nails . . . and house-hold repairs" while Babcock "found pleasure in home-keeping" and "domestic triumphs over the holes in stockings, over dust in corners," and over "recipes for cakes and puddings" that "satisfied her womanly nature."[26]

Michelson expressed concern and compassion for Clapp in enduring the loss of Babcock. The writer tenderly described the sad passing:

The wife of Miss Clapp was gasping, but she put her arms about the neck of the one who had cherished her so tenderly, so unselfishly, so gener-ously, and clung there with all the strength of her last breath. Her small, stiff white fingers had to be bent back, afterward, that of these two faithful comrades, the living might be separated from the dead.[27]

Michelson noted that the two women were inseparable until death took Babcock away. The communal outpouring of support helped console the grieving partner left behind.

When suffragist Lucy Diggs Slowe passed away in 1937, her partner Mary Burrill received hundreds of letters expressing condolences for her loss. The letter writers included a range of individuals from near strangers to the queer community they had built together. Marie Hardwick, a fellow unmarried suffragist and Howard University educator, expressed her deepest sympathy in a letter to Burrill, noting, "you will miss her as perhaps, no other person will. Your friendship reminded me of that of Jonathan's and David's."[28] Mollie Berrien's letter of condolence expressed similar sentiments: "My heart aches for you, for I know you two loved each other as only sisters could. I know your life will be sad and lonely without her sweet companionship but I pray that God will give you strength to endure the separation knowing that when God wills it, you two will be together once more never to be separated again."[29] Slowe's loss was deeply felt throughout the community.

Members of their chosen family shared in Burrill's grief. To keep the memory of her partner alive, Burrill kept a picture of Slowe on her piano with a silver vase filled with white carnations. In 1938, their friend Esther Popel wrote a poem entitled "White Carnations," noting the significance of Burrill's devotion for Slowe and the symbolism of the white carnations. She wrote that although Slowe "is not with us here, yet white carnations, somehow keep her near!"[30] Several years later, in 1941, Hilda Davis, Dean of Women at Howard University, wrote to Burrill expressing sorrow that Burrill had to give up living in the home she had shared with Slowe. Acknowledging the importance of the home and their relationship, Davis wrote, "It is hard to think of the Kearney Street house as the home of anyone but you and Miss Slowe, and I am sure that it was too full of memories of your friend to be a comfort to you alone."[31] These letters poignantly illustrate the importance of chosen family in both life and death.

Queering Memorials

Public memorials served as a way for queer suffragists to transform their personal grief into acts of service that honored their deceased loved one.

Following Lucy Diggs Slowe's death, Mary Powell Burrill ordered copies of her eulogy printed to serve as a more permanent record of her partner's life. Burrill wrote a foreword to the eulogy that read:

> Because I believe that Time, the unerring appraiser of all human values, will give Lucy D. Slowe a secure place among those great spirits who have wrought mightily for our race; and because the Eulogy by Dwight O. W. Holmes interprets her character and her work with such truth and beauty, I have given it something of permanency in these printed pages.
>
> May Lucy D. Slowe's spirit of helpfulness and courage and devotion to duty abide with us always.[32]

Burrill included a photograph of Slowe and mailed it out to many individuals and organizations. She hoped the book would preserve Slowe's memory. The bound eulogy not only gave permanency to Slowe's life but recorded Burrill's grief for perpetuity.

Some queer suffragists chose to memorialize their partner with funds that supported the causes that were most sacred to their loved one. Nevada suffragist Hannah Keziah Clapp donated money to ensure that a new kindergarten building be completed as a memorial to Eliza Babcock. The goal was to carry on the educational work that Babcock had committed to in life. The building was dedicated as the Babcock Memorial Kindergarten.[33] Alice P. Smyth decided that the best way to honor her partner Mary Askew Mather was with a public donation to create the New Castle County Free Library in Wilmington, Delaware. Mather had worked to establish and maintain the library system during her life. Smyth believed the memorial fund was therefore a fitting tribute to her in death. The memorial library was founded in 1927 and provided service to rural areas through a bookmobile.[34] California suffragist Gail Laughlin donated funds to refurbish the delivery room of the Florence Crittenton Home in Denver as a memorial to Dr. Mary Sperry. Sperry had volunteered her services as a physician to the women who lived there. Laughlin also offered to sponsor a scholarship in Dr. Sperry's honor to Mills College.[35]

Alice Morgan Wright and Edith Goode both agreed before their deaths to donate a substantial portion of their estates to the cause that they cared most deeply about: animal rights. After years of work for suffrage and women's rights on both the national and international stages, Wright and Goode turned to the cause of animal activism. They created the National Humane Education Society and devoted the remaining years of their life to this work. Prior to their deaths, they established an endowed trust under both of their names. The "Alice Morgan Wright–Edith Goode Fund" continues to support the work of the National Humane Education Society.[36]

Queering Probate

Rather than willing their property and possessions to male spouses or children, suffragists queered heteronormative death traditions by providing for their life partners. Alice Stone Blackwell made plans to provide for Katherine "Kitty" Blackwell in the event of her death. The daughter of Lucy Stone and Henry Blackwell, Alice Stone Blackwell carried on a family tradition by devoting her life to women's suffrage. She served as the editor of the *Women's Journal* and worked to reunite the American Woman Suffrage Association (AWSA) and the National Woman Suffrage Association (NWSA) into the National American Woman Suffrage Association (NAWSA). She remained active in NAWSA into the 1910s. Historian Lillian Faderman has speculated that Alice had a passionate relationship with Kitty Blackwell (her aunt Elizabeth Blackwell's adopted daughter). The two became companions in their later life.[37] In a 1934 version of her will, Alice Stone Blackwell made her wishes known:

> Whereas, it is my desire to assure Miss Katherine Barry Blackwell . . . of a comfortable subsistence for the rest of her life; Now, therefore, I hereby direct, bequeath and devise, that my executors shall . . . set aside out of my estate or the profit or incomes arising therefrom, a sufficient amount to suitably and properly maintain and care for said Katherine Barry Blackwell.[38]

Although Kitty passed away before Alice, the desire to provide for her partner upon her death was clear in these early drafts of her will.

Queer suffragists also wanted to ensure that their partners continued to have a place to call home. When Pennsylvania suffragist Leona Huntzinger passed away, she left everything, including the farm where they had lived together, to her companion Elizabeth Hopkinson. Mary Askew Mather similarly made sure to stipulate in her will that her partner, Alice P. Smyth, retained full ownership of the house they had purchased together to live in if she so chose. Nevada suffragist Eliza Babcock left her entire estate to Hannah Clapp. About eight years before Babcock's death, the couple had purchased a home in Palo Alto, California, where they planned to retire someday. After Babcock's burial, Clapp moved to their dream home alone.[39]

Annie Tinker was perhaps less concerned about providing for her former lover than she was with expressing her continued affection. After her work on the New York suffrage campaign, Tinker traveled to Europe during World War I to offer her services to the Red Cross. She met and apparently had a romantic relationship with Kate Darling Nelson. Their relationship ended and Tinker pursued relationships with other women. Nelson married a wealthy Parisian businessman named Bertolini. Still, Tinker left her entire estate to her in perhaps a final declaration of love. Tinker also requested that Nelson ensure that a house Tinker owned in Poquott, New York and a portion of her estate be used to establish a charity home for elderly women. This decision to entrust her estate to her former lover apparently caused quite a bit of tension in the Tinker family as they speculated about the nature of the relationship that had existed between the two. The Tinker family filed suit against Nelson in probate court to contest the will.[40]

Providing for lovers, partners, and chosen family after death often strained relationships between queer suffragists and their biological family. Dr. Mary Austin Sperry distanced herself from her family both before and after her death. Sperry was a noted physician in San Francisco who became intimately involved with suffrage organizer Gail Laughlin. NAWSA sent Laughlin to California, where she worked closely with Mary Simpson Sperry who was president of the California Woman's Suffrage Association and the mother of Dr. Sperry.[41] Mother Sperry was apparently irritated about the relationship that developed between Laughlin and her daughter and was enraged when the two decided to move away together to Denver, Colorado in 1907. Perhaps the move was precipitated by a desire to distance themselves somewhat from the Sperry family and live their own life free from familial intervention. They publicly indicated that they were simply eager to live in a progressive state where women enjoyed the liberty to exercise their social and political freedoms. Laughlin opened a law office and Sperry started a private medical practice.

Familial relationships were apparently mended somewhat in 1914 when Laughlin and Sperry moved back to San Francisco and moved in with Sperry's mother in the family home on Pacific Street. Laughlin continued to work as an attorney, opening a law office and then serving as a police court judge in San Francisco. Sperry worked as an obstetrical surgeon at the San Francisco Children's Hospital and served as a member of the Society of Women Physicians. Gail Laughlin, Dr. Mary Sperry, and Mary Simpson Sperry now devoted themselves to the national suffrage campaign. Laughlin served as the chairman and Dr. Sperry as the treasurer of the California Branch of the Congressional Union for Woman Suffrage (CUWS). They attended national conferences together and in 1915, marched side by side in the opening parade of the Panama Pacific International Exposition wearing the colors of the CUWS.[42]

Despite the appearance of harmony and unity, Mother Sperry continued to resent Laughlin's presence in her daughter's life. But it appears that she avoided direct, public condemnation, perhaps because of Laughlin's position as a beloved suffrage speaker or because of the potential negative attention that such a critique could bring to the suffrage cause. Private family disputes over this issue may have contributed to the younger Sperry's decision to strike her family out of her will in 1917. Yet, no word of this familial discontent leaked to the press until Dr. Sperry's tragic death on May 7, 1919. Upon the public reading of the will, the Sperry family was shocked to learn that Sperry left everything, including her body, to Laughlin. The will, written two years before her death, read: "I, Mary A. Sperry . . . give and bequeath my body to my friend Gail Laughlin."[43] She also willed her entire estate to Laughlin, leaving nothing to her mother and siblings. Dr. Sperry noted in the text that it was indeed her intention to "purposely omit" her mother, sister, and brothers from her will, indicating that they had the financial means to provide for themselves.

Sperry's attempt to permanently sever ties with her family in her will and provide for her life partner infuriated her mother. Court records attest to the bitterness of the dispute. Mother Sperry contested the will, arguing that her daughter was "not of sound mind and not mentally competent" at the time. But she struggled to offer any solid proof of this, given that Sperry was a well-respected and highly competent physician. Mary Simpson Sperry tried another tactic. Instead, she accused Laughlin of poisoning and prejudicing her daughter's mind and preventing her from interacting with the rest of the family. Laughlin vehemently denied these charges. The accusations reflected not only concern about Laughlin's influence over the younger Sperry but also hints at homosexual relations between them. Mother Sperry argued that Laughlin was "mannish" with a "domineering, masculine and assertive disposition." She told the judge that Laughlin was her daughter's "constant companion," even occupying "the same room and same bed."[44]

Gail Laughlin, however, seemed to care less about her own public image or the reputation of the suffrage movement itself than about the memory of her beloved partner whom Mary Simpson Sperry had described as mentally incompetent. Laughlin ignored the accusations of mannishness and implied sexual abnormality. Seeking to preserve the reputation of her partner, Laughlin insisted that disparaging remarks about Sperry's mental competency at the time of her death be expunged from the record. Defending her partner's reputation, Laughlin countered the claims that Sperry was sickly or weak of will, noting on the record that she was "a successful and beloved physician, of strong personality and determined will, sound judgment and strong mentality, not living secluded in her own room or elsewhere, but taking an active part in the life of the community, a member of the staff of the Children's Hospital for some time and up to the time of her last illness."[45]

Queering Interment

Queer suffragists thus fought to preserve the reputations of their partners and codify their relationships in death. Heterosexual couples often memorialized their relationship with a joint burial. Suffragists queered this tradition by requesting that they be buried next to their women partners. Although the right to legally marry in life was not available to them, there was no regulation against being joined together in death in this way. Carrying out Dr. Mary Austin Sperry's wishes, Gail Laughlin had Sperry's body cremated and kept her partner's ashes with her for life. Mary Simpson Sperry objected by inscribing her daughter's name on

Figure 6.3. Gail Laughlin requested in her will that upon her death her remains, along with those of Dr. Sperry, be interred together under a single headstone bearing their names. Photo by author. Laughlin family plot, Brooklawn Memorial Park, Portland, Cumberland County, Maine.

the family plot in Stockton, California with the phrase "in memoriam." This simple phrase suggested that although her daughter's body was not there, her rightful place remained with her kin. When Laughlin died in 1952, her will directed that she be laid to rest side by side with Sperry, interred in the same grave alongside other members of Laughlin's family cemetery in Maine. Laughlin noted in her will:

> I direct that my body be cremated and that my ashes, together with the ashes of my friend, Mary A. Sperry, be placed in my lot in Brooklawn Memorial Park to be marked by a tablet bearing only our names.[46]

In a very visible and public display of her affection, Laughlin insisted that both of their names be etched on a single grave marker as a way of commemorating their life together and their commitment to each other in this world and beyond.

Other queer suffragists also created joint burials. When NAWSA president Carrie Chapman Catt died in 1947, she requested to be buried next to her partner, Mary "Mollie" Garrett Hay, in Woodlawn Cemetery in New York City under a tombstone that reads: "Here lie two, united in friendship for 38 years through constant service to a great cause." Similarly, Pennsylvania suffragist Edna Schoyer and Annie Shelton Richardson were laid to rest in the same plot under the same headstone in Mountain Grove Cemetery in Bridgeport, Connecticut.

Nevada suffragist Eliza Babcock made it known before her death that she wished to be buried next to her partner. In 1899, Babcock told her companion Hannah Clapp that "when I die, bury me where your ashes may be laid upon my breast."[47] Nine years later, when Clapp passed away in 1908, her will fulfilled Babcock's final wish: "I direct that my body be cremated and that my ashes be put in a suitable urn, and that the same be placed on the grave of my dear deceased friend and companion Elizabeth A. Babcock."[48] Clapp and Babcock rest together at Mount Hope Cemetery in Bangor, Maine.[49]

In 1970, when New York suffragist Alice Morgan Wright lost her companion, Edith J. Goode, she was upset that they would not be interred together. As early as 1955, Wright had requested in various iterations of her will that the two women be buried next to each other in a plot in Albany Rural Cemetery. She left the decision up to Goode and her family:

> In case my friend Edith J. Goode should die either before or after or at the same time with me, unless she has declared to her Executors some other preference as to the disposition of her remains, it is my wish, as she knows, that they be interred in like fashion with mine on this lot and that a stone bearing her name and dates, 1882—be placed close to mine.[50]

But this never happened. A note in the back of Wright's address book reveals her deep grief and regret over the two of them not being buried together:

> My wanting leaves something to be desired. My writing leaves something to be desired but I should never forget these names, badly printed so they are. Edith Goode & Alice Wright . . . I believe there has never been a moment in all these years when I have not put together these two names. Why on earth didn't I enter these two names together the last time, not long ago when I last asked you to put us together.[51]

Alice Morgan Wright passed away five years later and was buried without her partner in her family plot in Albany Rural Cemetery, New York.

Queering the Afterlife

Suffragists queered death by finding ways to maintain connections to each other in the afterlife. Hannah Clapp continued to mourn the loss of Eliza Babcock for years after her death. In the last years of her life, Clapp wrote detailed letters to her niece Kate Baker Busey about her days. But tucked away in the envelopes with these standard letters were notes signed by the deceased Babcock. In April 1905, Clapp wrote to Busey: "I have enclosed a little communication from Miss Babcock which I am quite certain you would like to see. I would not send them to anyone else."[52] Clapp explained to Busey that Babcock and other departed relatives spoke to her from beyond the grave. Midway through a March 27, 1907 letter to Busey, Clapp stopped writing for a moment because she said that she felt the presence of her deceased niece and Busey's sister, Nellie Dunlap. Babcock wrote:

> I think she is here now. So she was. I got a piece of paper and sent you what was written. Sometimes I write automatically. Miss Babcock controls my hand. I do not know what is written till I see it.[53]

Clapp believed that Nellie, Babcock, and other spirits from the otherworld frequently spoke through her to communicate messages of support to her and the family. She enclosed the letters along with her own letters and sent them on to Busey. In a July 13, 1905 letter, Clapp included a note from the spirit of Babcock:

> We are often very near you, can see you, and often hear you talk. We know much that is going on in the earth life. You cannot tell the time of our coming. The vibrations do not rouse you.[54]

These spirit letters were generally affirming and loving, encouraging the living to carry on through their troubles. On May 21, 1905, a spirit letter from Babcock read:

I am here my dear to say to you that you are to have a better time from this on. You are to see things turn in your own way. The good things of life are coming to you. I cannot tell you just how, but I know they are. Keep up your courage and do the best you can. Love everybody. There is good in all only bring out the good. I love you all the same as when on earth. My soul is with you now. I do try to comfort you. Keep youthful and keep your health.[55]

Clapp and Busey were both adherents to spiritualism, a belief that the spirits of the dead could communicate with the living. By the late nineteenth century, spiritualism had become very popular in the United States, especially among middle- and upper-class reformers. Several women gained nationwide popularity as mediums that could communicate with the spirits. This imbued them with authority and provided a willing audience to communicate their message of women's rights. Spiritualism thus spread among suffragists.[56] As Clapp aged, she reflected on her days with Babcock. She frequently told family and friends that Miss Babcock had all her love and that she looked forward to seeing her again in the afterlife.[57] Clapp's communications with Babcock allowed her to feel connected to her partner long after her death.

Conclusion

Queer suffragists adopted, adapted, and queered heteronormative grieving and death rituals. The erection of physical memorials, monuments, and the dedication of buildings ensured that the memory of their partner and their connection to each other lived on. Suffrage couples chose to be laid to rest together in the same plot or under the same headstone in the manner typically associated with heterosexual couples. Legally codifying their relationships at death through the probate process was yet another strategy that queer suffragists used to memorialize their love. Rituals, prayers, memorials, and writings allowed suffragists to preserve the memory and remain connected to their partners even after death.

These queer death rituals allow for the possibility of resurrecting queer lives after death. Not all deaths were as publicly grievable as some of the examples in this chapter. Babcock and Clapp's story, for example, stands out as unique in the shared public grief over the death of Babcock and the outpouring of sympathy for Clapp. The loss of other queer lives passed quietly with private mourning rituals or none at all. But the desire of queer suffragists to care for each other before and after their passing and to preserve the memory of their partners has left evidence that allows perceptive historians and biographers to diffuse the murky obscurity that prevents us from seeing the true nature of their queer relationships. By piecing together the remnants of their lives and their deaths, we resist the historical erasure of these stories of queer love.

Conclusion

This book began with the simple premise that queer suffragists existed. This is an essential point to begin and end with because acknowledging the existence of queer suffragists also helps us come to terms with the systematic erasure of their existence (or at least of their queerness) from the historical record. Their gender-defying behavior and queer relationships have largely been expunged from the narrative of suffrage history. The erasure of the lives of queer women reveals the process that feminist scholars examined in depth in the 1970s and writer Adrienne Rich attributed to "compulsory heterosexuality." Rich noted that the destruction of letters, poems, and diaries providing evidence of love between women has rendered the lesbian possibility invisible by keeping women from the knowledge of the realities of lesbian love.[1] There has in fact been an extensive historical erasure of all queer identities. It is important to understand the how and the why of this, especially within the context of women's suffrage history.

The erasure of the queer history of the women's suffrage movement can be at least partially linked to the deliberate concealment of queerness in the campaign by the movement's leaders. As discussed in chapter 1, national, state, and local suffrage organizations launched publicity campaigns to counter depictions of mannish, man-hating suffragists by propping up images of gender-conforming and heterosexual suffragists. They sought to conceal individuals who deviated from socially accepted gender and sexual norms. This included minimizing the importance or entirely erasing queer individuals from the official published histories of the movement. Their goal was ultimately to make the suffrage movement more palatable to a mainstream audience in their own generation and beyond.

The efforts of individual suffragists to sanitize their own histories also partially accounts for the erasure of the queer history of the suffrage movement. For some women, the pathologizing of homosexuality and gender non-conformity in the early twentieth century, and especially in the decades immediately following the passage of the Nineteenth Amendment, led to an internalized homophobia and a sense of shame about any behavior that could be interpreted as deviating from a cisheterosexual norm. They could not or did not want to define themselves as a sexual invert or lesbian in part because the definition of the homosexual female that had emerged was of a pathologically deviant, abnormally developed woman. Some suffragists purged their personal files, destroying evidence of queer relationships in their past. Others refused to acknowledge their queer desire even to themselves. Suffragist Jeannette Marks for example defensively sought to distinguish her long-term committed relationship with Mary Woolley from the so-called unhealthy and abnormal infatuations described by sexologists. She distanced herself from the identity of lesbian because it was seen as a derisive label in mainstream society. In 1912, Alice Stone Blackwell was disgusted by Havelock Ellis's writings, no doubt unable to see her own relationships with women in the same light as the sexual inverts described in his research.[2]

Not all suffragists felt this way. As they engaged in open discussions about homosexuality, some queer women embraced the new labels used to classify their so-called abnormal sexuality. Edith Lees Ellis, the suffragist wife of sexologist Havelock Ellis, openly identified as a "sexual invert." She frequently spoke to women's groups, including members of the New York club Heterodoxy, about her views on love and marriage. Heterodoxy member and NAWSA leader Mary Ware Dennett also openly and publicly discussed sex and sexuality. In 1918, she wrote *The Sex Side of Life* in order to normalize discussions about sex.[3] Dennett appears to have identified as a heterosexual woman but lived with a group of suffragists who had relationships with other women.[4] She published her book to promote sex positivity and dispel myths about sexuality. When women wrote to her about their homosexual relationships, Dennett reassured them that homosexuality was common and recommended Edward Carpenter's book, *Love's Coming of Age*. One young woman wrote expressing concern about her romantic and physical feeling for another woman. At Dennett's recommendation, she read Carpenter's book and was relieved to learn there was such a thing as an "intermediate sex" noting that "it helps to classify oneself—it has helped me." The young woman acknowledged Dennett's advice about the primacy of heterosexual marriage and commented that she had "no mind-set against marriage at present should the man come into my life" but insisted that "men at present have no appeal whatsoever. The company of girls is so much more interesting!" She told Dennett that her relationship with her woman friend continued to enrich her life: "Life seems so sweet when we have each other." She also noted that the physicality between them had continued and, thanks to Dennett's advice, they now felt "fearless, shameless, and wholesome" about their relationship.[5]

But even if they embraced their sexuality in private, most women recognized that they had to continue to be careful about any public revelation of their sexuality. Especially in the shifting context of the post–World War era, the increasingly hostile attitude toward feminism and homosexuality created a stigma around women's relationships. Whereas these relationships endured perhaps less direct scrutiny in the late nineteenth and early twentieth centuries, by the mid-twentieth century they were largely seen as pathologically deviant. In the decades following the passage of the Nineteenth Amendment, a conservative backlash deified heterosexual families and demonized feminists and lesbians. This hostile attitude is clear in the reflections of aging suffragists during this era. In the 1940s and 1950s, former National Woman's Party member Doris Stevens implicated some of her former suffrage colleagues as lesbians. She recorded in her diary a conversation with a friend who suggested that Alice Paul was "a devotee of Lesbos." Stevens insisted that she herself was neither a "queerie" nor a "commie" but reported some of her former colleagues to the government and media as likely lesbians and/or communists.[6] In an interview conducted toward the end of her life, Alice Paul herself seemed to view homosexuality derisively. Other suffragists similarly tried to distance themselves from association with lesbianism.[7] Identifying as a bisexual or lesbian in this atmosphere required an individual to accept the label of homosexual and its negative association with criminality, deviancy, and pathological abnormality. Few suffragists were willing to do so. Thus, the burning of records sometimes occurred in the later years of a suffragist's life—in the 1940s, '50s, or '60s. Although some queer suffragists accepted their sexuality, others felt increasingly compelled to purge evidence of it, believing it was essential to protect their reputation. By denying access to their personal lives, they thus maintained some power and control over the story that would be told about them in the future.[8]

Former lovers also sometimes destroyed evidence of past queer relationships. Annie Tinker's life was subject to this process of erasure. Although there is limited existing evidence of her love life, it appears from a few letters written about Tinker after her death that she had engaged in romantic affairs with various women in Paris in the 1920s. Tinker willed the vast majority of her estate to her closest friend, Kate Darling Nelson Bertolini.[9] In a letter to lawyer William Woart Lancaster, Bertolini seemed to imply that her relationship with Tinker was not sexual, unlike Tinker's relationship with other women. She wrote: "It is curious, is it not, that all of Dan's friends in New York should have heard of me and should have understood that the friendship between Dan & myself was something quite different than that which existed between herself and other women, and yet her mother seemed to look upon me with the most awful suspicion."[10] But even if she had had a romantic relationship with Tinker in the past, Bertolini had strong motives for concealing such an affair. She had since married a wealthy Parisian businessman. This may explain why Bertolini convinced Lancaster that they should destroy all of Tinker's correspondence. Upset when Lancaster chose to take some of the letters with him, Bertolini chastised him for being careless. Lancaster agreed to send them back to her for destruction.[11] Thus, any evidence of Tinker's relationship with Bertolini or any other women has mostly been erased.

Uncovering evidence of suffragists' queer relationships therefore requires a sort of reading between the lines to bridge the gaps created by archival silences. Archival silences refer to the absence, destruction, or distortion of documentation that results in gaps in our understanding of the past. Researchers must read against the grain, examining texts for omissions in order to give voice to the silenced.[12] Susan Ware discussed the challenge this presented in her research on the lives of queer suffragists Molly Dewson and Polly Porter as she struggled to assemble the circumstantial evidence to write their biographies and complete a whole picture of their life together. Fragments of information proved crucial in piecing together the story of their relationship.[13]

The importance of reading against the grain is also illustrated by the story of Annie Tinker. Most of Tinker's personal correspondence was destroyed by Bertolini and Lancaster. In fact, they destroyed some of their letters to each other wherein they discussed Tinker's personal life. However, one surviving letter from Bertolini to Lancaster written a few weeks before Tinker's death hints at Tinker's sexuality. Bertolini wrote to Lancaster, apparently concerned about Tinker's excessive drinking and conveying details of an incident that had been related to her by Tinker's friend Frances Griffiths:

> While Mrs. Griffiths was away, two women friends of Dan's came to stay with her.—One a Dr. Hamilton and her 'life-long' friend Miss Madge Foussett (?).—Dan and Miss Foussett struck up a palship and Dr. Hamilton, mad, packed her Gladstone . . . and left for London. Apparently Miss F—repentant decides to follow, so two more Gladstones are packed and she and Dan start for London too.[14]

Bertolini asked Lancaster to destroy the letter after he read it, but clearly he did not in this case. Although Bertolini does not directly discuss Tinker's sexuality, the use of terms like "'life-long' friend" and "palship" in the context of the argument between Hamilton, Foussett, and Tinker implies relationships beyond the bounds of friendship. The whole incident is subject to interpretation, but within the broader context of Bertolini's concern that her relationship with Tinker not be misinterpreted and the destruction of Tinker's letters, it seems to suggest a deliberate attempt to conceal Tinker's queer life.

Reconstructing the lives of queer suffragists also requires much digging to understand why material is missing. Another example of this may be found in the story of Alice Morgan Wright. Her collection of personal papers at Smith College is quite extensive, but conspicuously missing is any correspondence between her and her partner, Edith Goode. In seeking to solve this mystery, I located a 1967 letter from Goode to a friend, Ruth Miner, who was caring for Wright in illness. Out of concern about her health, they began making plans for the future disposition of Wright's estate. Goode wrote to Miner: "I want to read every scrap of Alice's memoranda I have assembled as well as her correspondence with me over the years."[15] Perhaps Goode wanted to scrub material that might reflect unfavorably on her or prove too intimate or revealing to future generations. Goode's note to Miner tells us that these letters once existed. But, Goode did not want anyone to see the words they wrote to each other. Direct evidence of their relationship would not exist at all, therefore, if not for drafts of romantic poems to Goode that remained in Wright's old notebooks. Because queer history often happens in the in-between places, it is necessary to look deeper and in less obvious locations. Scribbled notes in the back of Wright's address book, crossed out drafts of poems, and initialed dedications offer a fuller picture of their queer life together.

The erasure of queer lives also often occurred generations after the death of the individual. Biographies written to memorialize suffragists frequently tried to explain away or normalize gender or sexual transgressions. Descendants and biographers burned love letters, photographs, and other evidence of gender non-conformity or queer desire. A sense of communal shame emanating from the larger cissexist and homophobic culture of the post–World War era led to attempts to conceal the queer aspects of a suffragist's life. Vague phrases such as "life-long companions" or "intimate friends" obscured the true nature of romantic and sexual relationships. Even after the public "coming out" of many individuals in the queer liberation movement of the 1970s, biographers perpetuated the process of erasure in an attempt to make the life stories of suffragists appealing to a wider public. In what feminist historian Blanche Wiesen Cook has referred to as the "historical denial of lesbianism," the romantic and sexual lives of queer suffragists have been purposely concealed or denied. Cook criticized Anna Mary Wells for her dismissal and disregard of clear evidence of a queer relationship in her 1978 biography of suffragists Jeannette Marks and Mary Woolley. Cook called for an immediate end to this process of erasure.[16]

A similar denial of lesbianism can be observed in the biography of suffragist Gail Laughlin. Ruth Sargent, Laughlin's niece, wrote a book in 1979 to honor the life of her aunt. But Sargent relegated Laughlin's partner, Dr. Mary Austin Sperry, to a passing reference, noting simply that the two women formed a "close friendship" in Colorado and then moved to California to live in the Sperry family home.[17] Sargent made no mention of their sixteen-year relationship, Sperry's decision to bequeath her entire estate to Laughlin upon her death, the subsequent controversy over the will, the court battle with the Sperry family, accusations of lesbianism, nor Sperry's final request that Laughlin care for her remains. It is tempting to give Sargent the benefit of the doubt and assume that she was not aware of all of these details. However, it seems likely she was aware of the fact that Laughlin and Sperry were buried together under the same headstone in the Laughlin family plot. Sargent never mentioned this in the book. Later biographical articles written about Laughlin replicated the narrative, neglecting to mention Sperry altogether, essentially erasing her and her significance in Laughlin's life from history.

The erasure of the queer lives of Black women, Indigenous women, and women of color is even more pronounced. Perceived gender and sexual deviance had greater implications for women whose racial identities already marked them as "other." Concealing or purging evidence of their sexual relationships may have seemed essential to maintaining their status as respectable women. Recovering evidence of their lives for this project posed a huge challenge largely due to disparities in the preservation of records. Whose story gets told depends in part on whose story was deemed worthy of preserving. Overlapping layers of power and privilege come into play here. Racism and classism meant that the records of the lives of elite white women were more likely to be documented and saved. Heterosexist assumptions and homophobia also play a role. The long history of the racialization of gender and sexuality perpetuated harmful stereotypes. Biographers and descendants may have worried about the implications of revealing details of suffragists' queer lives for fear of harming not only the individual's reputation but the reputation of the entire community.[18]

Given this long history of erasure, the reconstruction and retelling of the life histories of queer suffragists is a crucial first step in the process of recovering the queer history of the suffrage movement. This book is only a beginning. Much work remains to be done by future scholars to even begin to rectify this issue. Fleshing out the lives of these individuals is important in ensuring that their full stories be told, finally free from the shame and stigma that has haunted them in the past. But the importance of these queer suffragists also resonates far beyond the individual story to the story of the suffrage movement as a whole.

Queer suffragists pushed the boundaries of the gender and sexual norms of their era in simultaneously subtle and bold ways. Their presence deconstructs the cisheteronormative narrative that continues to frame our understanding of historical events and social movements to this day. They defied gender expectations through their appearance and behaviors. They contested heteronormative notions of domesticity and family through the creation of queer domestic arrangements, the formation of chosen families, and the cultivation of queer community. They built queer transatlantic alliances by forging important political and professional connections between American and British suffragists. They transformed sites that were formerly used to marginalize, restrain, or control them into spaces of queer resistance. They co-opted heteronormative mourning and death rituals ensuring that the memory of their queer lives and queer loves would live on.

Queer suffragists mattered to the suffrage movement because their unconventional lives and their experiences with marginalization made them more aware of larger structural inequities and often more committed to a broader vision of women's rights. Many of them lived daring lives breaking convention from their earliest days. After casting off restrictive gender and sexual norms in their private lives, they felt freer to advocate for larger social changes.

The suffrage movement mattered to queer suffragists because with the vote they hoped to begin to dismantle the structures of their oppression. Gender non-conforming suffragists contested the very notion of a binary seeking to obliterate the concept of normal versus abnormal. Spinsters and women who loved women challenged the idea that heterosexual marriage was essential or even necessarily desirable. Queer suffragists believed that with the vote, they could attain economic independence and status that would free women from forced dependency on men and marriage. They thus helped normalize the concept of women living together as couples or alone as unmarried women. This paved the way for future women to openly identify as lesbian, asexual, bisexual, or pansexual.

Queer suffragists found their voice through their activism. Some, like Dr. Mary Edwards Walker, boldly demanded that suffrage leaders fight for more progressive reforms. Walker and other suffragists like Annie Tinker publicly embraced their queerness, taking to the streets to help make the suffrage movement more visible and to attract more attention to the cause. Black queer suffragists and queer suffragists of color like Alice Dunbar Nelson, Mary Burrill, Lucy Diggs Slowe, and Margaret Chung impelled suffragists to take on issues such as segregation, racialized violence, and immigration exclusion. Queer suffragists like Margaret Foley, Kathleen De Vere Taylor, Anne Martin, and Mabel Vernon embraced revolutionary new tactics, from open-air speaking to heckling local politicians and directly calling out the president of the United States. Alice Morgan Wright, Zelie Emerson, Vida Milholland, and Paula Jacobi were among the first to put their bodies on the line and endure assault, arrest, imprisonment, hunger-striking, and force-feeding for the cause. Even though they did not realize all of their goals in their lifetime, their existence mattered as they opened the door for future reforms.[19]

But, queer suffragists were not a monolith. There was no consensus on issues related to gender and sexuality. Radical queer suffragists elicited the ire of more moderate or conservative queer suffragists. Leaders like Anna Howard Shaw and Carrie Chapman Catt advocated more subtle tactics as they foregrounded the fight for the vote. They downplayed their own queerness and the queerness of the movement as a whole in order to win popular support for the women's suffrage amendment.

Catering to the middle had long-term repercussions as suffragists steered away from radical reform in order to placate the mainstream. The suffrage movement ignored or more often perpetuated classism, racism, xenophobia, and homophobia. White queer suffrage leaders played a role in this. When faced with criticism, they responded defensively. They played respectability politics and marginalized non-conformists in the movement. They developed policies and tactics to win the vote that isolated and tokenized women of color, working-class, Black, Indigenous, immigrant women, and queer people. In order to deflect personal criticism away from their own lives and to win popular support for women's suffrage, they sacrificed pieces of themselves. This accommodationist approach led to the public silencing and erasure of the queer lives of radical suffragists, some of the most vocal advocates of reform within their movement. Yet, it was often the queer militant tactics and the visible queerness of the women's suffrage movement that attracted public attention and helped move the suffrage question into center view.

This tension between militancy and conformity would reemerge and divide organizers of civil rights movements in the mid-twentieth century. Subsequent generations of marginalized groups fighting for their rights likewise recognized the strategic importance of respectability politics with its emphasis on conformity to mainstream ideals. In their fight for gay and lesbian rights in the 1950s, the Mattachine Society and the Daughters of Bilitis adopted conformist tactics similar to those used by queer suffrage leaders. After their initial more radical tactics failed, the leaders of the homophile movement promoted less confrontational tactics. They encouraged their members to dress, act, and speak in a manner that would help win popular support. By adopting cishetero-sexual mores and projecting an appearance of middle-class normalcy, they hoped to win support for their cause. Historian Martin Meeker has pointed to the effectiveness of this strategy, insisting that the "Matta-chine Society's presentation of a respectable public face was a deliberate and ultimately successful strategy to deflect the antagonisms of its many detractors" by disarming anti-gay sentiment in the larger culture while defending and nurturing the gay world. Meeker argues that it served as a mask, behind which the members could engage in more daring ac-tivities.[20] Queer suffrage leaders had essentially invented this strategy of masking decades earlier. But it was fraught with inherent problems.

Feminists in the 1960s and 1970s similarly struggled to balance re-spectability politics with radical reform. The National Organization for Women (NOW) advocated upending the existing patriarchal system that continued to oppress women. Hearkening back to their suffragist ances-tors, they also promoted a conformist approach that supported white cisheterosexual women while ostracizing queer women, Black women, and women of color in the movement. NOW president Betty Friedan vocalized her concern that lesbians represented a "lavender menace" that posed a threat to the women's movement. Friedan and her allies tried to distance themselves from the queer women in the movement. They relied on derisive old stereotypes of "mannish" and "man-hating" lesbians originally used to invalidate suffragists and feminists (and es-pecially queer suffragists and feminists). This did more harm than good to the movement and led to the rebellion of lesbian feminists, who or-ganized a protest at the May 1970 Second Congress to Unite Women in New York City. Wearing T-shirts that read "Lavender Menace," approxi-mately three hundred women interrupted the meeting, declaring that they would no longer be in the closet for the women's movement. They demanded inclusion for lesbians and an end to homophobia. Black feminist lesbians organized in 1974 under the Combahee River Collective. They called out the sexism and homophobia in the civil rights movement and the racism and homophobia in the feminist movement. The collective highlighted the interlocking layers of oppression and called for an intersectional activism.[21]

Activists and scholars have debated the cost-benefits and long-term effects of accommodationist strategies. They acknowledge on the one hand the importance of the politics of respectability in gaining widespread support for civil rights reforms but recognize on the other hand the concessions that individuals often make by sacrificing their own identities and the radical elements of their movements. This approach typically leaves the most vulnerable members of the community behind. Left to fight an uphill battle for their rights, these marginalized folks are forced to wage their battle not only against the outside world but against those in their own community.

The gay liberation and lesbian feminist movements in the 1960s and 1970s rejected the conformist approach of the homophile movement and women's rights movement, preferring to push for fundamental change through direct action rather than assimilating to the status quo to gain acceptance. Building, in part, on the rights that prior generations of activists had earned for them, this younger generation of queer activists insisted that it was time to stop hiding and to instead "come out" of the closet. They succeeded in making the queer community visible. Yet, gay liberation and lesbian feminist movement leaders also failed to meet the needs of all the individuals in their community. As their movements became more accepted in the mainstream, they also became more exclusionary. Gay liberation leaders focused primarily on issues of concern to white middle-class cisgender gay men. Transphobic lesbians tried to drive out trans activists from their organizations. Working-class, trans, Black, Indigenous activists and people of color called out gay liberation and lesbian feminist leaders for marginalizing individuals based on their class, gender, and race. They demanded inclusion in mainstream organizations and launched their own groups to fight for their rights. Sylvia Rivera cofounded Street Transvestite Action Revolutionaries (STAR) with Marsha P. Johnson, took to the stage at the 1973 Christopher Street Liberation Day Rally in New York City and criticized gay liberation leaders for ignoring the issues faced by drag queens and trans people as well as impoverished, homeless, and imprisoned queer people—the most marginalized members of the community. Today, these problems are far from settled. Even as there have been significant gains in visibility and acceptance, the modern LGBTQIA+ rights movement and women's rights movements continue to reckon with similar issues of inclusion and exclusion within their organizations.[22]

Queer suffragists paved the way for future generations of LGBTQIA+ and feminist activists. The strategies that individual queer suffragists adopted to survive served as models for future queer activists fighting to survive in the homophobic post–World War era. The queer domesticities, chosen families, and queer communities they created to nurture each other would be replicated by feminist, homophile, and gay liberation leaders. The alliances they forged, the queer spaces they built, and the queer tactics they pioneered in the fight for the vote provided an organizational prototype for later groups to expand on. But, the mistakes that they made, and their failures, also served as examples. These represented the issues that subsequent generations of activists would inherit and need to address if they hoped to succeed. The work of queer suffragists thus provided a foundation to build on and, when necessary, to tear down and build again.

Most suffragists, queer or not, were fighting for much more than the right to vote. The women who fought for enfranchisement did not think that winning the vote would solve all of society's problems. They knew there was much more work to do. They hoped the vote would be a stepping-stone that would provide the power they needed to begin to dismantle the structures that denied them their full liberty. Queer suffragists hoped to break free from rigid gender and sexual norms that confined them to oppressive boxes. They hoped the vote would liberate them from dependence on a cissexist, racist, heteropatriarchal system. They hoped the vote would allow them to live their own lives, choose their own partners, and create their own families. They hoped the vote would give them the ability to care for each other in life, to tend one another in sickness, and to provide for each other in death. Perhaps most of all, they hoped that after the vote, when they were long gone, we would remember them, pick up the banner, and carry on their fight.

ACKNOWLEDGMENTS

This project was a labor of love that was unfortunately interrupted many times by various events ranging from personal crises to a global pandemic. There were times when I thought the book would never make it to final publication. I therefore want to begin by thanking all the folks at NYU Press who ultimately made this book possible—especially to Clara Platter, who believed in this book enough to give it a chance.

I am grateful for my colleagues at San Jose State University (SJSU) in the College of Social Sciences and the History department who provided the essential day-to-day support to balance the demands of teaching and research: Leslie Corona, Treina Bills, Glen Gendzel, Ron Rogers, Cami Johnson, Walt Jacobs, Wendy Thowdis, and Maria Alaniz. I relied on the financial assistance from the SJSU University Faculty RSCA Assigned Time Program, College of Social Sciences, and the Department of History in funding research and conference travel.

Research support for this project was also graciously provided by a Madeleine L'Engle Travel-To-Collections Grant from the Smith College Special Collections and a Mellon-Schlesinger Summer Research Grant from the Radcliffe Institute for Advanced Study at Schlesinger Library. Thank you to the archivists and staff at Smith College Archives: Elizabeth Myers, Nichole Calero, Amy Hague, and Mary Biddle. The folks at the Schlesinger Library especially worked overtime to make materials available to scholars remotely during the COVID-19 crisis. Thank you to Jane Kamensky, Ellen M. Shea, Jen Weintraub, Jennifer Fauxsmith, Samantha Mewhorter, Laurie Ellis, and Diana Carey.

I am grateful for the many fellow scholars who provided research advice, comments on conference papers, and feedback on various iterations of the manuscript draft: Pippa Holloway, Rachel Guberman, Susan Ware, Mary Ann Irwin, Michelle Moravec, Paula Lichtenberg, David Duffield, Rachel Corbman, Amanda Littauer, and Anya Jabour. I am most thankful for the various anonymous reviewers who have been so amazing throughout this process. You provided so much helpful guidance for revisions of the initial drafts of the manuscript and I am forever indebted to you.

Although I began the research years ago, this project was fueled by the enthusiasm and scholarship surrounding the centennial of the ratification of the Nineteenth Amendment in 2020. I have been so inspired by the recent research of suffrage scholars such as Allison K. Lange, Laura Prieto, Cathleen Cahill, Alison M. Parker, Martha S. Jones, Ellen DuBois, Anya Jabour, Liette Gidlow, Kelly Marino, Sherry L. Smith, Corinne Field, Kimberly Hamlin, Katherine Marino, Kate Clarke Lemay, Rachel Michelle Gunter, Christina Wolbrecht, Susan Ware, Page Harrington, and Lisa Tetrault.

Thank you also to the staff of the Women's Suffrage Centennial Commission and the National Park Service, who helped amplify the research of suffrage scholars during the centennial events. With gratitude to Kimberly Wallner, Stephanie Marsellos, Anna Laymon, and Candace Samuels. I especially want to honor the folks who are preserving and interpreting suffrage and LGBTQ history for future generations. Shout out to Megan Springate, Sylvea Hollis, and Susan Ferentinos for their important work.

I want to thank all the individuals who sent research hints or helped track down leads, especially Rachel B. Tiven, Catherine Tinker, Hilary McCollum, Sarah-Joy Ford, Paul Clarke, Harry Kollatz, Jane Laughlin, Diana E. McCarthy, Aracele Govea, Terry Hamburg, Judy Tzu-Chun Wu, Chris Ryon, and Susan Orifici. Marla McMackin, Nikita Shepard, and Hekang Yang assisted in searching nearly inaccessible archives for documents during the Covid-19 shutdown. Much appreciation also to Tilke Hill and Lukia Costello who helped make the history of queer suffragists come to life with their video-making genius.

Major research projects like this would not be possible without the support of friends who you know you can send a text to and commiserate with about research, political crises, and global pandemics. I am eternally grateful for conversations with Serene Williams, Kristen Kelly, Beth Slutsky, Stacey Greer, Lauren Peterson, and Nikki and Renee Smith. I also want to send my love to my queer chosen family who was there for me in all the ways. Thank you especially to Lauren Jensen for patiently and lovingly listening to me talk about this project.

My parents, Sherry, Denis, and Jennifer, have given so much to provide me with the opportunities I have had to pursue the academic life. Love to my family, especially: Bridget, Michelle, Catriona, Amanda, Patricia, Chuck, Mike, Richard, Cody, Devin, Brooke, Reilly, Logan, Lucien, Anthony, Salem, Nico, Emily, Jack, Lance, Diane, Henry, and George. Always grateful for my bestie Cab for sharing some of her "best day evers" with me.

I most wish to thank the queer suffragists whose life stories made this book possible. In delving into their private lives, I came to know them well beyond their suffrage work. I learned about their pain and their passion. The stories of these queer ancestors sometimes paralleled my own so closely that I found myself weeping over their diaries, letters, and poems. In reading and writing their stories, I realized I am not alone. I have never been alone. We all walk in the footsteps of our queer ancestors. Queer pain and queer love reverberate across the generations. Queer lives endure across time.

NOTES

INTRODUCTION

1 "From the Capital," *Buffalo Commercial*, January 17, 1873, 3.

2 Harris, *Dr. Mary Walker*, 142.

3 Ibid., 151–152.

4 Cott, *The Grounding of Modern Feminism*; "Interchange: Women's Suffrage, the Nineteenth Amendment, and the Right to Vote," 662–694; Du Bois, *Suffrage*; Jones, *Vanguard*; Cahill, *Recasting the Vote*; Lange, *Picturing Political Power*; Marino, *Feminism for the Americas*; Tetrault, *The Myth of Seneca Falls*; Lemay, *Votes for Women*; Cooper, *Beyond Respectability*; Lindsey, *Colored No More*.

5 Katz, *The Invention of Heterosexuality*, 83–112; D'Emilio, "Capitalism and Gay Identity," 100–113.

6 Fischer, *Pantaloons and Power*, 79–80, 91–94, 102–104.

7 "Although the number of women . . . ," *Detroit Free Press*, November 17, 1880, 4.

8 "Dr. Mary Walker," *Baltimore Sun*, July 24, 1873, 1.

9 Harris, *Dr. Mary Walker*, 186.

10 Susan B. Anthony Diary, January 19, 1873, Susan B. Anthony Papers.

11 Stanton, Anthony, and Gage, *History of Woman Suffrage*, 360.

12 Harris, *Dr. Mary Walker*, 147.

13 Letter from Anna Howard Shaw to Alice Paul, April 23, 1913, Folder: 002619-002-1260, National Woman's Party Papers.

14 Higginbotham, *Righteous Discontent*, 14–15.

15 D'Emilio, *Sexual Politics, Sexual Communities*, 75–91; Meeker, "Behind the Mask of Respectability," 81, 90; Meeker, *Contacts Desired*; Horowitz, *Betty Friedan and the Making of the Feminine Mystique*; Warner, *The Trouble with Normal*.

16 Franzen, *Anna Howard Shaw*, 42; Faderman, *To Believe in Women*, 41–42.

17 Franzen, *Anna Howard Shaw*, 57.

18 Ibid., 107; "Anna Howard Shaw Dies of Pneumonia," *New York Sun*, July 3, 1919, 9.

19 Faderman, *To Believe in Women*; Franzen, *Anna Howard Shaw*; Jabour, *Sophonisba Breckinridge*.

20 Franzen, *Anna Howard Shaw*; Jabour, *Sophonisba Breckinridge*; Faderman, *To Believe in Women*, 50–51; Rupp, "'Imagine My Surprise,'" 61–70.

21 Mrs. George F. Arnold, "Dr. Shaw's Lecture," *Houston Post*, April 8, 1917, 48.

22 Hull, *Give Us Each Day*, 250, 374–375; Hull, *Color, Sex, & Poetry*, 360–364, 374.

23 Frisken, *Victoria Woodhull's Sexual Revolution*, 40.

24 Horowitz, "Victoria Woodhull, Anthony Comstock, and Conflict," 413–415; Frisken, *Victoria Woodhull's Sexual Revolution*, 20, 26, 38.

25 Horowitz, "Victoria Woodhull, Anthony Comstock, and Conflict," 415–417, 428–429; Frisken, *Victoria Woodhull's Sexual Revolution*, 11, 28, 31, 46–53.

26 "Biography of Lucy Stone," General Correspondence, circa 1890–1947, Roderick, Virginia, 1930, Carrie Chapman Catt Papers.

27 The terms "mannish," "man-hating," and "abnormal" appear throughout this article because these were the most common terms used to describe queer suffragists in the popular press during the 1900–1920 period. Modern terms and identities were not in use at the time, but the use of these words indicates the increasing scrutiny of queer relationships and the pathologizing of queer individuals in society during this era.

28 Higginbotham, *Righteous Discontent*, 14–15.

CHAPTER 1. MANNISH WOMEN AND FEMININE MEN

1 Kroeger, *The Suffragents*, 157.

2 Welter, "The Cult of True Womanhood: 1820–1860," 151–174; Cott, *The Bonds of Womanhood*; Ryan, *Cradle of the Middle Class*; Mintz and Kellogg, *Domestic Revolutions*; Kessler-Harris, *Out to Work*, 90; Bederman, *Manliness and Civilization*, 18–20.

3 "Woman Suffrage Means the Disruption of the Home," *Ukiah Daily Journal*, September 8, 1911, 8; Goodier, *No Votes for Women*, 2–5; Franzen, *Spinsters and Lesbians*, 5–7.

4 Klein, *Practical Etiquette*, 67; Hall, *The Correct Thing in Good Society*, 307; Ordway, *The Etiquette of To-Day*, 113; *Correct Social Usage*, 39, 522.

5 Behling, *The Masculine Woman in America*, 2–4; Finnegan, *Selling Suffrage*, 71–72; Sheppard, *Cartooning for Suffrage*, 25, 122, 136, 142, 200; Kennedy, *Drawn to Purpose*, 148–149; Rauterkus, *Go Get Mother's Picket Sign*, 30–35, 37–48, 67–68; Lange, *Picturing Political Power*, 2, 148–149; Chapman, *Making Noise, Making News*, 32.

6 See for example "Dr. Mary Walker's Visit," Miriam and Ira D. Wallach Division of Art, Prints and Photographs: Print Collection; "A suggestion to the Buffalo Exposition;–Let us have a chamber of female horrors," Theodore Roosevelt Digital Library; Thomas E. Powers, "Twelve Great Men in History?" 1912, Caroline and Erwin Swann Collection of Caricature and Cartoon.

7 "Miss Mannish" (Chicago: H.G. Zimmerman & Co. Date unknown), Catherine Palczewski Suffrage Postcard Archive.

8 "I Don't Like to See a Woman Do a Man's Work," The Dovie Horvitz Collection, The Gender and Women's Studies Collection, University of Wisconsin Digital Collections.

9 Krafft-Ebing, *Psychopathia Sexualis*; Ellis, "Sexual Inversion in Women," 141–158; Ellis, *Studies in the Psychology of Sex*; Oosterhuis, *Stepchildren of Nature*; Carpenter, *Love's Coming of Age*; Bauer, *The Hirschfeld Archives*; McMurtrie, "Principles of Homosexuality and Sexual Inversion in the Modern Female," 146–148; Talmey,

Love: A Treatise on the Science of Sex-Attraction; Chauncey, "From Sexual Inversion to Homosexuality," 114–146.

10 Somerville, *Queering the Color Line*, 27–31; Terry, *An American Obsession*, 33–35, 86–87; Snorton, *Black on Both Sides*, 31–71.

11 Ellis, *Studies in the Psychology of Sex*, 147–148.

12 Lee, "Effeminate Men and Masculine Women," 686–687; Lee, *The Perverts*, 207–208.

13 Freud, "The Psychogenesis of a Case of Homosexuality in a Woman," 13–33; Chauncey, "From Sexual Inversion to Homosexuality," 137; Terry, *An American Obsession*, 35, 65.

14 "Opinions of Patriots Against Double Suffrage," *Lebanon Daily News*, October 9, 1915, 3.

15 Somerville, *Queering the Color Line*, 27–31; Terry, *An American Obsession*, 33–35, 86–87.

16 William W. Gregg, "The Third Sex," *New York Times*, August 4, 1918, Section 4, 2.

17 Eleanor Kinsella McDonald, "A Woman's Response," *New York Times*, August 11, 1918, Section 3, 2.

18 "Leader of Antis Opposes Poll Watching," *Pittsburgh Post-Gazette*, May 23, 1915, 2.

19 "Woman Suffrage Means the Disruption of the Home," *Ukiah Daily Journal*, September 8, 1911, 8.

20 Kroeger, *The Suffragents*, 4; Neuman, *Gilded Suffragists*, 129.

21 "Critic Fires Hot Blast at Suffragettes," *Inter Ocean*, April 14, 1909, 1, 3.

22 "Beard's Speech Hissed by Women," *Austin American-Statesman*, February 7, 1917, 2.

23 Nixola Greeley-Smith, "Typical Suffraget No Amazon," *Pittsburgh Press*, April 27, 1912, 9.

24 "Lovable Nature to Win Men in Vote War," *San Francisco Examiner*, April 6, 1913, 70.

25 Caroline Howlett and Katrina Rolley in their studies of the British Women's Social and Political Union noted that dress regulations were typically spread via word of mouth and suggestions. Howlett notes that "overt instructions" did not "appear in print, as this would have undermined the impression that suffragettes spontaneously dressed in a feminine way. Instead, suffragettes were guided into the appropriate self-image to cultivate" through fashion advertisements, advice columns, and verbal instructions. Howlett, "Femininity Slashed: Suffragette Militancy, Modernism and Gender," 73; Rolley, "Fashion, Femininity and the Fight for the Vote," 51–52.

26 "Campaigning with the Suffragists," *Pittsburgh Sunday Post*, January 14, 1912, 26.

27 Mrs. O. H. P. Belmont, "My New Idea for Women," *New York World Magazine*, December 3, 1911, 1, Department of Hygiene 1911–1913, Folder: 002615-169-0641, National Woman's Party Papers.

28 "A Beauty Shop for Suffragists," *Morning Telegram*, October 27, 1914, Department of Hygiene 1911–1913, Folder: 002615-169-0641, National Woman's Party Papers.

29 "Women Physicians Balk at Suffrage Beauty Treatment," *New York City American*, December 13, 1911, Department of Hygiene 1911–1913, Folder: 002615-169-0641, National Woman's Party Papers.

30 "Face Creams and Suffrage," *Times*, February 18, 1912, Department of Hygiene 1911–1913, Folder: 002615-169-0641, National Woman's Party Papers.

31 Sheppard, *Cartooning for Suffrage*, 25, 122, 136, 142, 200; Finnegan, *Selling Suffrage*, 71–72; Kennedy, *Drawn to Purpose*, 148–149; Rauterkus, *Go Get Mother's Picket Sign*, 30–35, 37–48, 67–68; Lange, *Picturing Political Power*, 2, 91, 97–98, 109, 111, 126–127, 139, 143–144, 159, 161, 177, 196–197; Chapman, *Making Noise, Making News*, 5.

32 Susan B. Anthony, "Homes of Single Women," 1877, Speeches and Writings, 1848–1895, Susan B. Anthony Papers.

33 For example, in 1901 the *Woman's Journal* disagreed with the assumption of an anti-suffrage writer that Womanly Women were doomed, agreeing with his point that "the law of natural selection will provide for the prevalence of womanly women, while mannish women, like effeminate men, will always remain abnormal exceptions." In 1910, the *Woman's Journal* referred to a photograph of New York delegates to the National Suffrage Convention as an image of "a fine, womanly-looking group, as different as possible from the misrepresentations of the old-time caricaturists." "Notes and News," *Woman's Journal* 32, no. 23 (June 8, 1901), 181; "The New York News-Letter . . ." *Woman's Journal* 41, no. 21 (May 21, 1910), 83.

34 *Muncy, Creating a Female Dominion in American Reform*; Mink, *The Wages of Motherhood*; Sheppard, *Cartooning for Suffrage*, 25, 122, 136, 142, 200; Finnegan, *Selling Suffrage*, 71–72; Kennedy, *Drawn to Purpose*, 148–149; Rauterkus, *Go Get Mother's Picket Sign*, 30–35, 37–48, 67–68; Lange, *Picturing Political Power*, 2, 91.

35 "The Mother and The Ballot," *State Journal*, July 2, 1913, 4.

36 Behling, *The Masculine Woman in America*, 39.

37 Hazel Hunkins to Anne Hunkins, March 10, 1918, Hazel Hunkins-Hallinan Papers.

38 Hazel Hunkins notes from picketing, "Early Suffrage Involvement," Hazel Hunkins-Hallinan Papers.

39 "A Tribute to All Women," *New York Tribune*, December 27, 1916, 8.

40 Letter from the Women's Club of Jefferson City, Missouri to the National Convention of the Women's Club July 23, 1895, *A History of the Club Movement Among the Colored Women of the United States of America*, 16.

41 Letter from John Albert Williams to the National Convention of Colored American Women, July 21, 1895, *A History of the Club Movement Among the Colored Women*, 22–23.

42 "Constitution of the National Association of Colored Women."

43 Hine, "Rape and the Inner Lives of Black Women in the Middle West," 912–920; Hine, "'We Specialize in the Wholly Impossible,'" 70–93; Higginbotham, *Righteous Discontent*, 14–15, 185–231; Terborg-Penn, *African American Women in the Struggle for the Vote*, 54–80; Jones, *All Bound Up Together*, 177; Materson, *For the Freedom of Her Race*, 15, Lange, *Picturing Political Power*, 126–127, 139, 143–144.

44 National Association of Colored Women, Convention Minutes, 1914, Folder: 001554-001-0406, Records of the National Association of Colored Women's Clubs.

45 "Woman's Case in Equity," *The Colored American*, February 17, 1900, 1.

46 Ibid.

47 Margaret Murray Washington quoted in Jones, *Vanguard*, 162.

48 Higginbotham, *Righteous Discontent*, 14–15; Hine, "Rape and the Inner Lives of Black Women," 912–920; Hine, "'We Specialize in the Wholly Impossible,'" 70–93.

49 Cooper, *Beyond Respectability*, 58, 64, 76; Jones, *Vanguard*, 7–10, 157–158; Parker, *Unceasing Militant*, 69–70, 90, 183, 289, 299–300.

50 "Some Knit; Others Plead," *Indiana Gazette*, March 15, 1911, 22.

51 Bederman, *Manliness and Civilization*, 18–20; Putney, *Muscular Christianity*, 99–126; Kimmel, *Manhood in America*, 168–169; Rotundo, *American Manhood*, 241–242.

52 George MacAdam, "Feminist Revolutionary Principle Is Biological Bosh," *New York Times*, January 18, 1914, Magazine Section, 2.

53 Ibid.

54 Dr. Frederick Peterson, "Woman's Uplift Means Man's Uplift," *New York Times*, February 15, 1914, Magazine Section, 4.

55 Empire State Campaign Committee, *The Biological Argument Against Woman Suffrage*.

56 Eastman, *Enjoyment of Living*, 316.

57 Jensen, *Mobilizing Minerva*, 6–8, 10, 40–41; "Staves Aided Boy Scouts," *Evening Star*, March 9, 1913, 17; "What the Boy Scouts Did at the Inauguration," 2–4; "Police Worse Than the Crowd," *Buffalo Commercial*, March 7, 1913, 2; Testimony of Mrs. Patricia M. Street, Mrs. Keppel Hall, and Philip Elliott, *Suffrage Parade: Hearings*, 69–76; "Hero Medals for Boy Scouts," *Baltimore Sun*, March 20, 1913, 1.

58 "Hail Columbia!" 289–290.

59 Ibid., 289.

60 Ibid., 290.

61 Cooper, *Beyond Respectability*, 3–4, 58, 88.

CHAPTER 2. QUEERING DOMESTICITY

1 Faderman, *To Believe in Women*, 6, 62–63; Rupp, "Sexuality and Politics in the Early Twentieth Century," 577–605.

2 Shah, *Contagious Divides*, 13–14.

3 For more, see Smith-Rosenberg, "The Female World of Love and Ritual"; Faderman, *Odd Girls and Twilight Lovers*; Faderman, *Surpassing the Love of Men*; Faderman, *To Believe in Women*; Rupp, *A Desired Past*; Rupp, *Sapphistries*.

4 "Would You Rather Have a Vote Than a Husband?" *Chicago Sunday Tribune*, June 22, 1913, 47.

5 Patterson, *The American New Woman Revisited*, 11–12; Elliott et al., *Historical Marriage Trends from 1890–2010*.

6   Franzen notes that the histories of these women have been largely neglected and the few women's historians who do "acknowledge the existence of never-married women—spinsters or lesbians—tend to relegate them to the margins of women's experience." Franzen, *Spinsters and Lesbians*, 1, 5.

7   Kimmel, *Manhood in America*, 90–91; Kevles, *In the Name of Eugenics*, 20, 74; Larson, *Sex, Race, and Science*, 19–22, 29.

8   Susan B. Anthony, *Homes of Single Women*, 1877, *Speeches and Writings*, 1895, Susan B. Anthony Papers; Behling, *The Masculine Woman in America*, 82–83; Franzen, *Spinsters and Lesbians*, 6, 72.

9   Squire, "What Women Want in Men," 906–910.

10   Davis, "'Not Marriage at All, but Simple Harlotry,'" 1137–1163; Coontz, *Marriage, a History*.

11   "Would You Rather Have a Vote Than a Husband?" 47.

12   "Prefixes Title 'Mrs.' Without a Husband," *Columbus Republican*, February 27, 1913, 8.

13   "Would You Rather Have a Vote Than a Husband?" 47.

14   "Suffrage Party on Way to Parade Splits Over 'Mrs.,'" *Chicago Tribune*, March 2, 1913, 1.

15   Stevens, *Jailed for Freedom*, 362; Jail Diary, November 1917, Elizabeth McShane Hilles Papers.

16   "Husband Gone; She Gets Divorce," *Chicago Tribune*, February 2, 1915, 3; "Aviation Is Safer than Marriage," *Evening World*, November 13, 1916, 5; *Leda Richberg Hornsby vs. Hubert Primm Hornsby*, Bill for Divorce, Circuit Court of Cook County, January 23, 1915, Cook County, Illinois.

17   "Drops Suffrage Petitions from Sky on President Wilson's Yacht," *Akron Beacon Journal*, December 15, 1916, 2; "Wind Brings Down Suff Bird Women," *The Sun*, December 3, 1916, 8; "Chicago Woman Here Would Fly Over Ocean," *Dayton Herald*, October 13, 1913, 15; "Aviatrix," *Dayton Daily News*, May 26, 1914, 15; "Mrs. L. Hornsby, Aviatrix, Sues for Separation," *Chicago Examiner*, January 23, 1915, 1; Edwards, *Orville's Aviators*, 11–12.

18   "Aviation Is Safer than Marriage," 5.

19   Grimké, *Selected Works of Angelina Weld Grimké*, 6–8; Bruce, *Archibald Grimké: Portrait of a Black Independent*, 30, 54–55; Perry, *Lift Up Thy Voice*, 257, 273.

20   Brown, "To Catch the Vision of Freedom," 67–69; Stevenson, *Life in Black and White*, 160–161, 325.

21   Honey, *Aphrodite's Daughters*, 55, 60–62; Perry, *Lift Up Thy Voice*, 297–299.

22   Letter from Mary Burrill to Angelina Weld Grimké, February 25, 1896, Angelina Weld Grimké Papers.

23   Ibid.

24   Grimké, *Selected Works of Angelina Weld Grimké*, 7.

25   Perry, *Lift Up Thy Voice*, 297–299.

26   1903 Diary, Angelina Weld Grimké Papers; Perry, *Lift Up Thy Voice*, 312–314; Beemyn, *A Queer Capital*, 73–76; Honey, *Aphrodite's Daughters*, 55, 88.

27 Grimké, *Selected Works of Angelina Weld Grimké*, 10.

28 Honey, *Aphrodite's Daughters*, 39.

29 Perry, *Lift Up Thy Voice*, 312–314; Beemyn, *A Queer Capital*, 73–76.

30 Honey, *Aphrodite's Daughters*, 40.

31 Mitchell, "Antilynching Plays," 210–230; Perry, *Lift Up Thy Voice*, 338.

32 Honey, *Aphrodite's Daughters*, 86; Perry, *Lift Up Thy Voice*, 219–221, 259–260; Terborg-Penn, *African American Women in the Struggle for the Vote*, 62–64.

33 US Bureau of the Census, Fifteenth Federal Census of the United States, 1930; US Bureau of the Census, Sixteenth Federal Census of the United States, 1940.

34 "Brunswick Brevities," *Chariton Courier*, December 5, 1913, 8: Letter from Alma B. Sasse to Anne Hunkins, August 13, 1913, Box 79, Folder 3, Hazel Hunkins Hallinan Papers; Letter from Hazel Hunkins to Anne Hunkins, September 22, 1913, Box 79, Folder 3, Hazel Hunkins Hallinan Papers; Letter from Hazel Hunkins to Anne Hunkins, January 15, 1914, Box 79, Folder 5, Hazel Hunkins Hallinan Papers; Letter from Hazel Hunkins to Anne Hunkins, October 11, 1914, Box 79, Folder 7, Hazel Hunkins Hallinan Papers.

35 Letter from Hazel Hunkins to Anne Hunkins, January 25, 1914, Box 79, Folder 5, Hazel Hunkins Hallinan Papers.

36 Steinhardt, *Ten Sex Talks to Girls*, 50.

37 Stage, "What 'Good Girls' Do," 151, 156–157.

38 Davis, *Factors in the Sex Life*, 248–249, 277.

39 "Missouri News," 690; "Will Help in Suffrage Campaign," *Evening Missourian*, July 7, 1916, 3; Letter from Hazel Hunkins to Anne Hunkins, August 11, 1916, Box 79, Folder 11, Hazel Hunkins Hallinan Papers.

40 Letter from Hazel Hunkins to Anne Hunkins, January 4, 1917, Box 80, Folder 1, Hazel Hunkins Hallinan Papers.

41 Letter from Hazel Hunkins to Anne Hunkins, January 19, 1917, Box 80, Folder 1, Hazel Hunkins Hallinan Papers.

42 Letter from Alma Sasse to Hazel Hunkins, n.d., Box 61, Folder 9, Hazel Hunkins Hallinan Papers.

43 Letter from Hazel Hunkins to Anne Hunkins, January 4, 1917, Box 80, Folder 1, Hazel Hunkins Hallinan Papers.

44 Incomplete Spring, May 8, 1917, Box 61, Folder 9, Hazel Hunkins Hallinan Papers.

45 Compensation, n.d., Box 61, Folder 9, Hazel Hunkins Hallinan Papers.

46 Letter from Alma Sasse to Hazel Hunkins, July 1917, Box 61, Folder 9, Hazel Hunkins Hallinan Papers.

47 Ibid.

48 Letter from Hazel Hunkins to Anne Hunkins, January 22, 1918, Box 80, Folder 5, Hazel Hunkins Hallinan Papers.

49 Letter from Hazel Hunkins to Anne Hunkins, July 5, 1917, Box 61, Folder 9, Hazel Hunkins Hallinan Papers.

50 Letter from Hazel Hunkins to Anne Hunkins, December 13, 1918, Box 80, Folder 7, Hazel Hunkins Hallinan Papers.

51 McCarthy, *Respectability & Reform*, 211–214.
52 Letter from Nellie Green to Margaret Foley, September 28, 1911, Correspondence/ Subject Files. Alphabetical, ca. 1903, 1910–1926, Margaret Foley Papers.
53 Letter from Ettie Lowell to Margaret Foley, October 18, 1912, Correspondence/ Subject Files. Alphabetical, ca. 1903, 1910–1926, Margaret Foley Papers.
54 Letter from Ben Reitman to Margaret Foley, August 31, 1916, Correspondence/ Subject Files. Alphabetical, ca. 1903, 1910–1926, Margaret Foley Papers.
55 Wexler, *Emma Goldman*, 139–161.
56 Letter from Ben Reitman to Margaret Foley, January 9, 1916, Correspondence/ Subject Files. Alphabetical, ca. 1903, 1910–1926, Margaret Foley Papers.
57 Letter from Ben Reitman to Margaret Foley, August 31, 1916, Correspondence/ Subject Files. Alphabetical, ca. 1903, 1910–1926, Margaret Foley Papers.
58 Letter from Helen Goodnow to her grandmother, May 16, 1916. Margaret Foley and Helen Elizabeth Goodnow Papers.
59 Letter from Helen Goodnow to her grandmother, June 1, 1916. Margaret Foley and Helen Elizabeth Goodnow Papers.
60 Re: estate of Foley, 1919–1973, Additional Papers of Margaret Foley, 1892–1974. "Bigger Share of Estate Asked by 12 Charities," *Boston Globe*, October 26, 1959, 32.
61 Garvey, "Alice Dunbar-Nelson's Suffrage Work," 311, 316.
62 Ibid.; Gaines, *Uplifting the Race*, 209–233.
63 "Delta Sigma Theta," 1, 4.
64 Neverdon-Morton, "Advancement of the Race through African American Women's Organizations in the South, 1895–1925," 125–128.
65 Hull, *Give Us Each Day*; Hull, *Color, Sex & Poetry*; Garvey, "Alice Dunbar-Nelson's Suffrage Work," 319–324.
66 Letter from Edwina Kruse to Alice Dunbar Nelson, November 4, 1907, Folder 193, Box 8, Alice Dunbar Nelson Papers.
67 Letter from Edwina Kruse to Alice Dunbar Nelson, October 5, 1907, Folder 192, Box 8, Alice Dunbar Nelson Papers.
68 Letter from Edwina Kruse to Alice Dunbar Nelson, October 18, 1907, Folder 191, Box 8, Alice Dunbar Nelson Papers.
69 Letter from Edwina Kruse to Alice Dunbar Nelson, November 19, 1907, Folder 195, Box 8, Alice Dunbar Nelson Papers.
70 Letter from Edwina Kruse to Alice Dunbar Nelson, November 30, 1907, Folder 195, Box 8, Alice Dunbar Nelson Papers.
71 Letter from Edwina Kruse to Alice Dunbar Nelson, October 19, 1907, Folder 191, Box 8, Alice Dunbar Nelson Papers.
72 Quoted by Kruse in letter from Edwina Kruse to Alice Dunbar Nelson, November 4, 1907, Folder 193, Box 8, Alice Dunbar Nelson Papers.
73 Quoted by Kruse in letter from Edwina Kruse to Alice Dunbar Nelson, November 19, 1907, Folder 195, Box 8, Alice Dunbar Nelson Papers.
74 Letter from Edwina Kruse to Alice Dunbar Nelson, Date unknown (January 1908), Folder 197, Box 8, Alice Dunbar Nelson Papers.

75 Letter from Edwina Kruse to Alice Dunbar Nelson, January 26, 1908, Folder 199, Box 8, Alice Dunbar Nelson Papers.

76 Letter from Edwina Kruse to Alice Dunbar Nelson, March 4, 1908, Folder 202, Box 8, Alice Dunbar Nelson Papers.

77 Diary entry of May 5, 1907, Alice Dunbar Nelson Diary, 1906–1907, Alice Dunbar Nelson Papers.

78 Hull, *Color, Sex, & Poetry*, 360–361, 363–364, 374.

79 Franzen, *Anna Howard Shaw*, 56; Faderman, *To Believe in Women*, 50–51; Rupp, "'Imagine My Surprise,'" 61–70.

80 Van Dyne, "Abracadabra," 291, 295.

81 Thwing, "Advice of a Father to a Daughter Entering College," 475. For a scholarly analysis of the history of crushes and concerns about these relationships, see Inness, "Mashes, Smashes, Crushes, and Raves," 48–68; Inness, *Intimate Communities*.

82 "A New Century Club," *Morning News*, March 2, 1894, 2; "Work of Y.W.C.T.U.," *Morning News*, October 2, 1895, 2; "Suffragettes Before Legislature Today," *Morning News*, February 9, 1915, 2; Will of Mary Askew Mather, May 13, 1925, County of New Castle, Wilmington, Delaware.

83 Newman, *White Women's Rights*, 7–10, 19–20, 23, 52–53; Sneider, *Suffragists in an Imperial Age*, 12–14; Mead, *How the Vote Was Won*, 6.

84 Broadfoot, "Interview with Adele Clark," 39–40; Friedman, "Interview with Adele Clark."

85 Broadfoot, "Interview with Adele Clark," 35–36.

86 Terborg-Penn, *African American Women in the Struggle for the Vote*, 10, 121; Jones, *Vanguard*, 175–177.

87 Higginbotham, "Clubwomen and Electoral Politics in the 1920s," 135–136, 147–150.

88 Terborg-Penn, *African American Women in the Struggle for the Vote*, 120. Terborg-Penn was directly responding to a defense of white suffragists by Lebsock, "Woman Suffrage and White Supremacy: A Virginia Case Study," 40.

89 Michel Foucault argued that "homosexuality threatens people as a 'way of life' rather than as a way of having sex." Kath Weston similarly argued that queer families challenged heterosexual hegemony while also ironically reinforcing the status quo. Foucault, "Friendship as a Way of Life," 135–140; Weston, *Families We Choose*.

CHAPTER 3. QUEERING FAMILY

1 Wylie, *My Life with George*, 164–177; Baker, *Fighting for Life*, 191–200, 216–219, 235; Grier and Reid, *Lesbian Lives*, 419–424.

2 Wylie, *My Life with George*, 344.

3 Ibid., 344–345.

4 Freedman, "Separatism as Strategy," 512–29; Rupp, "'Imagine My Surprise,'" 61–70; Rupp, "The Women's Community in the National Woman's Party," 715–740; Fou-

cault, "Friendship as a Way of Life," 135–140; Faderman, *To Believe in Women*, 4, 24–63; Franzen, *Spinsters and Lesbians*, 108, 163; Halberstam, *In a Queer Time and Place*.

5 Weston, *Families We Choose*.

6 Sargent, *Gail Laughlin*, 46–47.

7 "Transition," Carton 9, Folder 44, Diary 1, Personalia 1834–1951, Anne Martin Collection.

8 Ibid.

9 Howard, *The Long Campaign*, 5–9.

10 Telegram from Mabel Vernon to Anne Martin, April 12, 1918, Box 9, Folder 18, Vernon, Mabel 1914–1950, Correspondence 1892–1951, Anne Martin Collection.

11 Rupp, "'Imagine My Surprise,'" 65; Faderman, *To Believe in Women*, 82, 154–156.

12 US Bureau of the Census, Twelfth Census of the United States, 1900; US Bureau of the Census, Thirteenth Census of the United States, 1910; Huntzinger, "Why I Joined My Union," 312–313; "Suffrage Speaker Here This Evening," *Valley Independent*, August 23, 1915, 1; Moravec, Pettine, and Smalley, "Stunts and Sensationalism," 631–656.

13 Hopkinson, "Hoboing Across the Continent"; "Lace Curtain Makers Abandon Trade to Campaign for Suffrage," *Buffalo Times*, August 14, 1917, 6.

14 US Bureau of the Census, Fourteenth Census of the United States, 1920; US Bureau of the Census, Fifteenth Census of the United States, 1930.

15 "Miss Mary S. Malone," *Daily News [Lebanon, PA]*, June 14, 1913, 8; "Anna Woods Bird," 72; Author correspondence with Diana McCarthy, current homeowner of the Bird/Malone home, August 2020.

16 Nelson, "Nontraditional Adoption in Progressive-Era Orphan Narratives," 183.

17 Ibid.

18 Schwarz, *Radical Feminists of Heterodoxy*, 86–87; Waitt, "Katharine Anthony," 72.

19 Mrs. George F. Arnold, "Dr. Shaw's Lecture," *Houston Post*, April 8, 1917, 48.

20 Letter from Katharine Anthony to Ethel Sturgis Drummer, November 29, 1916, Ethel Sturgis Drummer Collection; "Elizabeth Howard Weston," 57; Simonson, "Féminisme Oblige," 220, 263.

21 Faderman, *Odd Girls and Twilight Lovers*, 24; Waitt, "Katharine Anthony," 73, 75; "Irwin, Elisabeth Antoinette," 107; New York State Census, 1915; US Bureau of the Census, Fourteenth Census of the United States, 1920; US Bureau of the Census, Fifteenth Census of the United States, 1930.

22 Faderman, *Odd Girls and Twilight Lovers*, 23; Waitt, "Katharine Anthony," 76; US Bureau of the Census, Sixteenth Census of the United States, 1940.

23 "Woman's Story of Life as Man," *Los Angeles Herald*, September 1, 1915, 1; *History of the City of Denver, Arapahoe County, and Colorado*, 306; Avery, "Vassar College," *The Education of American Girls*, 346–361; Avery, "Vassar College," *Sex and Education*, 191–195.

24 *History of the City of Denver*, 306; "Officers of the N.W.S.A. for 1877 and '78," *The New Northwest*, June 14, 1878, 3; Avery, "The Colorado Campaign," 24; "Bradley,

M. J.," *San Francisco Examiner*, January 14, 1892, 11; "Eugene De Forest," *San Francisco Call*, August 26, 1897, 13.

25   Avery was the treasurer of the Susan B. Anthony Club in San Francisco, a founding member and president of the San Jose Equality Club, the treasurer of the Santa Clara County Equal Suffrage Club, and a director of the California Woman Suffrage Association. Anthony and Harper, *History of Woman Suffrage*, 24, 483, 485; "Woman's State Suffrage," *San Francisco Call*, September 28, 1890, 3; "Woman Suffragists Discuss Vital Topics in Convention," *San Francisco Call*, October 19, 1901, 3.

26   "Bradley, M. J.," 11; "Eugene De Forest," 13; Crocker-Langley, *San Francisco City Directory, 1905*, 215, 560; "Death of John M. Hart," *Evening News*, July 24, 1893, 3; "Wears Men's Dress," *San Francisco Chronicle*, September 6, 1893, 3; "Woman's Story of Life as Man," 1.

27   Sears, *Arresting Dress*; "Eugenia De Forrest," *Evening News*, September 29, 1893, 2.

28   "A Certain Eugenia De Forest . . ." *The WASP* 31, no. 11 (September 9, 1893): 3.

29   "A Card," *Berkeley Advocate*, December 14, 1895, 2.

30   "An Enviable Record," *Berkeley Advocate*, December 14, 1895, 1.

31   "De Forest Is a Man," *Daily Morning Union*, December 15, 1895, 1.

32   "She's a Man," *Los Angeles Times*, December 15, 1895, 3.

33   Manion, *Female Husbands*, 262.

34   "Bradley, M. J.," 11; "Eugene De Forest," 13; Crocker-Langley, *San Francisco City Directory, 1905*, 215, 560.

35   Skidmore, *True Sex*, 89.

36   Sueyoshi, *Discriminating Sex*, 41.

37   "In Male Attire," *Evening News*, December 16, 1895, 4.

38   "Woman's Story of Life as Man," 1.

39   Both Avery and De Forrest were living at 816a Larkin Street, San Francisco in 1905. Crocker-Langley, *San Francisco City Directory, 1905*, 215; "On New Lines," *Evening News*, March 17, 1894, 4; "St. George's Hall," *San Francisco Examiner*, March 19, 1894, 8; Gullett, *Becoming Citizens*, 18, 22; "Dr. Alida C. Avery Is Buried in San Jose," *San Francisco Call*, September 25, 1908, 4.

40   On the marriage certificate, De Forrest changed his parents' last name from Bradley to De Forrest, claimed to be from Philadelphia, and changed his first name to Albert, perhaps in honor of his deceased brother. "Albert Edward De Forest & Margaret Barton Hawley," Marriage License, County of Santa Barbara, State of California. November 17, 1911; "Marriages, First Methodist Church, Santa Barbara," 153–156.

41   See Cleves, "'What, Another Female Husband?'" 1055–1081; Manion, *Female Husbands*; Sears, *Arresting Dress*; Skidmore, *True Sex*.

42   "Wooer Renounced by Fiancée When Police Bare True Sex," *Los Angeles Herald*, 1; "Remarkable Story of a Los Angeles Woman Who Posed as Man 22 Years as a Result of Pre Natal Influence," *Washington Post*, September 19, 1915, 3.

43   "Woman's Story of Life as Man," 1; "Remarkable Story of a Los Angeles Woman," 3.

44 Skidmore, *True Sex*, 89–94.

45 "De Forest School of Acting," *Los Angeles Herald*, August 18, 1917, 20; "Man by Nature, Really a Woman," *Los Angeles Times*, September 30, 1917, 76; "Albert E. De Forrest," Certificate of Death, October 8, 1917, California State Board of Health, Bureau of Vital Statistics, County of Los Angeles, City of Los Angeles.

46 The cremation record listed him as Albert E. De Forrest, Date of Death, Oct. 8, 1917, Age 68, White, Female, according to the records of Evergreen Cemetery, Los Angeles County, California. His cremated remains were interred at Cypress Lawn on November 15, 1917, according to the records at Cypress Lawn Cemetery in Colma, California.

47 Wu, *Doctor Mom Chung of the Fair-Haired Bastards*, 2, 9, 23, 44–45, 63–65.

48 Ibid.

49 "Chinese Women Want Ballot," *Indiana Weekly Messenger*, April 2, 1913, 3; "Chinese Girl Suffragist," *Los Angeles Evening Express*, May 6, 1912, 15; "The Ballot in China," *San Diego Union and Daily Bee*, October 6, 1912, Magazine Section, 3; Lee, *At America's Gates*, 115, 188, 202; Cahill, *Recasting the Vote*, 25–46.

50 "Chinese Girl Here Studying Medicine," *Los Angeles Evening Herald*, October 14, 1914, 8.

51 For more on the perpetual foreigner stereotype and the exoticizing of Chinese American women and children, see Okihiro, *Margins and Mainstreams*; Lee, *Orientals*; Wu, *Yellow*; Lee, Wong, and Alvarez, "The Model Minority and the Perpetual Foreigner," 69–84; Jorae, *Children of Chinatown*; Sueyoshi, *Discriminating Sex*.

52 Biographer Judy Tzu-Chun Wu has provided evidence of lesbian desire in Chung's pursuit of erotically charged relationships with women. But Wu has also concluded that a definitive determination of Chung's sexual identity remains elusive. Chung never married but was allegedly engaged to a man at one point in her life. Unlike other independent women of her era, she never lived with another woman. But there were rumors in the Chinese American community that Chung was a lesbian. Elsa Gidlow, an out lesbian, had a flirtatious friendship with Chung and declared Chung a "sister lesbian." In the 1940s, Chung engaged in a romantic friendship with Sophie Tucker. Her letters to Tucker suggest an emotional and perhaps physical intimacy between the two women. Yet, Wu concludes that Chung's hesitancy to fully commit to a lesbian relationship was perhaps a result of an "inability to reconcile a lesbian identity with her professional and social goals." Wu, "Was Mom Chung a 'Sister Lesbian'?" 58–82; Wu, *Doctor Mom Chung of the Fair-Haired Bastards*, 44–45, 103–116.

53 Van Hoosen, *Petticoat Surgeon*, 219; Wu, "Was Mom Chung a 'Sister Lesbian'?" 58–82; Wu, *Doctor Mom Chung of the Fair-Haired Bastards*, 44–45, 103–116; Yung, *Unbound Feet*, 142.

54 O'Gara, "The Ministering Angel of Chinatown," 28.

55 Wu, "Was Mom Chung a 'Sister Lesbian'?" 58–82; Wu, *Doctor Mom Chung of the Fair-Haired Bastards*, 119–154, 199; Yung, *Unbound Feet*, 271–272.

56 "Friends Meet Here," *Kenosha News*, October 22, 1925, 4; "Poor Haven't Much Room in This Model Tenement," *Buffalo Courier*, December 12, 1911, 5.

57 "Appointments," *Evening Star*, November 4, 1915, 3; "Public Schools," *Evening Star*, June 19, 1921, 19; "Paragraphic News," *Washington Bee*, June 27, 1908, 1; Miller and Pruitt-Logan, *Faithful to the Task at Hand*.

58 Miller and Pruitt-Logan, *Faithful to the Task at Hand*, 2, 27, 32, 34, 44, 271; Slowe, "After Commencement What?" 19–21.

59 Brown, "To Catch the Vision of Freedom," 67–69.

60 For more on the depiction of African American women, and queer Black women specifically, as inherently depraved, see Somerville, *Queering the Color Line*, 34; Somerville, "Scientific Racism and the Invention of the Homosexual Body," 241–261; Agyepong, "Aberrant Sexualities and Racialized Masculinization," 270–293; Woolner, "'Woman Slain in Queer Love Brawl,'" 406–427.

61 Olsen, "Remaking the Image," 418–459; Simmons, "Companionate Marriage and the Lesbian Threat," 56; Beemyn, *A Queer Capital*, 77–83.

62 Letter from Lucy D. Slowe to Abraham Flexner, June 2, 1933, Lucy Diggs Slowe Papers.

63 Beemyn, *A Queer Capital*, 77–83; Miller and S. Pruitt-Logan, *Faithful to the Task at Hand*, 184, 198–201; Lindsey, "Climbing the Hilltop," 281–282.

64 Smith, *Bohemians West*, 107; Eby, *Until Choice Do Us Part*, 87–88.

65 "Ex-Reporter and Author," *Washington Post*, June 30, 1966, B4; "Frances Maule," *Daily News [New York]*, June 30, 1966, 24; Arthur, *Radical Innocent*, 90; Frances Maule's Personnel File, September 27, 1920, J. Walter Thompson Company Archives.

66 Kelley, "Helicon Hall: An Experiment in Living," 29–51; Kaplan, "A Utopia During the Progressive Era," 59–73; Arthur, *Radical Innocent*, 85–102.

67 "Sinclair Sues," *San Francisco Examiner*, August 29, 1911, 1; "The Gospel of Free Love Is Preached in Greenwich Village," *New York Tribune*, January 8, 1918, 11; Kaplan, "A Utopia During the Progressive Era," 59–73; Arthur, *Radical Innocent*, 85–102; Eby, *Until Choice Do Us Part*, 107–152.

68 Letter from Frances Maule to Meta Fuller Sinclair, May 30, 1907, Folder 1888–1907, Papers of Meta Fuller Stone, Lilly Library.

69 Ibid.

70 Letter from Frances Maule to Meta Fuller Sinclair, September 9, 1907, Folder 1888–1907, Papers of Meta Fuller Stone, Lilly Library.

71 Letter from Frances Maule to Edwin Bjorkman, September 2, 1914, Personal Correspondence, Edwin Bjorkman Papers.

72 Letter from Frances Maule to Edwin Bjorkman, September 13, 1914, Personal Correspondence, Edwin Bjorkman Papers.

73 Letter from Frances Maule to Edwin Bjorkman, September 20, 1914, Personal Correspondence, Edwin Bjorkman Papers.

74 Letter from Frances Maule to Edwin Bjorkman, September 2, 1914, Personal Correspondence, Edwin Bjorkman Papers.

75 Letter from Frances Maule to Edwin Bjorkman, Gloversville, Sunday Evening, date unknown, Personal Correspondence, Edwin Bjorkman Papers.

76 Ibid.

77 Helen Resor note in Frances Maule's Personnel File, September 27, 1920, J. Walter Thompson Company Archives; "Ex-Reporter and Author," *Washington Post*, June 30, 1966, B4.

78 Frances Maule's Personnel File, September 27, 1920, J. Walter Thompson Company Archives; US Census Bureau, Fifteenth Census of the United States, 1930; US Census Bureau, Sixteenth Census of the United States, 1940; "Obituary: Frances Maule," *Daily News [New York]*, June 30, 1966, 24.

CHAPTER 4. QUEERING TRANSATLANTIC ALLIANCES

1 Suffragists Oral History Project, "Conversations with Alice Paul," 44–45; Wylie, *My Life with George*, 180–181.

2 For more on the international feminist movement and the significance of relationships between women, see Rupp, *Worlds of Women*; Marino, *Feminism for the Americas*.

3 "Suffragists go to England," 1911, Suffrage. General: clippings, most re: Foley and suffrage, 1909–1913, Margaret Foley Papers.

4 Ibid.; Journal re: International Woman Suffrage Alliance Conference, Florence Luscomb Papers; Strom, *Political Woman*, 77–83; Strom, "Leadership and Tactics in the American Woman Suffrage Movement," 312–313.

5 Cresswell, "Mobilising the Movement," 450–451; Strom, "Leadership and Tactics in the American Woman Suffrage Movement," 310–313.

6 "Claims Policeman Was Brutal to Her," *Boston Globe*, September 26, 1911, 11.

7 Ibid.

8 Ibid.; "Police Warning to Miss Foley," *Boston Globe*, September 26, 1911, 4.

9 "Girls Get Langtry's Goat," *The Sun*, October 12, 1911, 2.

10 "Our First Suffragette," *Transcript*, September 30, 1911, part 3, 16.

11 "She Talked Suffrage," *Boston Globe*, July 18, 1911, 13.

12 Letters from Helen Elizabeth Goodnow to her grandmother, April–June 1916, Margaret Foley and Helen Elizabeth Goodnow Papers.

13 Howard, *The Long Campaign*, 66–70.

14 Ibid.

15 "Thousands of Suffragettes Clash with Police," *Tonopah Daily Bonanza*, November 18, 1910, 1.

16 Letter from Joseph C. Hopper to Anne Martin, November 19, 1910, Anne Martin Collection.

17 Letter from Emmeline Pethick Lawrence to Anne Martin, November 13, 1911, Anne Martin Collection.

18 Martin Pugh and June Purvis disagree on the extent of lesbianism in the suffragette movement. See Pugh, *The Pankhursts*, 153, 212–213; Purvis, *Emmeline Pankhurst*, 4, 145, 393–394.

19 Atkinson, *Rise Up, Women!* 152–3.

20 Letter from Nurse Pitfield to Anne Martin, December 7, 1911, Anne Martin Collection.

21 "Anne Martin Is Again in Reno," *Nevada State Journal*, December 13, 1911, 8.

22 Letter from Evelina Haverfield to Anne Martin, November 28, 1911.

23 "Anne Martin Is Again in Reno," *Nevada State Journal*, December 13, 1911, 8.

24 Day letter from S. H. Friedlander to Anne Martin, January 17, 1912, Box 10, Folder 26, Correspondence 1892–1951, Anne Martin Collection.

25 Night lettergram from Annie Kenney to Anne Martin, October 17–18, 1914, Box 5, Folder 2, Correspondence 1892–1951, Anne Martin Collection.

26 Kenney, *Memories of a Militant*, 263; "Christabel Pankhurst on Nevada," *Gazette-Journal [Reno]*, February 24, 1912, 2; Day letter from S. H. Friedlander to Anne Martin, January 17, 1912, Box 10, Folder 26, Correspondence 1892–1951, Anne Martin Collection; Night lettergram from Annie Kenney to Anne Martin, October 17–18, 1914, Box 5, Folder 2, Correspondence 1892–1951, Anne Martin Collection.

27 Howard, *The Long Campaign*, 112.

28 "Alice Wright Hardworker," Newspaper Clipping, Series V. Subject Files, Clippings 1912–17, Alice Morgan Wright Papers.

29 Letter from Alice Morgan Wright to Edith Shepard, December 10, 1909, Correspondence, Letters to Edith Shepard, Alice Morgan Wright Papers.

30 Ibid.

31 Ibid.

32 Dennison, "The American Girls' Club in Paris," 32–37; M.F.T., "Intelligent Gentlewomen in Marble," 32–33.

33 Letter from Alice Morgan Wright to Edith Shepard, December 10, 1909, Correspondence, Letters to Edith Shepard, Alice Morgan Wright Papers.

34 Letters from Emmeline Pankhurst to Alice Morgan Wright, March 8, 1911 and June 26, 1911, Correspondence, Letters to Emmeline Pankhurst, Alice Morgan Wright Papers.

35 Letter from Emmeline Pankhurst to Alice Morgan Wright, September 18, 1911, Correspondence, Letters to Emmeline Pankhurst, Alice Morgan Wright Papers.

36 Letter from Alice Morgan Wright to Edith Shepard, October 21, 1911, Correspondence, Letters to Edith Shepard, Alice Morgan Wright Papers.

37 Letters from Emmeline Pankhurst to Alice Morgan Wright, December 13, 1911 and December 23, 1911, Correspondence, Letters to Emmeline Pankhurst, Alice Morgan Wright Papers.

38 Letter from Emmeline Pankhurst to Alice Morgan Wright, February 11, 1912, Correspondence, Letters to Emmeline Pankhurst, Alice Morgan Wright Papers.

39 Letter from Alice Morgan Wright to Margaret Grierson, February 18, 1952, Series II Correspondence, Alice Morgan Wright Papers.

40 Pankhurst, *My Own Story*, 212–213.

41 "London Police Hunt Mrs. Pankhurst," *Bennington Evening Banner*, March 7, 1912, 1; "Advance Obit, Alice Morgan Wright, Prepared 10/17/67 by S. Armstrong," Se-

ries I, Biographical Materials, Obituaries, 1967–75, Alice Morgan Wright Papers; Suffragettes Arrested, 1906–1914, Home Office 45, 24665, Suffragettes: Amnesty of August 1914, Index of Women Arrested, 1906–1914.

42 "American Girl Toils in Jail as Suffragette," *Trenton Evening Times*, March 6, 1912, 1.

43 "Hope to Free Miss Wright," *Bennington Banner*, March 7, 1912, 1.

44 "To the Editor," Suffrage, Prison in England—Notes, Writing and Memorabilia, Alice Morgan Wright Papers.

45 Decades later, Wright donated two bronze casts of the sculpture to a London museum and to the Sophia Smith Collection at her alma matter. See correspondence between Wright and Smith College archivist Margaret Grierson. Letter from Alice Morgan Wright to Margaret Grierson, February 18, 1952, Series II Correspondence, Alice Morgan Wright Papers; Letter from Alice Morgan Wright to Stella Newsome, December 2, 1952, Series II Correspondence, Alice Morgan Wright Papers; Pankhurst, *My Own Story*, 220.

46 Verse written in Holloway, March 1912, Series IV Artwork, Verse by AMW, n.d. Alice Morgan Wright Papers.

47 Ibid.

48 Miscellaneous Newspaper Clippings, 1912–1917, Series V Subject Files, Clippings, Alice Morgan Wright Papers.

49 Letter from Mrs. F. W. Pethick Lawrence to Alice Morgan Wright, April 24, 1912, Series II Correspondence, Pethick Lawrence, Emmeline, 1912, Alice Morgan Wright Papers.

50 "To the Editor," Suffrage, Prison in England—Notes, Writing and Memorabilia, Alice Morgan Wright Papers.

51 See letters and "Memorial to the Rt. Hon. H. H. Asquith on behalf of Emmeline Pankhurst, Emmeline Pethick Lawrence and Frederick Pethick Lawrence," Suffrage, Prison in England—Notes, Writing and Memorabilia, Alice Morgan Wright Papers.

52 "A Branch Formed," 3; Letter from Alice Morgan Wright to Edith Shepard, September 22, 1912, Correspondence, Letters to Edith Shepard, Alice Morgan Wright Papers; Letter from Emmeline Pankhurst to Alice Morgan Wright, February 15, 1913, Correspondence, Letters to Emmeline Pankhurst, Alice Morgan Wright Papers.

53 "Souvenir Program," Women Suffrage Parade, New York, October 27, 1917, National Woman's Party Papers.

54 "Three Capitol Women in Votes Trip Party," *Washington Herald*, March 26, 1916, 4; "Will Care for Suffragists Who Attend Inauguration," *Brooklyn Daily Eagle*, February 28, 1917, 28; "Suffragists Seek Vote of Californians," *San Francisco Chronicle*, April 26, 1916, 13; "Eastern Envoys to the West of the 'Suffrage Special' Sent by the Congressional Union For Woman Suffrage, April 9 to May 16, 1916," National Woman's Party Papers.

55 "United Plea Brought U.N. Step on Equal Rights, Sculptor Says," *Knickerbocker News*, May 23, 1946, B-3. For more on the struggle to create the Commission on the Status of Women, see Laville, "A New Era in International Women's Rights?" 34–56.

56 "Girl of Wealth Scrubs Floors," *Muncie Evening Press*, January 30, 1912, 5; Winslow, *Sylvia Pankhurst*, 34.

57 Emerson, "My Prison Experiences," 25–27, 56–57.

58 Ibid., "American Woman Punches English Officer in Face," *Pittsburgh Post-Gazette*, February 15, 1913, 6; "In the Courts," 8; Letter from Zelie Emerson to Keir Hardie, February 26, 1913, Independent Labour Party Archive; E. Sylvia Pankhurst, "Forcibly Fed," 87–93; Report of Mr. Forward, Deputy Medical Officer of Holloway Prison, Zelie Emerson, Lillian Lenton's Case, July 7, 1913, House of Commons Papers, 52, no. 190.

59 "American Girl Serenaded in London Bastile," *Gazette Journal* [Reno], March 29, 1913, 1; "News of Miss Emerson," 410; "Jail Term Made Her Ill," *Harrisburg Daily Independent*, April 15, 1913, 9; "Miss Emerson Released," 424; "Rush to Hospital Follows Release," *Topeka Daily Capital*, April 9, 1913, 1.

60 "Suffragettes and Officers Fight Battle," *Arizona Daily Star*, October 14, 1913, 1; "American Militant Dangerously Hurt," *Pittsburgh Press*, November 11, 1913, 5; American Militant is Assaulted, *Buffalo Enquirer*, November 6, 1913, 15.

61 "Zelie Emerson," 636–639.

62 "Conversation like this . . . ," 772.

63 "Forcible Feeding," 190.

64 "Miss Emmeline Pankhurst," *Times Herald*, November 12, 1913, 6.

65 Emerson, "My Prison Experiences," 27.

66 "Militant Troops Study Jiu Jitsu," *Chicago Examiner*, November 18, 1913, 1.

67 "Case of Inspector Potter," 11.

68 "American Arrested in London," *Calgary Herald*, December 27, 1913, 18.

69 "More About Government Methods," 412; "May Deport Miss Emerson," *Sioux City Journal*, February 27, 1914, 5; "Militant Fears Deportation by British Court," *Calgary Herald*, February 17, 1914, 5; "Militants Fight London Officers," *Rock Island Argus*, March 9, 1914, 1; "Miss Zelie Emerson Rests on Her Laurels," *Times Herald*, June 1, 1914, 6.

70 Winslow, *Sylvia Pankhurst*, 41–75; Zelie Emerson to Sylvia Pankhurst, no date, circa 1914, Sylvia Pankhurst Papers.

71 Zelie Emerson to Sylvia Pankhurst, n.d., ca. 1914, Sylvia Pankhurst Papers.

72 Winslow, *Sylvia Pankhurst*, 34.

CHAPTER 5. QUEERING SPACE

1 "In Saddle for Votes," *Washington Post*, February 11, 1912, 8.

2 "Here and There Under the 'Votes for Women' Banners," *New York Times*, May 11, 1913, 18.

3 Matthew Cottrill defined queer space as "spaces that critique the divisions of sexuality, gender, class and race through political, cultural, social, real, ephemeral, geographic and historical contexts." Natalie Oswin has suggested we move beyond a narrow "focus on 'queer' lives and an abstract critique of the heterosexualization of space" to a more complex deconstruction of the "hetero/homo binary" and examination of "sexuality's deployments in concert with racialized, classed and gendered processes." Cottrill, *Queering Architecture*, 359. See also Bell and Valentine, *Mapping Desire*; Oswin, "Critical Geographies and the Uses of Sexuality," 100.

4 For more on the significance of homosocial spaces to the women's movement see: Freedman, "Separatism as Strategy," 512–529; Rupp, "The Women's Community in the National Woman's Party," 715–40.

5 "With the Members Sworn to Secrecy," *New York Tribune*, November 24, 1914, 7; Schwarz, *Radical Feminists of Heterodoxy*, 14, 44–45.

6 "With the Members Sworn to Secrecy," 7; "By-laws of Heterodoxy," December 12, 1932, Heterodoxy, 1930–1938, Papers of Mary Ware Dennett.

7 Ellis, *My Life*; "How to Be Happy Though Married," *Boston Globe*, April 30, 1914, 13; "With the Members Sworn to Secrecy," 7.

8 Schwarz, *Radical Feminists of Heterodoxy*, 107.

9 Heterodoxy to Marie, [1920], Papers of Inez Haynes Gillmore.

10 "Miss Taylor Dies, 76, in Village," *Kingston Daily Freeman*, November 8, 1949, 13; "Defy Wintry Blasts," *Brooklyn Citizen*, March 3, 1915, 7; "Girls Invade Wall Street," *Austin American Statesman*, May 2, 1928, 3; "Women Plunge in Stocks as Market Prices Soar," *Brooklyn Daily Eagle*, March 27, 1928, 3; "Ticker Tape Instead of the Bargain Counter," *Courier-Journal*, May 5, 1929, 90; Marguerite Mooers Marshall, "'Wall Street' Women Who Found Stocks and Bonds Way to Top," *Evening World*, March 27, 1919, 24.

11 Schwarz, *Radical Feminists of Heterodoxy*, 108.

12 Terborg-Penn, *African American Women in the Struggle for the Vote*, 97–105, 122–123; Davis, *Lifting as They Climb*, 116–117; Materson, *For the Freedom of Her Race*, 81, 187; "The Alpha Suffrage Club," 1.

13 "The Alpha Suffrage Club," 1; Terborg-Penn, *African American Women in the Struggle for the Vote*, 97–99, 122–123.

14 Faderman, *To Believe in Women*, 155.

15 "J. E. Milholland Regrets Slight to Colored Race," *Brooklyn Daily Eagle*, August 18, 1924, 2.

16 "National Womans Party Head Snubs Race," *The Advocate*, August 30, 1924, 1.

17 "White Women Slight Negro in Memorial to Inez Milholland," *New York Age*, August 23, 1924, 3.

18 "Remarks of Dr. Emmett J. Scott," Meadowmount, New York, August 17, 1924, Box 90, Folder 1, Lucy Diggs Slowe Papers, Moorland-Spingarn Research Center; "Dr. Emmett J. Scott Did Speak at Grave of Inez Milholland," *New York Age*, September 6, 1924, 2.

19 Sloan, "Sexual Warfare in the Silent Cinema," 412–436.

20 "Miss Friganza a Suffragette," *New York Tribune*, October 15, 1908, 7; "Trixie Friganza Is a Suffragette," *Tribune*, January 17, 1909, 7; "'Be Fat: Secret of Youth,' So Trixie Friganza Says," *Reno Evening Gazette*, March 6, 1915, 9.

21 Furth, Moran, and Heelan, *No Wedding Bells for Me*.

22 Ibid.

23 "'I Wouldn't Marry the Best Man Living'—Trixie Friganza," *Davenport Democrat and Leader*, March 5, 1911, 15.

24 "Trixie Friganza's Husband Abused Her," *San Francisco Examiner*, November 1, 1914, 22.

25 Hurewitz, *Bohemian Los Angeles and the Making of Modern Politics*, 31.

26 Wolf, "The Sort of Fellow Julian Eltinge Really Is," 793, 802–803.

27 "Julian Eltinge's Ideal Husband and Wife," *Julian Eltinge Magazine* (date unknown), 50, Townshend Walsh Collection.

28 Wolf, "The Sort of Fellow Julian Eltinge Really Is," 793, 802–803.

29 Hurewitz, *Bohemian Los Angeles and the Making of Modern Politics*; Casey, *The Prettiest Girl on Stage Is a Man*, 37–76.

30 *A Busy Day* [Film], Keystone Company, 1914; *A Cure for Suffragettes* [Film], Biograph, 1912; Sloan, "Sexual Warfare in the Silent Cinema," 412–436.

31 "Women's Play Ready," *Washington Post*, February 15, 1914, 6; "Wit in Suffrage Play," *Washington Post*, February 21, 1914, 14; "Suffragists Seek Vote of Californians," *San Francisco Chronicle*, April 26, 1916, 13; "Eastern Envoys to the West of the 'Suffrage Special' Sent by the Congressional Union For Woman Suffrage, April 9 to May 16, 1916," National Woman's Party Papers.

32 Letters between Edith J. Goode to Olive Chapin Higgins, 1904–1905, Olive Higgins Prouty Papers.

33 Hatton, *Before Sunrise*, 8.

34 Hamilton and St. John, *How the Vote Was Won*, 17.

35 Ibid.

36 Hatton, *Before Sunrise*, 14.

37 Christian, *Marriage and Late-Victorian Dramatists*, 189–190; Ricketts, "The Fractured Pageant," 82–94; Pugh, *The Pankhursts*, 94; Cockin, "Charlotte Perkins Gilman's *Three Women*," 74–92.

38 *80 Million Women Want—?*, [Film], Unique Film Company, 1913; Stamp, *Movie Struck Girls*, 154–194.

39 Cahill, *Recasting the Vote*, 32. For more on women claiming public space, see McCammon, "'Out of the Parlors and into the Streets,'" 787–818; Sewell, *Women and the Everyday City*. Studies on modern pride parades similarly reflect on this idea of queering the streets. See Johnston, *Queering Tourism*; Bruce, *Pride Parades*.

40 "How to Dress for Suffrage Parade," *Brooklyn Daily Eagle*, May 1, 1912, 24.

41 "Judging from the women . . . ," 4.

42 "Boots and Breeches for Suffrage Amazons," *Pittsburgh Post-Gazette*, February 11, 1912, 1.

43 "Chinese Suffragist on Horseback," *Brooklyn Daily Eagle*, April 23, 1912, 24.

44 "Chinese Talk Suffrage," *New York Tribune*, April 11, 1912, 3.

45 "Chinese Suffragist on Horseback," 24.

46 Cahill, *Recasting the Vote*, 25–46, 148–160, 180–183. For more on the perpetual foreigner stereotype and the exoticizing of Chinese American women and children, see Okihiro, *Margins and Mainstreams*; Lee, *Orientals*; Wu, *Yellow*; Lee, Wong, and Alvarez, "The Model Minority and the Perpetual Foreigner," 69–84; Jorae, *Children of Chinatown*; Sueyoshi, *Discriminating Sex*.

47 "An Indian Suffragist," *Brooklyn Daily Eagle*, March 3, 1913, 26; "Indian Girls to Ride in Parade," *Boston Globe*, February 9, 1913, 6.

48 "Young Indian Princess Has Many Admirers," *Neenah Times*, January 23, 1913, 3.

49 "Indian Women the First Suffragists and Used Recall, Chippewa Avers," *Washington Times*, August 3, 1914, 9; "Indians Were Suffragists," *Brooklyn Daily Eagle*, December 31, 1911, 6; Cahill, *Recasting the Vote*, 11–24, 71–82, 100–102, 131–141.

50 "Sum Up Day's Work," *Washington Post*, March 4, 1913, 3; "Colored Women in Parade," *Star Tribune*, March 2, 1913, 6; "Suffrage Paraders," 296.

51 Alice Paul to Alice Stone Blackwell, January 15, 1913, National Woman's Party Papers.

52 Alice Paul to Marie I. Hardwick, Chairman Procession Committee, January 28, 1913, NWP Suffrage Correspondence, National Woman's Party Papers.

53 Nellie M. Quander to Alice Paul, February 15, 1913, National Woman's Party Papers.

54 Nellie M. Quander to Alice Paul, February 17, 1913 and Alice Paul to Nellie Quander, Chairman Procession Committee, February 23, 1913, National Woman's Party Papers.

55 Anna Howard Shaw to Alice Paul, February 28, 1913, Telegram, National Woman's Party Papers.

56 "Colored Women in Parade," 6; "Sum Up Day's Work," 3; "Suffrage Paraders," 296; Terborg-Penn, *African American Women in the Struggle for the Vote*, 98–99, 122–124; Higginbotham, "In Politics to Stay," 212–213; Cahill, *Recasting the Vote*, 104–108.

57 "Suffrage Paraders," 296.

58 Julius F. Taylor, "The Equal Suffrage Parade," *Broad Ax*, March 8, 1913, 1.

59 "'Who's Afraid!' Cry Suffragets Who Make Headquarters in Haunted House," *Muskogee Daily Phoenix and Times-Democrat*, April 6, 1916, 1; Vice Chairman to Mrs. Lawrence Lewis, June 17, 1915, National Woman's Party suffrage correspondence, National Woman's Party Papers.

60 "Hospitality to Prevail in Old Cameron House," *Evening Star*, December 27, 1916, 4; "Brilliant Meeting at Cameron House," 8; "First National Convention of the Congressional Union," 5; Mrs. Ella M. Dean of Montana, [ca. 1915–1916 Mar. 11], Records of the National Woman's Party.

61 Vernon, Milholland, and Martin all were in Boston marriages and had romantic relationships with women at some point in their lives. For more on the queer lives

of these women, see Rupp, "Imagine My Surprise," 65; Faderman, *To Believe in Women*, 82, 154–156.

62 Stevens, *Jailed for Freedom*, 43, 75–78.

63 Mary Kimmell Plough to National Woman's Party, January 27, 1919, National Woman's Party suffrage correspondence, National Woman's Party Papers.

64 Florence Whitehouse to Alice Paul, October 25, 1917, correspondence on Alice Paul's imprisonment, National Woman's Party Papers.

65 Letter from Mary Craven Johnson to Alice Paul, October 21, 1917, National Woman's Party Correspondence on sentencing of Alice Paul, National Woman's Party Papers.

66 Letter from Katharine Fisher to Mabel Vernon, June 27, 1917, National Woman's Party Correspondence on Branch Organization Activities and Public Reaction to Picketing, Arrests, and Imprisonment of Picketers, National Woman's Party Papers.

67 Stevens, *Jailed for Freedom*, 364, 365, 368–369.

68 Affidavit of Julia Emory, National Woman's Party correspondence on suffrage prisoner accounts of conditions and brutal treatment at DC jail and Occoquan Workhouse, National Woman's Party Papers.

69 I do not know if Elizabeth McShane and Mary Ingham ever had a romantic relationship. I do know that Ingham and McShane lived together and were each other's chosen family during this period of time.

70 Telegram to Virginia Arnold from Mary Ingham, November 22, 1917, National Woman's Party Correspondence on Brutal Treatment of Imprisoned Suffragists," National Woman's Party Papers.

71 Letter from Elizabeth McShane to Mary Ingham, ca. November 25, 1917, National Woman's Party press releases on organization and suffrage movement activities, National Woman's Party Papers.

72 Ibid.

73 Elizabeth McShane Hilles, Prison Notes, Woman Suffrage-Vassar College, Folder 5.23.

74 Ibid.

75 "Suffs, Out of Jail, Hailed as Heroines," *Evening Sun*, June 29, 1917, 1; "Suffragettes Protest When Freed from Jail," *Fort Worth Star-Telegram*, November 28, 1917, 2.

76 "Pistol Fired as 5,000 Mob 'Suffs,' Destroy 37 Banners," *Washington Herald*, August 15, 1917, 1; "Pelt Cameron House," *Washington Post*, August 15, 1917, 1; "A Congressional Investigation of the Lawless Attack on the Suffrage Picket Demanded," 5.

77 "President Onlooker at Mob Attack on Suffragists," 7.

78 Letter from Betty Gram Swing to Fellow Picket, November 26, 1937, National Woman's Party Fundraising and Advocacy Activities, National Woman's Party Papers.

CHAPTER 6. QUEERING DEATH

1 The bench was relocated to Golden Gate Park in the 1940s. Park & Recreation Commission Minutes, San Francisco, California. September 12, 1933; "A Last-

ing Tribute to a Friend," *San Francisco Examiner*, October 18, 1934, 20; "Teacher Left $43,000 in Will," *Oakland Tribune*, July 5, 1933, 9; "Career is Monument to Beloved Educator," *San Francisco Examiner*, June 27, 1933, 9.

2 Radomska, Mehrabi, and Lykke, "Queer Death Studies," 6.

3 Butler, *Frames of War*, 38.

4 See poems to Edith in Verse by AMW, n.d., Series IV Artwork, Alice Morgan Wright Papers.

5 No title, February 1932, Verse by AMW, n.d., AMW Collection, Series IV Artwork, Alice Morgan Wright Papers.

6 Alice Morgan Wright to Marine Leland, September 13, 1956, Box 3, Folder 7, Series II: Correspondence, Alice Morgan Wright Papers.

7 Letters from Paula Jakobi to Rose Pastor Stokes, 1932, Medical Matters Folder, Rose Pastor Stokes Papers.

8 "Marie Jenney Howe to Fola La Follette," December 13, 1933, quoted in Schwarz, *Radical Feminists of Heterodoxy*, 101.

9 Brooks, Spottswood, and Spottswood, *Lost Sounds*, 254–258; Snyder, *Harry T. Burleigh*, 167–168; "Woman of Rare Musical Talent," *Pittsburgh Courier*, October 18, 1912, 1.

10 Snyder, *Harry T. Burleigh*, 168; "Nearly Ten Thousand Take Part in Big Silent Protest," *New York Age*, August, 2, 1917, 1; "4th Educational Recital," *New York Age*, April 27, 1918, 6; "A Series of Five Educational Recitals," *New York Age*, February 23, 1918, 6; "Club Women Have Interesting Session," *Daily Standard Union*, July 2, 1914, 6; "Female Smokers Are Criticized," *New York Age*, July 10, 1913, 1; "Colored Women Elect Officers for State Body," *Buffalo Morning News*, July 6, 1913, 52; "Anti-Lynching Mass Meeting on Nov. 12," *New York Age*, November 11, 1922, 1.

11 "Summer Visitors Throng Sag Harbor, Long Island," *New York Age*, August 9, 1924, 5; "St. Mark's Church Lyceum," *New York Age*, November 7, 1925, 5.

12 "In Memory of," *New York Age*, February 6, 1926, 10.

13 "Miss Edna Schoyer," *Pittsburgh Post-Gazette*, August 22, 1915, 12; "Pittsburg Suffragists Are to Speak," *Pittsburgh Press*, November 20, 1912, 3; "Suffragists Prepare for Big Convention," *Pittsburgh Daily Post*, October 26, 1913, 4; "County League of Voters Holds Ridgefield Meet," *Bridgeport Telegram*, April 8, 1925, 9; "Miss Edna Schoyer," *Pittsburgh Press*, August 7, 1946, 32.

14 "Bequests Made by Ridgefielder," *Bridgeport Post*, August 26, 1965, 42.

15 Ibid.

16 Hall, *Give Us Each Day*, 374–375.

17 "This Lofty Oak," Box 14–16, Alice Dunbar Nelson Papers.

18 Totton, "Hannah Keziah Clapp," 169, 170–173; Miriam Michelson, "Nevada's Feminine David and Jonathan: A Sketch from Life," *Bulletin*, October 8, 1899, 9–10; "Sierra Seminary," *Daily Appeal*, December 31, 1876, 1; Anthony and Harper, *History of Woman Suffrage*, 810–811; "The Woman Suffrage Convention . . . ," *Weekly Independent*, November 3, 1895, 3.

19 "Companions for Years Separated by Death," *San Francisco Call*, December 23, 1899, 16.

20 Resolution, October 5, 1899, The Woman's Guild of Trinity Parish, Reno, Nevada, Folder 3, Hannah Keziah Clapp and Elizabeth Cecilia Babcock Collection.

21 "Death of Miss E. C. Babcock," *Reno Evening Gazette*, September 19, 1899, 3.

22 Ibid., 2.

23 "For Auld Lang Syne in the Sagebrush State," *Reno Evening Gazette*, June 3, 1904, 3.

24 Letter to Hannah Clapp from Miriam Michelson, September 26, 1899, San Francisco, California, Folder 3, Clapp, Hannah Keziah and Elizabeth Cecilia Babcock Collection.

25 Galpin, "A Theme for a Poet"; "About Two Nevada Women," *Reno Evening Gazette*, October 9, 1899, 3.

26 Michelson, "Nevada's Feminine David and Jonathan," 9–10.

27 Ibid.

28 Letter from Marie Hardwick to Mary Burrill, December 20, 1937, Lucy Diggs Slowe Papers.

29 Letter from Mollie T. Berrien to Mary Burrill, October 23, 1937, Box 90, Folder 1, Lucy Diggs Slowe Papers.

30 Poem by Esther Popel, May 25, 1938, Box 90, Folder 1, Lucy Diggs Slowe Papers.

31 Letter from Hilda A. Davis to Mary Burrill, December 8, 1941, Lucy Diggs Slowe Papers.

32 Mary P. Burrill, Foreword in the "Eulogy by Dwight O.W. Holmes at the Obsequies of Lucy D. Slowe." October 25, 1937, Lucy Diggs Slowe Papers; Miller and Pruitt-Logan, *Faithful to the Task at Hand*, 232.

33 Totton, "Hannah Keziah Clapp," 177–178; "Hannah K. Clapp," *San Francisco Chronicle*, December 23, 1899, 12; "Babcock Memorial," *Reno Evening Gazette*, September 8, 1900, 3.

34 "Local Library Circulation Is Over 500,000," *Evening Journal*, July 28, 1927, 8.

35 Wilson, *Fifty Years Work with Girls*, 268; Letter from Aurelia Hendry Reinhardt of Mills College to Gail Laughlin, February 3, 1921, Aurelia Henry Reinhardt Papers.

36 Letter from Alice Morgan Wright, January 1963, "Will and Instructions to Executors, 1954–67," Series I, Biographical Materials, Alice Morgan Wright Papers.

37 Faderman, *To Believe in Women*, 37.

38 Alice Stone Blackwell Will, 1934, Miscellany, Wills, Alice Stone Blackwell Papers.

39 Last Will and Testament of Leona Huntzinger, August 22, 1922, Bacton, East Whiteland Township, Chester County, Pennsylvania; Will of Mary Askew Mather, May 13, 1925, County of New Castle, Wilmington, Delaware; Totton, "Hannah Keziah Clapp," 177; "Hannah K. Clapp," *San Francisco Chronicle*, December 23, 1899, 12; "Babcock Memorial," *Reno Evening Gazette*, September 8, 1900, 3.

40 Will of Annie Tinker, June 27, 1918, Correspondence between Tinker estate heir Kate Bertolini and lawyer William Woart Lancaster, 1921–1924, Records of the Annie Tinker Association for Women.

41 "Hearst Plea for Women Is Indorsed," *San Francisco Examiner*, July 2, 1918, 5; Gullett, "Constructing the Woman Citizen," 581–582; Gullett, *Becoming Citizens*, 3, 94.

42 *Annual Report of the Children's Hospital of San Francisco, 1918*, 6; "Dr. Mary Sperry is Seriously Ill," *San Francisco Examiner*, May 8, 1919, 6; Telegram from Margaret Fay Whittemore to Alice Paul, February 20th, 1915, National Woman's Party Papers.

43 Superior Court of the State of California in and for the City and County of San Francisco, "In the Matter of the Estate of Mary A. Sperry," June 23, 1919, Will Proof and Certificate, Book D of Wills, no. 443, p. 254.

44 Superior Court of the State of California, "Estate of Mary A. Sperry"; "Sperry Will Contest Case Compromised," *San Francisco Chronicle*, November 30, 1920, 3.

45 Superior Court of the State of California, "Estate of Mary A. Sperry."

46 Court of Cumberland County, Portland, Maine, "Last Will and Testament of Gail Laughlin," August 4, 1950, vol. 790, p. 303; author's email correspondence with Judy Jensen, Brooklawn Memorial Park, January 22, 2019.

47 Michelson, "Nevada's Feminine David and Jonathan," 9–10.

48 Hannah K. Clapp, Last Will and Testament, February 21, 1908, Will Books and Probate Records, Ca. 1850–1912, Superior Court, Santa Clara County, California.

49 Elizabeth C. Babcock and Hannah K. Clapp, Mount Hope Cemetery, Bangor, Maine.

50 Alice Morgan Wright's note to her executors, December 15, 1955, "Will and Instructions to Executors, 1954–67," Series I, Biographical Materials. Alice Morgan Wright Papers.

51 Green Address Book, circa 1960s, Series I, Biographical Materials, Alice Morgan Wright Papers.

52 Hannah Keziah Clapp to Kate Baker Busey, April 21, 1905, Kate Baker Busey Papers, Baker-Busey-Dunlap Family Papers.

53 Hannah Keziah Clapp to Kate Baker Busey, March 27, 1907, Kate Baker Busey Papers, Baker-Busey-Dunlap Family Papers.

54 Hannah Keziah Clapp to Kate Baker Busey, July 13, 1905, Kate Baker Busey Papers, Baker-Busey-Dunlap Family Papers.

55 Hannah Keziah Clapp to Kate Baker Busey, May 21, 1905, Kate Baker Busey Papers, Baker-Busey-Dunlap Family Papers.

56 For more on the association between Spiritualism and suffrage, see Goldsmith, *Other Powers*; Braude, *Radical Spirits*.

57 Letter from Sarah Jane Crosswell to Kate Baker Busey, January 19, 1909, Kate Baker Busey Papers, Baker-Busey-Dunlap Family Papers.

CONCLUSION

1 Rich, "Compulsory Heterosexuality and Lesbian Existence," 647–649. See also Cook, "The Historical Denial of Lesbianism," 60–65; Faderman, "Who Hid Lesbian History?" 74–76; Rupp, "'Imagine My Surprise,'" 61–70; Smith-Rosenberg, "The Female World of Love and Ritual," 1–29.

2 Jeannette Marks, "Unwise College Friendships," 1908, Jeannette Marks' Papers; Marks, *A Girl's Student Days and After*, 35–37; Letter from Alice Stone Blackwell to Kitty Barry Blackwell, March 1, 1912, Blackwell Family Papers; Faderman, *Surpassing the Love of Men*, 229–230, 309; Franzen, *Spinsters and Lesbians*, 104, 173–175; Faderman, *To Believe in Women*, 37.

3 Dennett, *The Sex Side of Life*.

4 Dennett had gone through a very public divorce after her husband embraced free love principles and began a relationship with another woman against her will. Dennett was very open about sexuality but did not adhere to her husband's definition of free love. She believed sex should be free from state regulation and could occur outside of marriage but also believed in consensual, monogamous relationships. Dennett moved to Greenwich Village where she lived with a chosen family of queer suffragists and continued her work for NAWSA.

5 Letter from unknown woman in Buffalo, New York, April 19, 1925, Folder 467, Papers of Mary Ware Dennett.

6 Rupp, "'Imagine My Surprise,'" 66–67; Doris Stevens to Westbrook Pegler, May 3, 1946, Box 34, Folder 15, Doris Stevens Papers; Diary Entry, December 1, 1945, Box 6, Folder 2, Doris Stevens Papers.

7 Suffragists Oral History Project, "Conversations with Alice Paul," 196; Suffragists Oral History Project, "The Suffragists: From Tea Parties to Prison," 196, 3–39.

8 Estelle Freedman described how Miriam Van Waters, a prison reformer under investigation for allegedly condoning homosexual behavior among inmates, chose to burn letters to purge evidence of her lesbian relationship with her partner of over 22 years. Freedman, "'The Burning of Letters Continues,'" 181–200. For a similar discussion of how queer women of this era purged or concealed evidence of their relationships, see Orleck, *Common Sense and a Little Fire*, 310. Rodney Carter discusses how marginalized individuals "deny the archives their records as a way to exercise their power over the powerful." Carter, "Of Things Said and Unsaid," 215–233; Rich, "The Cartographies of Silence," 17.

9 Will of Annie Tinker, June 27, 1918, Records of the Annie Tinker Association for Women.

10 Letter from Kate Bertolini to William Woart Lancaster, March 16, 1924, Correspondence between Tinker estate heir Kate Bertolini and lawyer William Woart Lancaster, 1921–1924, Records of the Annie Tinker Association for Women.

11 Letter from Kate Bertolini to William Woart Lancaster, June 13, 1924, Correspondence between Tinker estate heir Kate Bertolini and lawyer William Woart Lancaster, 1921–1924, Records of the Annie Tinker Association for Women.

12 For more on this see Trouillot, *Silencing the Past*; Carter, "Of Things Said and Unsaid," 215–233.

13 Ware, "Unlocking the Porter-Dewson Partnership," 51–64; Ware, *Partner and I*, 58–59.

14 Letter from Kate Bertolini to William Woart Lancaster, February 10, 1924, Correspondence between Tinker estate heir Kate Bertolini and lawyer William Woart Lancaster, 1921–1924, Records of the Annie Tinker Association for Women.

15 Letter from Edith J. Goode to Ruth Miner, November 16, 1967, "Will and Instructions to Executors, 1954–67," Series I, Biographical Materials. Alice Morgan Wright Papers.

16 Cook, "The Historical Denial of Lesbianism," 60–65; Wells, *Miss Marks and Miss Woolley*; Faderman, "Who Hid Lesbian History?" 74–76.

17 Sargent, *Gail Laughlin*, 99.

18 Beemyn, *A Queer Capital*, 67.

19 Franzen, *Anna Howard Shaw*; Jabour, *Sophonisba Breckinridge*; Faderman, *To Believe in Women*, 50–51; Rupp, "'Imagine My Surprise,'" 61–70.

20 D'Emilio, *Sexual Politics, Sexual Communities*, 75–91; Meeker, "Behind the Mask of Respectability," 81, 90; Meeker, *Contacts Desired*; Horowitz, *Betty Friedan and the Making of the Feminine Mystique*; Warner, *The Trouble With Normal*.

21 Strub, "Gay Liberation (1963–1980)," 87; Faderman, *The Gay Revolution*, 235–237; Jay, *Tales of the Lavender Menace*.

22 Strub, "Gay Liberation (1963–1980)," 82–94; Stryker, *Transgender History*, 87.

BIBLIOGRAPHY

PRIMARY SOURCES

80 Million Women Want—? [Film]. Unique Film Company. 1913.

A Busy Day [Film]. Keystone Company. 1914.

"A Branch Formed." *Suffragette* 1, no. 19 (February 21, 1913): 3.

"A Certain Eugenia De Forest . . ." *The WASP* 31, no. 11 (September 9, 1893): 3.

"A Congressional Investigation of the Lawless Attack on the Suffrage Picket Demanded." *Suffragist* 5, no. 83 (August 25, 1917): 5.

A Cure for Suffragettes [Film]. Biograph, 1912.

A History of the Club Movement Among the Colored Women of the United States of America. Washington, DC: National Association of Colored Women's Clubs, Inc., 1902.

"Albert E. De Forrest." Certificate of Death. October 8, 1917. County of Los Angeles. California State Board of Health, Bureau of Vital Statistics.

"Albert Edward De Forest & Margaret Barton Hawley." November 17, 1911. Marriage License. County of Santa Barbara. State of California.

"Anna Woods Bird." *Vassar Quarterly* 3, no. 1 (November 1, 1917): 72.

Annual Report of the Children's Hospital of San Francisco, 1918. San Francisco: The James H. Barry Company, 1919.

Anthony, Susan B. and Ida Husted Harper, editors. *History of Woman Suffrage.* Vol. 4. Indianapolis, IN: Hollenbeck Press, 1902.

Avery, Alida C. "The Colorado Campaign." *The Woman's Journal* 8, no. 3 (January 20, 1877): 24.

———. "Vassar College." In *The Education of American Girls,* edited by Anna Callender Brackett, 346–361. New York: G.P. Putnam's Sons, 1874.

———. "Vassar College." In *Sex and Education: A Reply to Dr. E. H. Clarke's "Sex in Education,"* edited by Julia Ward Howe, 191–195. Boston: Roberts Brothers, 1874.

Baker, Josephine. *Fighting for Life.* New York: Macmillan Co, 1939.

"Brilliant Meeting at Cameron House." *The Suffragist* 4, no. 49 (December 2, 1916): 8.

Broadfoot, Winston. "Interview with Adele Clark." February 28, 1964. Southern Oral History Program. Southern Historical Collection. University of North Carolina at Chapel Hill.

Carpenter, Edward. *Love's Coming of Age.* Manchester: Labour Press, 1896.

"Case of Inspector Potter." *Votes for Women* 7, no. 309 (February 6, 1914): 11.

"Constitution of the National Association of Colored Women." *The Woman's Era* 3, no. 4 (November 1896).

"Conversation like this . . ." *Life Magazine* 61, 1590 (April 17, 1913): 772.

Correct Social Usage. New York: New York Society of Self-Culture, 1906.

Crocker-Langley. *San Francisco City Directory, 1905.* San Francisco: H. S. Crocker Company.

Davis, Katharine Bement. *Factors in the Sex Life of Twenty-Two Hundred Women.* New York: Arno Press & the New York Times, 1972.

"Delta Sigma Theta." *Howard University Journal* 13, no. 14 (February 11, 1916): 1, 4.

Dennett, Mary Ware. *The Sex Side of Life: An Explanation for Young People.* New York: n. p., 1918.

Eastman, Max. *Enjoyment of Living.* New York: Harper & Brothers, 1948.

"Elizabeth Howard Weston." *Smith Alumnae Quarterly* 7, no. 1 (November 1915): 57.

Ellis, Havelock. *My Life.* Boston: Houghton Mifflin, 1939.

———. *Studies in the Psychology of Sex. Vol. 1: Sexual Inversion.* London: University Press, 1900.

———. "Sexual Inversion in Women." *Alienist and Neurologist* 16, no. 2 (April 1895): 141–58.

Emerson, Zelie. "My Prison Experiences." *Metropolitan Magazine* 38, no. 6 (October 1913): 25–27, 56–57.

Empire State Campaign Committee. *The Biological Argument Against Woman Suffrage.* New York: National Woman Suffrage Publishing Company, 1914.

"First National Convention of the Congressional Union." *The Suffragist* 3, no. 44 (October 30, 1915): 5.

"Forcible Feeding." *Life and Labor* 3, no. 6 (June 1913): 190.

Freud, Sigmund. "The Psychogenesis of a Case of Homosexuality in a Woman." 1920. In *That Obscure Subject of Desire: Freud's Female Homosexual Revisited,* edited by Ronnie C. Lesser and Erica Schoenberg, 13–33. New York: Routledge, 1999.

Friedman, Belinda. "Interview with Adele Clark." January 22, 1978. Southern Oral History Program. Southern Historical Collection. University of North Carolina at Chapel Hill.

Furth, Seymour, E. P. Moran, and Will A. Heelan. *No Wedding Bells for Me.* New York: Shapiro Music Publisher Corporation, 1906.

Galpin, Kate Tupper. "A Theme for a Poet." Circa 1875. In *Nevada Poems.* Reno: Reno Print Company, c. 1927.

Grimké, Angelina Weld. *Selected Works of Angelina Weld Grimké.* New York: Oxford University Press, 1991.

"Hail Columbia!" *The Crisis* 5, no. 6 (April 1913): 289–90.

Halberstam, J. Jack. *In a Queer Time and Place: Transgender Bodies, Subcultural Lives.* New York: New York University Press, 2005.

Hall, Florence Howe. *The Correct Thing in Good Society.* Boston: Dana Estes & Company, 1902.

Hamilton, Cicely and Christopher St. John. *How the Vote Was Won.* London: Woman's Press, 1909.

Hatton, Bessie. *Before Sunrise.* London: Privately Printed, c. 1909.

History of the City of Denver, Arapahoe County, and Colorado. Chicago: O.L. Baskin & Co., 1880.

Hopkinson, Elizabeth. "Hoboing Across the Continent," *Life and Labor* 7, no. 6–10 (June–October 1917).

Hornsby, Leda Richberg vs. Hubert Primm Hornsby. Bill for Divorce. January 23, 1915. Circuit Court. Cook County, Illinois.

Huntzinger, Leona. "Why I Joined My Union, and What It Has Done for Me." *Life and Labor* 10, no. 10 (December 1920): 312–313.

"In the Courts." *Votes for Women* 6, no. 259 (February 21, 1913): 8.

In the Matter of the Estate of Mary A. Sperry. June 23, 1919. Will Proof and Certificate. Book D of Wills, no. 443, 254. Superior Court of the State of California in and for the City and County of San Francisco.

"Irwin, Elisabeth Antoinette." *Bulletin of Smith College. Alumnae Biographical Register, 1871–1935,* 30, no. 1 (November 1935): 107.

"Judging from the women . . ." *Town Topics* 69, no. 19 (May 8, 1913): 4.

Kenney, Annie. *Memories of a Militant.* London: Edward Arnold & Co., 1924, 263.

Klein, Nora C. *Practical Etiquette.* Chicago: A. Flanagan Co., 1899.

Krafft-Ebing, Richard von. *Psychopathia Sexualis.* New York: Rebman Company, 1906.

Last Will and Testament of Gail Laughlin. August 4, 1950. vol. 790, 303. Court of Cumberland County. Portland, Maine.

Last Will and Testament of Hannah K. Clapp. February 21, 1908. Will Books and Probate Records, Circa 1850–1912. Superior Court. Santa Clara County, California.

Last Will and Testament of Leona Huntzinger. August 22, 1922. Bacton, East Whiteland Township. Chester County, Pennsylvania.

Lee, William Howard. *The Perverts.* New York: G. W. Dillingham Company, 1901.

———. "Effeminate Men and Masculine Women." *New York Medical Journal* 71 (May 5, 1900): 686–87.

Marks, Jeannette. *A Girl's Student Days and After.* New York: Fleming H. Revell Company, 1911.

M.F.T. "Intelligent Gentlewomen in Marble." *Smith Alumnae Quarterly* 27 no. 11 (November 1935): 32–33.

"Miss Emerson Released." *Suffragette* 1, no. 26 (April 11, 1913): 424.

"Missouri News." *The Woman Citizen* 3, no. 34 (January 18, 1919): 690.

"More About Government Methods." *Suffragette* 2, no. 71 (February 20, 1914): 412.

"News of Miss Emerson." *Suffragette* 1, no. 25 (April 4, 1913): 410.

New York State Census. 1915.

"Notes and News." *Woman's Journal* 32, no. 23 (June 8, 1901): 181.

O'Gara, Gerald J. "The Ministering Angel of Chinatown." *Sunset Magazine* 53, no. 12 (December 1924): 28–29.

Ordway, Edith B. *The Etiquette of To-Day.* New York: Sully and Kleinteich, 1913.

Pankhurst, Emmeline. *My Own Story.* New York: Hearst's International Library Company, 1914.

Pankhurst, E. Sylvia. "Forcibly Fed: The Story of My Four Weeks in Holloway Gaol." *McClure's Magazine* 41, no. 8 (August 1913): 87–93.

Park & Recreation Commission Minutes. San Francisco, California. September 12, 1933.

"President Onlooker at Mob Attack on Suffragists." *Suffragist* 5, no. 82 (August 18, 1917): 7.

Report of Mr. Forward. Deputy Medical Officer of Holloway Prison. Zelie Emerson and Lillian Lenton's Case. July 7, 1913. House of Commons Papers, 52, no. 190.

Slowe, Lucy D. "After Commencement What?" *Howard University Record* 12, no. 7 (December 1918): 19–21.

Squire, Belle. "What Women Want in Men." *The Delineator* 69, no. 5 (May 1907): 906–10.

Steinhardt, Irving David. *Ten Sex Talks to Girls*. Philadelphia: J. B. Lippincott Company, 1914.

Stevens, Doris. *Jailed for Freedom*. New York: Boni & Liveright Publishing Corporation, 1920.

Suffrage Parade: Hearings before a Subcommittee of the Committee on the District of Columbia, United States Senate. Sixty-Third Congress, Special Session of the Senate under S. Res. 499, pt. 1, March 6–17, 1913. Washington, DC: Government Printing Office, 1913.

"Suffrage Paraders." *The Crisis* 5, no. 6 (April 1913): 296.

Suffragettes Arrested, 1906–1914. Home Office 45, 24665. Suffragettes: Amnesty of August 1914. Index of Women Arrested, 1906–1914. The National Archives. UK, Kew, Surrey, England.

Suffragists Oral History Project. "Conversations with Alice Paul: Woman Suffrage and the Equal Rights Amendment—Alice Paul." An Interview Conducted by Amelia R. Fry, 1972–1973. Regional Oral History Office. Bancroft Library, University of California, Berkeley, 1977.

———. "The Suffragists: From Tea Parties to Prison, Miriam Allen DeFord, In the Streets." An Interview Conducted by Sherna Gluck, 1973. Regional Oral History Office, Bancroft Library. University of California, Berkeley, 1975.

Talmey, Bernard S. *Love: A Treatise on the Science of Sex-Attraction*. 4th rev. ed. New York: Eugenics Publishing Company, 1919.

"The Alpha Suffrage Club." *The Alpha Suffrage Record* 1, no. 1 (March 18, 1914): 1.

"The New York News-Letter . . ." *Woman's Journal* 41, no. 21 (May 21, 1910): 83.

Thwing, Charles F. "Advice of a Father to a Daughter Entering College." *The Independent* 71, no. 3273 (August 31, 1911): 473–477.

US Bureau of the Census. Sixteenth Federal Census of the United States. 1940.

———. Fifteenth Federal Census of the United States. 1930.

———. Fourteenth Federal Census of the United States. 1920.

———. Thirteenth Census of the United States. 1910.

———. Twelfth Census of the United States. 1900.

———. Tenth Federal Census of the United States. 1880.

Van Hoosen, Bertha. *Petticoat Surgeon*. Chicago: Pellegrini & Cudahy, 1947.

"Votes for Women." *The Moving Picture World* 12, no. 13 (June 29, 1912): 1267.

"What the Boy Scouts Did at the Inauguration." *Boys Life Magazine* 3, no. 2 (April 1913): 2–4.

Will of Mary Askew Mather. May 13, 1925. County of New Castle. Wilmington, Delaware.

Wilson, Otto. *Fifty Years Work with Girls, 1883–1933*. Alexandria, VA: The National Florence Crittenton Mission, 1933.

Wolf, Rennold. "The Sort of Fellow Julian Eltinge Really Is." *The Green Book Magazine* 10, no. 11 (November 1913): 793–803.

Wylie, Ida Alexa Ross. *My Life with George*. New York: Random House, 1940.

"Zelie Emerson." *The Forum* 49, no. 5 (May 1913): 636–639.

NEWSPAPERS

Advocate (Portland, OR)

Akron Beacon Journal (Akron, OH)

Arizona Daily Star (Tucson, AZ)

Austin American-Statesman (Austin, TX)

Baltimore Sun (Baltimore, MD)

Bennington Evening Banner (Bennington, VT)

Berkeley Advocate (Berkeley, CA)

Boston Globe (Boston, MA)

Bridgeport Post (Bridgeport, CT)

Bridgeport Telegram (Bridgeport, CT)

Broad Ax (Chicago, IL)

Brooklyn Citizen (Brooklyn, NY)

Brooklyn Daily Eagle (Brooklyn, NY)

Buffalo Commercial (Buffalo, NY)

Buffalo Courier (Buffalo, NY)

Buffalo Enquirer (Buffalo, NY)

Buffalo Morning News (Buffalo, NY)

Buffalo Times (Buffalo, NY)

Bulletin (San Francisco, CA)

Calgary Herald (Calgary, Canada)

Chariton Courier (Keytesville, MO)

Chicago Examiner (Chicago, IL)

Chicago Tribune (Chicago, IL)

Colored American (Washington, DC)

Columbus Republican (Columbus, OH)

Courier-Journal (Louisville, KY)

Daily Appeal (Carson City, NV)

Daily Morning Union (Grass Valley, CA)

Daily News (Lebanon, PA)

Daily News (New York, NY)

Daily Standard Union (Brooklyn, NY)

Davenport Democrat and Leader (Davenport, IA)

Dayton Daily News (Dayton, OH)

Dayton Herald (Dayton, OH)

Detroit Free Press (Detroit, MI)

Evening Journal (Wilmington, DE)

Evening Missourian (Columbia, MO)

Evening News (San Jose, CA)

Evening Star (Washington, DC)

Evening Sun (Baltimore, MD)

Evening World (New York, NY)

Fort Worth Star-Telegram (Fort Worth, TX)

Gazette Journal (Reno, NV)

Harrisburg Daily Independent (Harrisburg, PA)

Houston Post (Houston, TX)

Indiana Gazette (Indiana, PA)

Indiana Weekly Messenger (Indiana, PA)

Inter Ocean (Chicago, IL)

Kenosha News (Kenosha, WI)

Kingston Daily Freeman (Kingston, NY)

Knickerbocker News (Albany, NY)

Lebanon Daily News (Lebanon, PA)

Los Angeles Evening Express (Los Angeles, CA)

Los Angeles Evening Herald (Los Angeles, CA)

Los Angeles Herald (Los Angeles, CA)

Los Angeles Times (Los Angeles, CA)

Morning News (Wilmington, DE)

Morning Telegram (Minneapolis, MN)

Muncie Evening Press (Muncie, IN)

Muskogee Daily Phoenix and Times-Democrat (Muskogee, OK)

Neenah Times (Neenah, WI)

Nevada State Journal (Reno, NV)

New Northwest (Portland, OR)

New York Age (New York, NY)

New York City American (New York, NY)

New York Sun (New York, NY)

New York Times (New York, NY)

New York Tribune (New York, NY)

New York World (New York, NY)

Oakland Tribune (Oakland, CA)

Pittsburgh Courier (Pittsburgh, PA)

Pittsburgh Post (Pittsburgh, PA)

Pittsburgh Post-Gazette (Pittsburgh, PA)

Pittsburgh Press (Pittsburgh, PA)
Reno Evening Gazette (Reno, NV)
Rock Island Argus (Rock Island, IL)
San Diego Union and Daily Bee (San Diego, CA)
San Francisco Call (San Francisco, CA)
San Francisco Chronicle (San Francisco, CA)
San Francisco Examiner (San Francisco, CA)
Sioux City Journal (Sioux City, IA)
Star Tribune (Minneapolis, MN)
State Journal (Jefferson City, MO)
Sun (New York, NY)
Times (Jacksonville, FL)
Times Herald (Port Huron, MI)
Tonopah Daily Bonanza (Tonopah, NV)
Topeka Daily Capital (Topeka, KS)
Transcript (Boston, MA)
Trenton Evening Times (Trenton, NJ)
Tribune (Scranton, PA)
Ukiah Daily Journal (Ukiah, CA)
Valley Independent (Monessen, PA)
Washington Bee (Washington, DC)
Washington Herald (Washington, DC)
Washington Post (Washington, DC)
Washington Times (Washington, DC)
Weekly Independent (Elko, NV)

ARCHIVAL COLLECTIONS
Alice Dunbar Nelson Papers. Special Collections Department, University of Delaware Library, Newark, Delaware.
Alice Morgan Wright Papers. Sophia Smith Collection, Smith College Archives, Northampton, Massachusetts.
Alice Stone Blackwell Papers, 1848–1957. Blackwell Family Papers, Library of Congress, Washington, DC.
Angelina Weld Grimké Papers. Moorland-Spingarn Research Center, Manuscript Division, Howard University, Washington DC.
Anne Martin Collection, Bancroft Library, University of California, Berkeley.
Aurelia Henry Reinhardt Papers, 1877–1948. F. W. Olin Library, Mills College, Oakland, California.
Baker-Busey-Dunlap Family Papers, 1866–1933. Illinois History and Lincoln Collections, University of Illinois at Urbana Champaign.
Blackwell Family Papers. Schlesinger Library, Radcliffe Institute, Harvard University, Cambridge, Massachusetts.

Caroline and Erwin Swann Collection of Caricature and Cartoon. Library of Congress, Prints and Photographs Division, Washington, DC.

Carrie Chapman Catt Papers. Library of Congress, Washington, DC.

Catherine Palczewski Suffrage Postcard Archive. University of Northern Iowa. Cedar Falls, Iowa.

Doris Stevens Papers. Schlesinger Library, Radcliffe Institute, Harvard University, Cambridge, Massachusetts.

Dovie Horvitz Collection. The Gender and Women's Studies Collection, University of Wisconsin Digital Collections, Madison, Wisconsin.

Edwin Bjorkman Papers, 1855–1954. The Southern Historical Collection, Louis Round Wilson Special Collection Library, University of North Carolina, Chapel Hill.

Elizabeth McShane Hilles Papers. Schlesinger Library, Radcliffe Institute, Harvard University, Cambridge, Massachusetts.

Ethel Sturgis Drummer Collection. Schlesinger Library, Radcliffe Institute, Harvard University, Cambridge, Massachusetts.

Florence Luscomb Papers, 1856–1987. Schlesinger Library, Radcliffe Institute, Harvard University, Cambridge, Massachusetts.

Hannah Keziah Clapp and Elizabeth Cecilia Babcock Collection, Nevada Historical Society, Reno, Nevada.

Hazel Hunkins-Hallinan Papers, Schlesinger Library, Radcliffe Institute, Harvard University, Cambridge, Massachusetts.

Independent Labour Party Archive. London School of Economics Archives, London, England.

J. Walter Thompson Company Archives. Duke University Library, Durham, North Carolina.

Jeannette Marks' Papers. Williston Memorial Library, Mt. Holyoke College, South Hadley, Massachusetts.

Lucy Diggs Slowe Papers. Moorland-Spingarn Research Center, Howard University, Washington, DC.

Margaret Foley Papers. Schlesinger Library, Radcliffe Institute, Harvard University, Cambridge, Massachusetts.

Margaret Foley and Helen Elizabeth Goodnow Papers. Schlesinger Library, Radcliffe Institute, Harvard University, Cambridge, Massachusetts.

Miriam and Ira D. Wallach Division of Art, Prints and Photographs: Print Collection. New York Public Library Digital Collections.

National Woman's Party Papers. Library of Congress, Washington, DC.

Olive Higgins Prouty Papers. Clark University Archive, Clark University, Worcester, Massachusetts.

Papers of Inez Haynes Gillmore, 1872–1945. Schlesinger Library, Radcliffe Institute, Harvard University, Cambridge, Massachusetts.

Papers of Mary Ware Dennett, 1874–1945. Schlesinger Library, Radcliffe Institute, Harvard University, Cambridge, Massachusetts.

Papers of Meta Fuller Stone. Lilly Library, Indiana University, Bloomington, Indiana.

Records of the Annie Tinker Association for Women, 1903–2013. Schlesinger Library, Radcliffe Institute, Harvard University, Cambridge, Massachusetts.

Records of the National Association of Colored Women's Clubs, 1895–1992. Washington, DC.

Rose Pastor Stokes Papers. Yale University Library, New Haven, Connecticut.

Susan B. Anthony Papers. Library of Congress, Washington, DC.

Sylvia Pankhurst Papers. International Institute of Social History, Amsterdam, Netherlands.

Theodore Roosevelt Digital Library. Dickinson State University, Dickinson, North Dakota.

Townshend Walsh Collection. New York Public Library, New York.

SECONDARY SOURCES

Agyepong, Tera. "Aberrant Sexualities and Racialized Masculinization: Race, Gender and the Criminalization of African American Girls at the Illinois Training School for Girls at Geneva, 1893–1945." *Gender & History* 25, no. 2 (August 2013): 270–293.

Arthur, Anthony. *Radical Innocent: Upton Sinclair*. New York: Random House, 2006.

Atkinson, Diane. *Rise Up, Women!: The Remarkable Lives of the Suffragettes*. London: Bloomsbury, 2018.

Bauer, Heike. *The Hirschfeld Archives: Violence, Death, and Modern Queer Culture*. Philadelphia: Temple University Press, 2017.

Bederman, Gail. *Manliness and Civilization: A Cultural History of Gender and Race in the United States, 1880–1917*. Chicago: University of Chicago Press, 1995.

Beemyn, Genny. *A Queer Capital: A History of Gay Life in Washington DC*. New York: Routledge, 2014.

Behling, Laura L. *The Masculine Woman in America, 1890–1935*. Urbana: University of Illinois Press, 2001.

Bell, David and Gill Valentine, editors. *Mapping Desire: Geographies of Sexualities*. New York: Routledge, 1995.

Braude, Anne. *Radical Spirits: Spiritualism and Women's Rights in Nineteenth Century America*. 2d ed. Bloomington: Indiana University Press, 2001.

Brooks, Tim, Richard Keith Spottswood, and Dick Spottswood. *Lost Sounds: Blacks and the Birth of the Recording Industry, 1890–1919*. Urbana: University of Illinois Press, 2004.

Brown, Elsa Barkley. "To Catch the Vision of Freedom: Reconstructing Southern Black Women's Political History, 1865–1880." In *African American Women and the Vote, 1847–1965*, edited by Ann D. Gordon and Bettye Collier-Thomas, 66–99. Amherst: University of Massachusetts Press, 1997.

Bruce, Jr., Dickson D. *Archibald Grimké: Portrait of a Black Independent*. Baton Rouge: Louisiana State University Press, 1993.

Bruce, Katherine McFarland, *Pride Parades: How a Parade Changed the World*. New York: New York University Press, 2016.

Butler, Judith. *Frames of War: When Is Life Grievable?* London: Verso, 2009.

Cahill, Cathleen D. *Recasting the Vote: How Women of Color Transformed the Suffrage Movement*. Chapel Hill: University of North Carolina Press, 2020.

Carter, Rodney G. S. "Of Things Said and Unsaid: Power, Archival Silences, and Power in Silence." *Archivaria* 61 (September 2006): 215–233.

Casey, Kathleen B. *The Prettiest Girl on Stage Is a Man: Race and Gender Benders in American Vaudeville*. Knoxville: University of Tennessee Press, 2015.

Chapman, Mary. *Making Noise, Making News: Suffrage Print Culture and U.S. Modernism*. Oxford: Oxford University Press, 2014.

Chauncey, Jr., George. "From Sexual Inversion to Homosexuality: Medicine and the Changing Conceptualization of Female Deviance." *Salmagundi* 58–59 (Fall 1982–Winter 1983): 114–146.

Christian, Mary. *Marriage and Late-Victorian Dramatists*. London: Palgrave Macmillan, 2020.

Cleves, Rachel Hope. "'What, Another Female Husband?': The Prehistory of Same-Sex Marriage in America." *Journal of American History* 101, no. 4 (March 2015): 1055–1081.

Cockin, Katharine. "Charlotte Perkins Gilman's *Three Women*: Work, Marriage, and the Old(er) Woman." In *Charlotte Perkins Gilman: Optimist Reformer*, edited by Jill Rudd and Val Gough, 74–92. Iowa City: University of Iowa Press, 1999.

Cook, Blanche Wiesen. "The Historical Denial of Lesbianism." *Radical History Review* 20, no. 1 (Spring/Summer 1979): 60–65.

Coontz, Stephanie. *Marriage, a History: From Obedience to Intimacy, or How Love Conquered Marriage*. New York: Viking, 2005.

Cooper, Brittney C. *Beyond Respectability: The Intellectual Thought of Race Women*. Urbana: University of Illinois Press, 2017.

Cott, Nancy F. *The Grounding of Modern Feminism*. New Haven, CT: Yale University Press, 1987.

———. *The Bonds of Womanhood: "Woman's Sphere" in New England, 1778–1835*. New Haven, CT: Yale University Press, 1973.

Cottrill, J. Matthew. *Queering Architecture: Possibilities of Space(s)*. Master's Thesis, Miami University, 2006.

Cresswell, Tim. "Mobilising the Movement: The Role of Mobility in the Suffrage Politics of Florence Luscomb and Margaret Foley, 1911–1915." *Gender, Place and Culture* 12, no. 4 (December 2005): 447–461.

Davis, Elizabeth Lindsay. *Lifting as They Climb*. Chicago: National Association of Colored Women, 1933. Reprinted. New York: G. K. Hall, 1996.

Davis, Rebecca L. "'Not Marriage at All, but Simple Harlotry': The Companionate Marriage Controversy." *Journal of American History* 94, no. 4 (March 2008): 1137–1163.

D'Emilio, John. "Capitalism and Gay Identity." In *Powers of Desire: The Politics of Sexuality*, edited by Ann Snitow, Christine Stansell, and Sharon Thompson, 100–113. New York: Monthly Review Press, 1983.

———. *Sexual Politics, Sexual Communities: The Making of a Homosexual Minority in the United States, 1940–1970*. Chicago: University of Chicago Press, 1983.

Dennison, Mariea Caudill. "The American Girls' Club in Paris: The Propriety and Imprudence of Art Students, 1890–1914." *Woman's Art Journal* 26, no. 1 (Spring–Summer 2005): 32–37.

DuBois, Ellen Carol. *Suffrage: Women's Long Battle for the Vote.* New York: Simon & Schuster, 2020.

Eby, Clare Virginia. *Until Choice Do Us Part: Marriage Reform in the Progressive Era.* Chicago: University of Chicago Press, 2014.

Edwards, John Carver. *Orville's Aviators: Outstanding Alumni of the Wright Flying School, 1910–1916.* Jefferson, NC: McFarland & Company, 2009.

Elliott, Diana B., Kristy Krivickas, Matthew W. Brault, and Rose M. Kreider. *Historical Marriage Trends from 1890–2010: A Focus on Race Differences.* Presented at the annual meetings of the Population Association of America. San Francisco, CA, May 3–5, 2012.

Faderman, Lillian. *The Gay Revolution: The Story of the Struggle.* New York: Simon & Schuster, 2015.

———. *To Believe in Women: What Lesbians Have Done for America—A History.* Boston: Houghton Mifflin, 1999.

———. *Odd Girls and Twilight Lovers: A History of Lesbian Life in Twentieth-Century America.* New York: Columbia University Press, 1991.

———. *Surpassing the Love of Men: Romantic Friendship and Love Between Women from the Renaissance to the Present.* New York: William Morrow, 1981.

———. "Who Hid Lesbian History?" *Frontiers* 4, no. 3 (Autumn 1979): 74–76.

Finnegan, Margaret. *Selling Suffrage: Consumer Culture & Votes for Women.* New York: Columbia University Press, 1999.

Fischer, Gayle V. *Pantaloons and Power: Nineteenth-Century Dress Reform in the United States.* Kent, OH: Kent State University Press, 2001.

Foucault, Michel. "Friendship as a Way of Life." Interview with Michel Foucault by R. de Ceccaty, J. Danet, and J. Le Bitoux. Translated by John Johnston. *Gai Pied* (April 1981). Reprinted in *Michel Foucault: Ethics Subjectivity and Truth*, volume 1, edited by Paul Rabinow, 135–140. New York: New Press, 1994.

Frančíková, Dáša. "Romantic Friendships: Exploring Modern Categories of Sexuality, Love, and Desire Between Women." In *Understanding and Teaching U.S. Gay, Lesbian, Bisexual, and Transgender History*, edited by Leila J. Rupp and Susan Freeman, 143–152. Madison: University of Wisconsin Press, 2014.

Franzen, Trisha. *Anna Howard Shaw: The Work of Woman Suffrage.* Urbana: University of Illinois Press, 2014.

———. *Spinsters and Lesbians: Independent Womanhood in the United States.* New York: New York University Press, 1996.

Freedman, Estelle. "'The Burning of Letters Continues': Elusive Identities and the Historical Construction of Sexuality." *Journal of Women's History* 9, no. 4 (Winter 1998): 181–200.

———. "Separatism as Strategy: Female Institution Building and American Feminism, 1870–1930." *Feminist Studies* 5, no. 3 (1979): 512–529.

Frisken, Amanda. *Victoria Woodhull's Sexual Revolution: Political Theater and the Popular Press in Nineteenth-Century America.* Philadelphia: University of Pennsylvania Press, 2004.

Gaines, Kevin K. *Uplifting the Race: Black Leadership, Politics, and Culture in the Twentieth Century.* Chapel Hill: University of North Carolina Press, 1996.

Garvey, Ellen Gruber. "Alice Dunbar-Nelson's Suffrage Work: The View from Her Scrapbook." *Legacy* 33, no. 2 (2016): 310–335.

Goldsmith, Barbara. *Other Powers: The Age of Suffrage, Spiritualism, and the Scandalous Victoria Woodhull.* New York: Alfred A. Knopf, 1998.

Goodier, Susan. *No Votes for Women: The New York State Anti-Suffrage Movement.* Bloomington: University of Illinois Press, 2013.

Grier, Barbara and Coletta Reid. *Lesbian Lives: Biographies of Women from the Ladder.* Baltimore, MD: Diana Press, 1976.

Gullett, Gayle. *Becoming Citizens: The Emergence and Development of the California Women's Movement, 1880–1911.* Urbana: University of Illinois Press, 2000.

———. "Constructing the Woman Citizen and Struggling for the Vote in California, 1896–1911." *Pacific Historical Review* 69, no. 4 (November 2000): 573–593.

Harris, Sharon M. *Dr. Mary Walker: An American Radical, 1832–1919.* New Brunswick, NJ: Rutgers University Press, 2009.

Higginbotham, Evelyn Brooks. "Clubwomen and Electoral Politics in the 1920s." In *African American Women and the Vote, 1847–1965,* edited by Ann D. Gordon and Bettye Collier-Thomas, 134–155. Amherst: University of Massachusetts Press, 1997.

———. *Righteous Discontent: The Women's Movement in the Black Baptist Church, 1880–1920.* Cambridge, MA: Harvard University Press, 1993.

———. "In Politics to Stay: Black Women Leaders and Party Politics in the 1920s." In *Women, Politics, and Change,* edited by Louise A. Tilly and Patricia Gurin, 199–220. New York: Russell Sage Foundation, 1990.

Hine, Darlene Clark. "'We Specialize in the Wholly Impossible': The Philanthropic Work of Black Women." In *Lady Bountiful Revisited: Women, Philanthropy, and Power,* edited by Kathleen D. McCarthy, 70–93. New Brunswick, NJ: Rutgers University Press, 1990.

———. "Rape and the Inner Lives of Black Women in the Middle West: Thoughts on the Culture of Dissemblance." *Signs* 14, no. 4 (Summer 1989): 912–920.

Honey, Maureen. *Aphrodite's Daughters: Three Modernist Poets of the Harlem Renaissance.* New Brunswick, NJ: Rutgers University Press, 2016.

Horowitz, Daniel. *Betty Friedan and the Making of the Feminine Mystique: The American Left, the Cold War, and Modern America.* Amherst: University of Massachusetts Press, 1998.

Horowitz, Helen Lefkowitz. "Victoria Woodhull, Anthony Comstock, and Conflict over Sex in the United States in the 1870s." *Journal of American History* 87, no. 2 (September 2000): 403–434.

Howard, Anne Bail. *The Long Campaign: A Biography of Anne Martin.* Reno: University of Nevada Press, 1985.

Howlett, Caroline. "Femininity Slashed: Suffragette Militancy, Modernism and Gender." In *Modernist Sexualities*, edited by Hugh Stevens and Caroline Howlett, 72–91. Manchester: Manchester University Press, 2000.

Hull, Gloria T. *Color, Sex, & Poetry: Three Women Writers of the Harlem Renaissance.* Bloomington: Indiana University Press, 1987.

———. *Give Us Each Day: The Diary of Alice Dunbar-Nelson.* New York: W. W. Norton, 1984.

Hurewitz, Daniel. *Bohemian Los Angeles and the Making of Modern Politics.* Berkeley: University of California Press, 2008.

Inness, Sherrie A. *Intimate Communities: Representation and Social Transformation in Woman's College Fiction, 1895–1910.* Bowling Green, OH: Bowling Green State University Popular Press, 1995.

———. "Mashes, Smashes, Crushes, and Raves: Woman-to-Woman Relationships in Popular Women's College Fiction, 1895–1915." *NWSA Journal* 6, no. 1 (Spring 1994): 48–68.

"Interchange: Women's Suffrage, the Nineteenth Amendment, and the Right to Vote." *Journal of American History* 106, no. 3 (December 2019): 662–694.

Jabour, Anya. *Sophonisba Breckinridge: Championing Women's Activism in Modern America.* Urbana: University of Illinois Press, 2019.

Jay, Karla. *Tales of the Lavender Menace: A Memoir of Liberation.* New York: Basic Books, 1999.

Jensen, Kimberly. *Mobilizing Minerva: American Women in the First World War.* Urbana: University of Illinois Press, 2008.

Johnston, Linda. *Queering Tourism: Paradoxical Performances of Gay Pride Parades.* New York: Routledge, 2005.

Jones, Martha S. *Vanguard: How Black Women Broke Barriers, Won the Vote, and Insisted on Equality for All.* New York: Basic Books, 2020.

———. *All Bound Up Together: The Woman Question in African American Public Culture, 1830–1900.* Chapel Hill: University of North Carolina Press, 2007.

Jorae, Wendy Rouse. *Children of Chinatown: Growing up Chinese American in San Francisco's Chinatown, 1850–1920.* Chapel Hill: University of North Carolina Press, 2009.

Kaplan, Lawrence. "A Utopia During the Progressive Era: The Helicon Home Colony, 1906–1907." *American Studies* 25, no. 2 (Fall 1984): 59–73.

Katz, Jonathan Ned. *The Invention of Heterosexuality.* New York: Dutton Books, 1995.

Kelley, Edith Summers. "Helicon Hall: An Experiment in Living." *Kentucky Review* 1, no. 3 (Spring 1980): 29–51.

Kennedy, Martha H. *Drawn to Purpose: American Women Illustrators and Cartoonists.* Jackson: University Press of Mississippi, 2018.

Kessler-Harris, Alice. *Out to Work: A History of Wage-Earning Women in the United States.* New York: Oxford University Press, 1982.

Kevles, Daniel J. *In the Name of Eugenics: Genetics and the Uses of Human Heredity.* New York: Alfred A. Knopf, 1985.

Kimmel, Michael. *Manhood in America: A Cultural History*. New York: Free Press, 1996.

Kroeger, Brooke. *The Suffragents: How Women Used Men to Get the Vote*. Albany: State University of New York Press, 2017.

Lange, Allison K. *Picturing Political Power: Images in the Woman's Suffrage Movement*. Chicago: University of Chicago Press, 2020.

Larson, Edward J. *Sex, Race, and Science: Eugenics in the Deep South*. Baltimore, MD: Johns Hopkins University Press, 1995.

Laville, Helen. "'A New Era in International Women's Rights?': American Women's Associations and the Establishment of the UN Commission on the Status of Women." *Journal of Women's History* 20, no. 4 (Winter 2008): 34–56.

Lebsock, Suzanne. "Woman Suffrage and White Supremacy: A Virginia Case Study." In *Taking Off the White Gloves: Southern Women and Women Historians*, edited by Michele K. Gillespie and Catherine Clinton, 28–42. Columbia: University of Missouri Press, 1998.

Lee, Erika. *At America's Gates: Chinese Immigration during the Exclusion Era, 1882–1943*. Chapel Hill: University of North Carolina Press, 2003.

Lee, Robert G. *Orientals: Asian Americans in Popular Culture*. Philadelphia: Temple University Press, 1999.

Lee, Stacey J., Nga-Wing Anjela Wong, and Alvin N. Alvarez. "The Model Minority and the Perpetual Foreigner: Stereotypes of Asian Americans." In *Asian American Psychology: Current Perspectives*, edited by Nita Tewari and Alvin N. Alvarez, 69–84. New York: Routledge, 2009.

Lemay, Kate Clarke. *Votes for Women: A Portrait of Persistence*. Princeton, NJ: Princeton University Press, 2019.

Lindsey, Treva B. *Colored No More: Reinventing Black Womanhood in Washington, D.C.* Urbana: University of Illinois Press, 2017.

———. "Climbing the Hilltop: In Search of a New Negro Womanhood at Howard University." In *Escape from New York: The New Negro Renaissance Beyond Harlem*, edited by Davarian L. Baldwin and Minkah Makalani, 271–290. Minneapolis: University of Minnesota Press, 2013.

Manion, Jen. *Female Husbands: A Trans History*. New York: Cambridge University Press, 2020.

Marino, Katherine M. *Feminism for the Americas: The Making of an International Human Rights Movement*. Chapel Hill: University of North Carolina Press, 2019.

"Marriages, First Methodist Church, Santa Barbara." *Ancestors West: Santa Barbara Genealogical Society* 20, no. 3 (Spring 1994): 153–156.

Materson, Lisa G. *For the Freedom of Her Race: Black Women and Electoral Politics in Illinois, 1877–1932*. Chapel Hill: University of North Carolina Press, 2009.

McCammon, Holly J. "'Out of the Parlors and into the Streets': The Changing Tactical Repertoire of the U.S. Women's Suffrage Movements." *Social Forces* 81, no. 3 (March 2003): 787–818.

McCarthy, Tara M. *Respectability & Reform: Irish American Women's Activism, 1880–1920*. Syracuse, NY: Syracuse University Press, 2018.

McMurtrie, Douglas C. "Principles of Homosexuality and Sexual Inversion in the Female." *American Journal of Urology* 9, no. 3 (March 1913): 144–153.

Mead, Rebecca J. *How the Vote Was Won: Woman Suffrage in the United States, 1868–1914*. New York: New York University Press, 2006.

Meeker, Martin. *Contacts Desired: Gay and Lesbian Communications and Community, 1940s–1970s*. Chicago: University of Chicago Press, 2006.

———. "Behind the Mask of Respectability: Reconsidering the Mattachine Society and Male Homophile Practice, 1950s and 1960s." *Journal of the History of Sexuality* 10, no. 1 (January 2001): 78–116.

Miller, Carroll L. L. and Anne S. Pruitt-Logan. *Faithful to the Task at Hand: The Life of Lucy Diggs Slowe*. Albany: State University of New York Press, 2012.

Mink, Gwendolyn. *The Wages of Motherhood: Inequality in the Welfare State, 1917–1942*. Ithaca, NY: Cornell University Press, 1996.

Mintz, Steven and Susan Kellogg. *Domestic Revolutions: A Social History of American Family Life*. New York: Free Press, 1988.

Mitchell, Koritha A. "Antilynching Plays: Angelina Weld Grimké, Alice Dunbar-Nelson, and the Evolution of African American Drama." In *Post-Bellum, Pre-Harlem: African American Literature and Culture*, edited by Barbara McCaskill and Caroline Gebhard, 210–230. New York: New York University Press, 2006.

Moravec, Michelle Katherine Pettine, and Hope Smalley. "Stunts and Sensationalism: The Pennsylvania Progressive-Era Campaign for Women's Suffrage." *Pennsylvania History: A Journal of Mid-Atlantic Studies* 87, no. 4 (Autumn 2020): 631–656.

Muncy, Robyn. *Creating a Female Dominion in American Reform, 1890–1935*. New York: Oxford University Press, 1991.

Nelson, Claudia. "Nontraditional Adoption in Progressive-Era Orphan Narratives." *Mosaic: An Interdisciplinary Critical Journal* 34, no. 2 (June 2001): 181–197.

Neuman, Johanna. *Gilded Suffragists: The New York Socialites Who Fought for Women's Right to Vote*. New York: New York University Press, 2017.

Neverdon-Morton, Cynthia. "Advancement of the Race through African American Women's Organizations in the South, 1895–1925." In *African American Women and the Vote, 1837–1965*, edited by Ann D. Gordon and Bettye Collier-Thomas, 120–133. Amherst: University of Massachusetts Press, 1997.

Newman, Louise Michelle. *White Women's Rights: The Racial Origins of Feminism in the United States*. New York: Oxford University Press, 1999.

Okihiro, Gary Y. *Margins and Mainstreams: Asians in American History and Culture*. Seattle: University of Washington Press, 1994.

Olsen, Deborah M. "Remaking the Image: Promotional Literature of Mount Holyoke, Smith and Wellesley Colleges in the Mid-to-Late 1940s." *History of Education Quarterly* 40, no. 4 (Winter 2000): 418–459.

Oosterhuis, Harry. *Stepchildren of Nature: Krafft-Ebing, Psychiatry and the Making of Sexual Identity*. Chicago: University of Chicago Press, 2000.

Orleck, Annelise. *Common Sense and a Little Fire*, 2d ed. Chapel Hill: University of North Carolina Press, 2017.

Oswin, Natalie. "Critical Geographies and the Uses of Sexuality: Deconstructing Queer Space." *Progress in Human Geography* 32, no. 1 (2008): 89–103.

Parker, Allison M. *Unceasing Militant: The Life of Mary Church Terrell*. Chapel Hill: University of North Carolina Press, 2020.

Patterson, Martha H. *The American New Woman Revisited, A Reader, 1894–1930*. New Brunswick, NJ: Rutgers University Press, 2008.

Perry, Mark. *Lift Up Thy Voice: The Sarah and Angelina Grimké Family's Journey from Slaveholders to Civil Rights Leaders*. New York: Penguin Books, 2001.

Pugh, Martin. *The Pankhursts: The History of One Radical Family*. London: Vintage Books, 2008.

Purvis, June. *Emmeline Pankhurst: A Biography*. London: Routledge, 2003.

Putney, Clifford. *Muscular Christianity: Manhood and Sports in Protestant America, 1880–1920*. Cambridge, MA: Harvard University Press, 2001.

Radomska, Marietta, Tara Mehrabi, and Nina Lykke. "Queer Death Studies: Coming to Terms with Death, Dying and Mourning Differently." *Women, Gender and Research* nos. 3–4 (September 2019): 6.

Rauterkus, Cathleen Nista. *Go Get Mother's Picket Sign: Crossing Spheres with the Material Culture of Suffrage*. Lanham, MD: University Press of America, 2010.

Rich, Adrienne. "Compulsory Heterosexuality and Lesbian Existence." *Signs* 5, no. 4 (Summer 1980): 631–660.

———. "The Cartographies of Silence." In *The Dream of a Common Language: Poems 1974–1977*. New York: W. W. Norton, 1978.

Ricketts, Ellen. "The Fractured Pageant: Queering Lesbian Lives in the Early Twentieth Century." *Peer English* 10 (2015): 82–94.

Rolley, Katrina. "Fashion, Femininity and the Fight for the Vote." *Art History* 13, no. 1 (March 1990): 47–71.

Rotundo, E. Anthony. *American Manhood: Transformations in Masculinity from the Revolution to the Modern Era*. New York: Basic Books, 1993.

Rupp, Leila J. *Sapphistries: A Global History of Love between Women*. New York: New York University Press, 2009.

———. *A Desired Past: A Short History of Same-Sex Love in America*. Chicago: University of Chicago Press, 1999.

———. "Sexuality and Politics in the Early Twentieth Century: The Case of the International Women's Movement." *Feminist Studies* 23, no. 3 (Fall 1997): 577–605.

———. *Worlds of Women: The Making of an International Women's Movement*. Princeton, NJ: Princeton University Press, 1997.

———. "The Women's Community in the National Woman's Party, 1945 to the 1960s." *Signs* 10, no. 4 (Summer 1985): 715–740.

———. "'Imagine My Surprise': Women's Relationships in Historical Perspective." *Frontiers* 5, no. 3 (Fall 1980): 61–70.

Rupp, Leila J. and Susan Freeman, editors. *Understanding and Teaching U.S. Gay, Lesbian, Bisexual, and Transgender History*. Madison: University of Wisconsin Press, 2014.

Ryan, Mary P. *Cradle of the Middle Class: The Family in Oneida County, New York, 1790–1865*. New York: Cambridge University Press, 1981.

Sargent, Ruth Sexton. *Gail Laughlin: ERA's Advocate*. Portland, ME: House of Falmouth, 1979.

Schwarz, Judith. *Radical Feminists of Heterodoxy*. Norwich, VT: New Victoria Publishers, 1986.

Sears, Clare. *Arresting Dress: Cross-Dressing, Law, and Fascination in Nineteenth-Century San Francisco*. Durham, NC: Duke University Press, 2015.

Sewell, Jessica Ellen. *Women and the Everyday City: Public Space in San Francisco, 1890–1915*. Minneapolis: University of Minnesota Press, 2011.

Shah, Nayan. *Contagious Divides: Epidemics and Race in San Francisco's Chinatown*. Berkeley: University of California Press, 2001.

Sheppard, Alice. *Cartooning for Suffrage*. Albuquerque: University of New Mexico Press, 1994.

Simmons, Christina. "Companionate Marriage and the Lesbian Threat." *Frontiers* 4, no. 3 (Fall 1979): 54–49.

Simonson, Anna C. "Féminisme Oblige: Katharine Susan Anthony and the Birth of Modern Feminist Biography, 1877–1929." PhD Dissertation, City University of New York, 2017.

Skidmore, Emily. *True Sex: The Lives of Trans Men at the Turn of the Century*. New York: New York University Press, 2017.

Sloan, Kay. "Sexual Warfare in the Silent Cinema: Comedies and Melodramas of Woman Suffragism." *American Quarterly* 33, no. 4 (Autumn 1981): 412–436.

Smith, Sherry L. *Bohemians West: Free Love, Family, and Radicals in Twentieth-Century America*. Berkeley, CA: Heyday Books, 2020.

Smith-Rosenberg, Carroll. "The Female World of Love and Ritual: Relationships Between Women in Nineteenth-Century America." *Signs* 1, no. 1 (Autumn 1975): 1–29.

Sneider, Allison L. *Suffragists in an Imperial Age: U.S. Expansion and the Woman Question, 1870–1929*. New York: Oxford University Press, 2008.

Snorton, C. Riley. *Black on Both Sides: A Racial History of Trans Identity*. Minneapolis: University of Minnesota Press, 2017.

Snyder, Jean E. *Harry T. Burleigh: From the Spiritual to the Harlem Renaissance*. Urbana: University of Illinois Press, 2016.

Somerville, Siobhan B. *Queering the Color Line: Race and the Invention of Homosexuality in American Culture*. Durham, NC: Duke University Press, 2000.

———. "Scientific Racism and the Invention of the Homosexual Body." In *Queer Studies: A Lesbian, Gay, Bisexual and Transgender Anthology*, edited by Brett Beemyn and Mickey Eliason, 241–261. New York: New York University Press, 1996.

Stage, Sarah. "What 'Good Girls' Do: Katharine Bement Davis and the Moral Panic of the First U.S. Sexual Survey." In *The Moral Panics of Sexuality*, edited by Breanne Fahs, Mary L. Dudy, and Sarah Stage, 151–163. New York: Palgrave Macmillan, 2013.

Stamp, Shelley. *Movie Struck Girls: Women and Motion Picture Culture After the Nickelodeon*. Princeton, NJ: Princeton University Press, 2000.

Stanton, Elizabeth Cady, Susan B. Anthony, and Matilda Joslyn Gage. *History of Woman Suffrage*. Vol. 2, 1861–1876. New York: Fowler and Wells, 1881.

Stevenson, Brenda E. *Life in Black and White: Family and Community in the Slave South*. New York: Oxford University Press, 1996.

Strom, Sharon Hartman. *Political Woman: Florence Luscomb and the Legacy of Radical Reform*. Philadelphia: Temple University Press, 2001.

———. "Leadership and Tactics in the American Woman Suffrage Movement: A New Perspective from Massachusetts." *Journal of American History* 62, no. 2 (September 1975): 296–315.

Strub, Whitney. "Gay Liberation (1963–1980)." In *Routledge History of Queer America*, edited by Don Romesburg, 82–94. New York: Routledge, 2019.

Stryker, Susan. *Transgender History: The Roots of Today's Revolution*, 2d ed. New York: Seal Press, 2017.

Sueyoshi, Amy. *Discriminating Sex: White Leisure and the Making of the American "Oriental."* Bloomington: University of Illinois Press, 2018.

Terborg-Penn, Rosalyn. *African American Women in the Struggle for the Vote, 1850–1920*. Bloomington: University of Indiana Press, 1998.

Terry, Jennifer. *An American Obsession: Science, Medicine, and Homosexuality in Modern Society*. Chicago: University of Chicago Press, 1999.

Tetrault, Lisa. *The Myth of Seneca Falls: Memory and the Women's Suffrage Movement, 1848–1898*. Chapel Hill: University of North Carolina Press, 2014.

Tinker, Catherine. "Annie Rensselaer Tinker (1884–1924) Of East Setauket and NYC: Philanthropist, Suffragist, WWI Volunteer in Europe." *Long Island History Journal* 26, no. 1 (2017). http://lihj.cc.stonybrook.edu

Totton, Kathryn Dunn. "Hannah Keziah Clapp: The Life and Career of a Pioneer Nevada Educator, 1824–1908." *Nevada Historical Society Quarterly* 20, no. 3 (Fall 1977): 167–183.

Trouillot, Michel-Rolph, *Silencing the Past: Power and the Production of History*. Boston, MA: Beacon Press, 1995.

Van Dyne, Susan. "Abracadabra: Intimate Inventions by Early College Women in the United States." *Feminist Studies* 42, no. 2 (2016): 280–310.

Waitt, Alden. "Katharine Anthony: Feminist Biographer with the 'Warmth of an Advocate.'" *Frontiers: A Journal of Women Studies* 10, no. 1 (1988): 72–77.

Ware, Susan. "Unlocking the Porter-Dewson Partnership: A Challenge for the Feminist Biographer." In *The Challenge of Feminist Biography: Writing the Lives of Modern American Women*, edited by Sara Alpern, Joyce Antler, Elisabeth I. Perry, and Ingrid W. Scobie, 51–64. Urbana: University of Illinois Press, 1992.

———. *Partner and I: Molly Dewson, Feminism, and New Deal Politics*. New Haven, CT: Yale University Press, 1987.

Warner, Michael. *The Trouble with Normal: Sex, Politics, and the Ethics of Queer Life*. New York: Free Press, 1999.

Wells, Anna Mary. *Miss Marks and Miss Woolley*. New York: Houghton Mifflin, 1978.

Welter, Barbara. "The Cult of True Womanhood: 1820–1860." *American Quarterly* 18, no. 2 (Summer 1966): 151–174.

Weston, Kath. *Families We Choose: Lesbians, Gays, Kinship.* New York: Columbia University Press, 1991.

Wexler, Alice R. *Emma Goldman: An Intimate Life.* New York: Pantheon Books, 1984.

Winslow, Barbara. *Sylvia Pankhurst: Sexual Politics and Political Activism.* New York: St. Martin's, 1996.

Woolner, Cookie. "'Woman Slain in Queer Love Brawl': African American Women, Same-Sex Desire, and Violence in the Urban North, 1920–1929." *Journal of African American History* 100, no. 3 (Summer 2015): 406–427.

Wu, Frank H. *Yellow: Race in America Beyond Black and White.* New York: Basic Books, 2002.

Wu, Judy Tzu-Chun. *Doctor Mom Chung of the Fair-Haired Bastards: The Life of a Wartime Celebrity.* Berkeley: University of California Press, 2005.

———. "Was Mom Chung a 'Sister Lesbian'? Asian American Gender Experimentation and Interracial Homoeroticism." *Journal of Women's History* 13, no. 1 (Spring 2001): 58–82.

Yung, Judy. *Unbound Feet: A Social History of Chinese Women in San Francisco.* Berkeley: University of California Press, 1995.

INDEX

ABOUT THE AUTHOR

WENDY L. ROUSE is Associate Professor in the Department of History at San Jose State University. Her scholarly research focuses on the history of women, children, gender, and sexuality during the Progressive Era. Rouse is also the author of *Children of Chinatown: Growing Up Chinese American in San Francisco, 1880–1920* and *Her Own Hero: The Origins of the Women's Self-Defense Movement.*